JUDGES

First published April 2015
ISBN: 978-0-9893098-9-9
Visit us on the web!
www.mindijofurby.com
Published by: KingsWynd

KingsWynd exists to fight biblical illiteracy in the church and world. Our goal is to help others love God and become more like Jesus through His Word. We accomplish this through publishing books, articles, curriculum, and Bible studies used by individuals and churches throughout the world.

For more information about KingsWynd, visit www.KingsWynd.com

Printed in the United States of America
Scripture, unless otherwise noted, taken from the NEW AMERICAN STANDARD BIBLE®, Copyright © 1960, 1962, 1963, 1968, 1971, 1972, 1973, 1975, 1977, 1995 by The Lockman Foundation. Used by permission.

Author: Mindi Jo Furby
Edited by: Christina Miller
Formatted by: Polgarus Studio

CONTENTS

MAKE Bible Studies

The goal of every Christian is to glorify God and become more like Jesus. The process of realizing this goal is discipleship. Christ chose twelve disciples during His years of ministry on earth and commissioned them to continue the process of making disciples—of helping people become more like Him.

Since I am a disciple of Christ, my prayer is to do the same.

Some try to squeeze the process of discipleship into a concise list with check-off boxes in front of the tasks "read your Bible," "attend church regularly," etc. While we encourage such spiritual disciplines, by themselves they don't make disciples. We may gain knowledge, but the end product will mirror the Pharisees more than Jesus.

If we intend to become more like Jesus and help others do the same, we must do as He did. Jesus' method for discipleship was quite simple. He used relationships fueled by God's Word to produce disciples.

Jesus didn't instruct His disciples to check off behavioral boxes as they went about their lives. He didn't assign homework involving endless questions and intense reading before they could come back and talk to Him. He *lived* with them—pouring into their lives and using their relationships (with Him and each other) as the conduit for spiritual growth and maturity.

If that's how He produced disciples, that's how we should too.

MAKE Bible Studies exist to make disciples by igniting relationships fueled by God's Word. These studies are intensely practical and life applicable. They're intentionally designed with relationships in mind—first your relationship with God, then your relationships with others in a group setting.

MAKE studies work because they're simple and fiercely poignant. They're designed to be the launching point for discussion, action, and transformation—merging God's truth with life in practical, engaging ways. Be as involved as you want. You have the option of engaging in the personal Bible study and commentary as your group moves through the group study, or simply show up on group nights for discussion. (Homework is not necessary, though it is helpful.)

The following resources are available for your convenience: an Introduction to Judges, personal Bible study questions, and passage commentaries for each week. A special note to group leaders: read through the commentary and study guides prior to your group meeting. Pray over the material, make notes, and think of ways to instigate further discussion. Also, before beginning every week, discuss how your group members incorporated the prior week's challenges into their lives and faith. A leader's guide for the group studies is available at www.mjfpublishing.com.

Enjoy the journey of becoming more like Jesus through this study of Judges. Keep your eyes open and your heart hungry for His transforming power in your life and the lives of your group members!

Introduction to Judges

Judges is one of the darkest, most intense books in the Bible. Few books expose the depths of human depravity like Judges, and through it God reminds us of our dire need for Him.

We find several well-known stories and characters within the pages of this book—from Gideon testing God with fleece to the incomprehensible strength (and subsequent foolhardiness) of Samson. The stories that fill Judges leave us engaged, but when we submerge beneath the surface of entertainment, the black reality of sin hits us hard.

Fortunately, God gives us this book to help us savor His grace and learn from others' mistakes. Through our journey through Judges, we'll witness God's unrelenting faithfulness, mercy, and justice—all of which juxtapose Israel's degenerative cycle of spiritual fervor: their faith*less*ness, selfishness, and injustice.

HISTORY

```
        ┌─────────────────┐
        │    ABRAHAM      │
        │    & SARAH      │
        └─────────────────┘
                 │
                 ▼
        ┌─────────────────┐
        │     ISAAC       │
        │   & REBECCA     │
        └─────────────────┘
           │         │
           ▼         ▼
      ┌────────┐ ┌────────┐
      │  ESAU  │ │ JACOB  │
      └────────┘ └────────┘
                     │
                     ▼
        12 TRIBES OF ISRAEL
```

REUBEN	JOSEPH	DAN	GAD
SIMEON	BENJAMIN	NAPHTALI	ASHER
LEVI	ZEBULUN	ISSACHAR	JUDAH

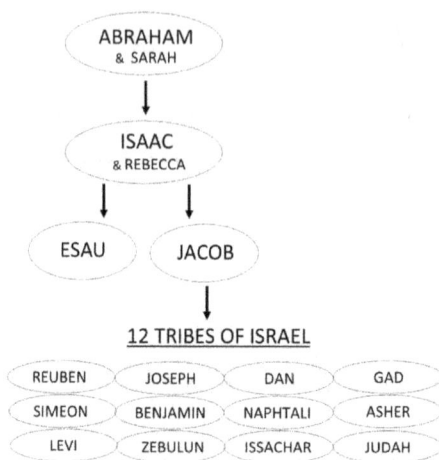

The best place to begin a study is at the beginning. We're going to back up before Judges and look at the beginning of the Bible, tracking Israel's history to see how their past influenced who they are when Judges begins.

We learn a lot from our past. While we're inevitably products of it, we don't have to be its victims. Israel would have done well to learn this lesson.

Our journey begins in Genesis 12, when God promises a man named Abram that he would be the father of a great and mighty nation. God enters this covenant with Abram and even gives him a fancy name-change, Abraham, to reflect the gravity of His promise. Abraham would be the father of a new nation (land included), one that was supposed to represent God to the world and bring peoples from all over to worship and adore the one true God.[1]

Way beyond childbearing years, Abraham and his wife, Sarah, have a son named Isaac. Years later, Isaac marries a woman named Rebecca and bears twin sons, Esau and Jacob. God chooses Jacob as the heir of His covenant, and Jacob becomes the father of twelve sons, who become the patriarchal leaders of the twelve tribes of Israel.

During Jacob's time as father to his twelve sons, the earth endures an incapacitating drought that forced people from several countries to travel to Egypt. God uses one of Jacob's sons, Joseph, to save multitudes from starvation and death. Joseph's high-ranking position in Egypt enables him not only to provide for his family, but also to bring them to live with him in security and stability within the borders of Egypt.

Unfortunately, when the reigning Pharaoh dies, his successor neglects to remember the favor of Joseph and his family. This Pharaoh feels threatened by the growing population of the Hebrews (Israel, Abraham's descendants) and decides to control the situation by enslaving them.

The Hebrews remain enslaved to the Egyptians for four hundred years. But God hears their cries of desperation (they are His chosen people, after all) and He raises up a man to deliver them from Egypt. Though an unlikely candidate, Moses is used by God to deliver Israel from their captivity and sets them on their way to the land promised by God to Abraham several hundred years prior.

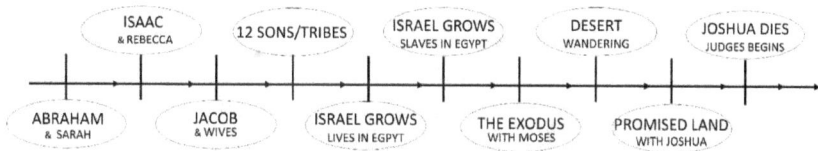

ISAAC & REBECCA · 12 SONS/TRIBES · ISRAEL GROWS SLAVES IN EGYPT · DESERT WANDERING · JOSHUA DIES JUDGES BEGINS

ABRAHAM & SARAH · JACOB & WIVES · ISRAEL GROWS LIVES IN EGYPT · THE EXODUS WITH MOSES · PROMISED LAND WITH JOSHUA

If only Israel had chosen gratitude rather than grumbling. As it turns out, as soon as they are freed from Pharaoh's grasp, Israel turns against Moses (and God by extension) with their complaining and grumbling. Their selfishness and lack of faithfulness induce a great punishment from God—they are banned to roam the desert for forty years and won't enter the Promised Land until that sinful generation dies off.

The next generation is finally led into the much-anticipated land by Joshua, Moses' successor. Joshua maintained a close relationship with God, and although he didn't accomplish all he set out to do (clearing out the Promised Land and establishing it as Israel's), he does manage to end his life and leadership on a solid note. Upon his death, Israel recommits their lives to following God and to finishing what they began—taking the Promised Land as their own as God commanded.

At this point, the book of Judges begins. Israel is without a single prominent (human) leader for the first time in two generations and seems eager and ready to conquer the remaining land.

POLITICS

Because Israel has no formal leader and they've been a free nation for only two generations, they're fragile politically. God has always been their true leader; now is the time for them to revel in that and follow Him with all their hearts. Increased awareness of our dependence tends to drive us toward the One we're dependent on. Israel would do good to understand this. They've had human leaders until this point, but Moses and Joshua represented their true leader (God) to them. Now Israel can skip a step and simply follow God, if they're wise.

But they're different than other nations, and they find this fact difficult to overlook. Most nations have a human king (or a recognized set of leaders) who rule with complete power. Their words are law, and everyone bows to their authority. Israel has no such leader, which is especially difficult since until this point, they've had clearly established human leadership.

Along with no leader, Israel also has no military to speak of. Again, they were slaves for much of their ancestry; now they're desert nomads who have only recently accrued select portions of land. They're not warriors and they have precious little experience in battle following Joshua's lead. Now they're expected to continue their mission without a specified leader—a daunting task indeed!

They don't know how to exist without a human authority figure, though they aren't without instruction. God wants to be their leader (politically and otherwise). And like everyone else, they're given a chance to follow Him…which they hardly do.

SPIRITUALLY

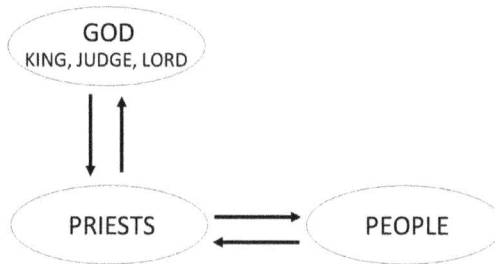

Israel fails to realize that their lack of a human leader leaves that much more room for their heavenly one to exercise His sovereign control over their lives. Their spiritual heritage is a bit flimsy as well. Though they know they belong to Yahweh and have a spectacular history of His involvement in their lives, He's very different than the gods other nations worship. He doesn't have an image they can recreate and bow down to, and He can't be manipulated through the giving of offerings and sacrifices. This God is different and demands an entirely new structure of worship than they're used to.

God knows this will be a challenge for them, so he provides them with priests—specifically ordained people who spend their lives studying His law, serving in His tabernacle, and giving spiritual guidance to His people. Israel was never left alone in their unique predicament. God gives them people to help lead them to Him—people who could be advocates on His behalf.

Israel's spiritual state may be fledgling, but it has the potential to thrive if only they'll abide by the words of their God.

CULTURALLY

The Israelites at this time are a new nation trying to merge their identity with what God has revealed to them. They are set apart from their pagan counterparts in diet, worship practices, the treatment of women, family structures, economics, and internal laws. God calls them to be as unique to the world as He is to the idols of it. By obeying God through their cultural practices, they revealed Him to a world completely lost without Him.

Israel is in a special position at this time in their history—one that we Americans can hardly identify with comprehensively. We don't understand what it's like to move to a foreign land with the intent to make it ours. Some of our ancestors may have experienced such a situation, but the concept is far removed from our comfortably established lives. For this study, let's place ourselves in the shoes of the Israelites as best we can. Let's tune into their situations and experience their stories as if we are one of them—all the while praying that God will reveal His heart so we can apply His truth to our lives today.

TITLE

Names and titles are significant, and we must exercise caution in gleaning meaning from them. The English term "judges" is a translation of the Hebrew word *soptim*, meaning both "deliverers" and "saviors."[2] Those referred to as judges within this book of the Bible should not be thought of like our modern courtroom judges. Rather, they are people whom God chose to rescue His people, Israel, from their enemies.

As far as we can tell from Scripture, Israel is left without a human leader after Joshua's death, since didn't he mentor a successor. Instead, they wisely attempt letting God reign as King and their Leader.

We learn quickly that this method didn't work for long. Left on their own, Israel is an uninspiring bunch, falling into cycles of degeneration that lead them further away from God, not toward Him.

To uphold His covenant and display His unending mercy, God intervenes over and over again. He chooses to raise up judges to deliver Israel from the oppressors who have enslaved them. Not only do these judges save Israel politically, they also lead (or try to lead) God's people morally and spiritually for a time. Judges were to lead Israel as God's chosen leaders, most doing so until they died.

Twelve judges are mentioned throughout the book. Six of these are minor or noncyclical judges, and the other six are major or cyclical judges. Cyclical and noncyclical refer to the judge story's adherence to the "Cycle of Degeneration" present within the book of Judges (see Week One Commentary). Cyclical judges follow the cycle to some degree with mention of at least one component of the cycle. Noncyclical judge stories neglect to include components of the cycle, dubbing them "out of the cycle" or "noncyclical."

We should not assume these judges were necessarily of high moral aptitude and impeccable integrity. What *ought* to be isn't a reality for the judges any more than it is for us today. In fact, their moral decay often makes them resemble Israel rather than God in His holiness. Nevertheless, God uses them (and uses us despite our many faults) to accomplish His great purposes to His glory and our good.

MAJOR THEMES

The (human) author of Judges chooses to remain anonymous, but we can stand confident in the book's validity as a part of the Canon. The Holy Spirit inspired the composition of Judges as He did the other sixty-five books of the Bible, and if we lean on Him, He'll ignite our reading, interpretation, and application of its passages to our lives (2 Tim 3:16-17).

Several major themes are present within this rich book, but three stand out with blinding clarity:

1. Israel's Degenerating Faith (and its consequences)
2. God's Unrelenting Faithfulness (and its ramifications)
3. God's Ability to Use Any Amount of Faith for His Glory

Israel's strongest moment resides within the first couple of verses of the book. From that point on, they find themselves falling deeper and deeper into the pit of their own destruction. They persistently disobey God—neglecting to follow and obey Him despite clear commands to do otherwise. As the book progresses, we witness their faith degenerating because of their constant disobedience to God, and it all but disappears by the end of the book.

Situated in dire contrast to Israel's unimpressive state is God's unrelenting faithfulness. He can and does use any amount (even almost nonexistent amounts) of faith for His glory. Even though Israel's actions deserve severe retribution, God extends grace, mercy, and lovingkindness, almost to the point of nausea for the reader. Our sense of justice burns against Israel with increasing frustration as we watch them deliberately forfeit favor with God only to be given grace time and again. Yet He still uses them and creates beauty from the ashes they give Him. Our anger seethes against Israel, but only until we realize, quite regrettably, that we're often of no greater standing in our faith than they are. But we're getting ahead of ourselves.

Prepare for an awakening to the utter depravity of human nature apart from God as well as to the unrelenting faithfulness of God our Savior, the ultimate Judge.

WEEK ONE:
Failure

JUDGES 1:1-3:6
PERSONAL STUDY QUESTIONS

1. Who is the first tribe of Israel to go against the Canaanites? (1:2)

2. How do you think you would've responded to such a call?

3. Do they completely obey God in going? Why or why not? (1:3)

4. Do you believe delayed or incomplete obedience is true disobedience? Why or why not?

5. Does the tribe of Benjamin succeed in driving out the Jebusites from their allotted territory? (1:21)

6. What tactic does the tribe of Joseph use to conquer Bethel (formerly known as Luz)? (1:23-25)

7. While their strategy seems to work, ultimately it fails. They destroyed one city only to have another pagan one spring up. Who built the twin city to the one Joseph destroyed? (1:25-26)

8. List the tribes that fail to drive out the people in their God-given land: (1:27-35)

   -
   -
   -
   -
   -
   -

9. How does Israel disobey God? (2:1-2)

10. What is Israel's punishment for disobedience? (2:3)

11. What's one reason the Israelites fall away from God? (2:10-13)

12. What causes you to slip away from God? What distracts you from total devotion to Him?

13. List three nations/peoples God causes to remain in the Promised Land. (3:3)

    -
    -
    -

14. Why were these nations allowed to remain? (3:4)

15. Has God allowed something difficult to remain in your life (a "thorn in your flesh") in order to drive you closer to Him? If so, what is it? Do you find yourself moving toward God because of it or slipping further away from Him?

COMMENTARY

Like most books, Judges begins with an introduction. Two, actually. The first (1:1-2:5) gives us Israel's perspective of their current situation, and the second (2:6-3:6) gives us God's perspective, along with a spiritual overview of what's to come in the book.

SECTION ONE (JUDGES 1:1-2:5)

The first introduction connects seamlessly with the conclusion of Joshua, as if the two books were written as one. Joshua is dead and Israel decides to capitalize on their spiritual momentum by going out to conquer the remaining people in the Promised Land.

Israel starts well by asking God which tribe should go first in their conquest against the Canaanites (1:1). The term "Canaanites" here is a generic name for the gentiles (or non-Jews) living in the land.[3] Israel's question may seem insignificant, but since their past is colored with the sin of taking matters into their own hands, it's quite noteworthy that they paused and asked God what to do before taking action.

God responds immediately, blessing their decision to involve Him from the start. He answers their question by calling Judah to go first and also makes them a promise—they'll be victorious (1:2). (Little side note: the tribes of Israel are named after the sons of Jacob, and the Bible authors often refer to them as individuals, i.e. "Judah said to Simeon his brother." While sounding like the individuals, we should read these references as if they were written, "The *tribe* of Judah said to Simeon *their brothers*," since the original twelve sons have long since passed away by this point.)

The tribe of Judah never asked who would win the battle; they asked who should go first. But God extends a guarantee of victory nonetheless. Their faith must have experienced a wonderful boost!

Well, their faith *should* have experienced a boost. God's response should have infused Judah with confidence and adrenaline—readying them to take on their enemies. But their bold request of faith disintegrates within moments of God's reply. Instead of relishing God's promise, they undercut it by asking their brother tribe, Simeon, to go with them to battle (1:3). If Simeon will help, Judah promises to return the favor when Simeon conquers their own land.

Can you imagine the scene?

God just told Judah, the largest tribe of Israel, to step up and conquer His enemies with blazing glory. Instead of pounding their chests and storming the front lines, Judah turns aside to ask Simeon, one of the smallest tribes, to hold their hands during battle. Picture a grown man asking a little boy to help him cut down a tree with an ax. Utterly ridiculous! That's not to mention that this tactic completely undermines what God just said. It seems Judah trusts Simeon more than they trust God, the One who created both Judah and Simeon, as well as the entire universe they were standing in. Not off to a great start, Judah.

It's easy to bash Judah for their failure to trust God. But before you do, ask yourself this: *How often do we do the same?* When God calls us to tithe more consistently, tell someone about Jesus, or go on that mission trip, we doubt, question, and do everything we can to make excuses for not doing it. If we're honest, we're hardly more impressive than Judah. Don't let our differing circumstances blind us from our own weak faith and lack of trust.

Using Simeon as a crutch, Judah musters enough confidence to go to battle. What happens? Why, exactly what God said would happen. Victory! Judah conquers the Canaanites and Perizzites, killing ten thousand men (1:4). But victory isn't complete without the capture of the enemy's leader, which is exactly what they do (1:5). Adoni-Bezek, the leader of the Canaanites and Perizzites, flees when he realizes that he and his troops don't stand a chance against Israel (1:6). But he doesn't make it far before Judah catches and captures him. In a showcase of domination over him,

Judah cuts off Adoni-Bezek's thumbs and big toes. While this may sound disturbing to us, captives were often mutilated and abused in that day. In fact, the Assyrian king Ashurnasirpal II boasted of his inhumane treatment of captives:

> In strife and conflict I besieged (and) conquered the city [Tela]. I felled 3,000 of their fighting men with the sword. I carried off prisoners, possessions, oxen, (and) cattle from them. I burnt many captives from them. I captured many troops alive: from some I cut off of some their arms (and) hands; from others I cut off their noses, ears, (and) extremities. I gouged out the eyes of many troops. I made one pile of the living (and) one of heads. I hung their heads on trees around the city.[4]

As you can see, inhumane treatment of captives was not only accepted, it was expected. Even Adoni-Bezek isn't surprised to lose his thumbs and big toes. He observes irony in his life, saying, "Seventy kings with their thumbs and their big toes cut off used to gather up scraps under my table; as I have done, so God has repaid me" (1:7a). He gives us a glimpse into Solomon's wisdom expressed in Ecclesiastes—there's nothing new under the sun (Ecclesiastes 1:9). At some point, we all come to our end; for Adoni-Bezek, the end involved retribution for the actions he conducted while living. After being mutilated, he goes with the Israelites to Jerusalem to die.

Judah continues their conquest in Jerusalem (1:8). This Jerusalem predates the one most familiar to us. While it is the same geographical location, at this time, it is likely a Jebusite border city located between Judah and Benjamin. Judah captures and burns it but probably doesn't preserve ownership very long before the Jebusites resume custody.[5]

After the Jerusalem raid, Judah heads down to fight against the Canaanites who lived in the hill country of the Negev, which was a vast desert lot located in the southern part of Judah (1:9).[6] They continue on and strike several more cities with death and destruction, including Sheshai, Ahiman, and Talmai (1:10).

These battles yield an awfully large slaughter, begging the age-old question: *Isn't this murder? Why did God tell Israel to kill off thousands of innocent people?*

Time forbids us from elaborating thoroughly on the subject, but since this is a repeating issue in Judges, we mustn't neglect it. Let's briefly explore this topic of apparent genocide by observing several key truths.

What is justice?

First things first. The slaughter ordained by God isn't technically a genocide. Genocide is defined as "the deliberate killing of people who belong to a particular racial, political, or cultural group."[7] God's command to wipe out the Canaanites isn't racially, culturally, or politically driven. Rather, it's morally or spiritually driven. God is exacting justice on a people consumed by evil; thus, we should call it judgment rather than genocide.

God is just. Justice is as much a part of the fabric of His being as are mercy, omniscience, and omnipotence. It's a part of who He is, and He executes justice completely and thoroughly. The problem isn't His justice; it's our perspective of it. We need to reevaluate and redefine justice in order to understand how righteous and just He is.

Webster defines justice as:

"The process or result of using laws to fairly judge and punish crimes and criminals."[8]

In other words, justice is righting wrongs. It has both positive and negative ramifications, depending on the side you're on. The negative side of justice is making people pay for their wrongs. When someone breaks a law, justice demands he make restitution. Thus, if a man steals from his company, justice requires that he pay back the money and then serve time in prison as punishment.

The positive side of justice is defending those who have been wronged. The thief who stole from his company robbed a single mother of her retirement funds. Justice demands that she be defended and her money reinstated.

Justice makes things right. It rights all wrongs.

Nothing seems right about killing, which is why we detest it so much. What could possibly be right about slaying thousands of people? It seems completely void of justice, which is why many people remain far from God. They don't want to be close to a God who kills on a whim. A God like that doesn't seem fair, so why should I trust Him with my life?

Such reasoning reveals the underlying issue: our fallibility. With our limited perspectives, we have a difficult time grasping the full prisms of truth. So when we hear about events like mass killings, we automatically attribute it to evil and unjustness. But what if it's not? *What if God was just to use Israel to kill thousands of people?*

I propose that very claim. The judgment against the Canaanites was necessary and just. To prove this, we must first have a standard by which to judge. The standards in our society are its laws. If the speed limit is 45 mph and we go 55 mph, we run the risk of getting a ticket. The speed limit is the standard of justice by which our behaviors are measured.

Sin is far more than just a "mistake."

So whose standard are we using in our study? God's. God's truth (as shown in His Word) is our ultimate standard of justice, and by it, our behaviors are judged. It's the most intense standard in existence…because it's perfection.[9] According to Scripture, God created a perfect world with perfect people (Adam and Eve) who never sinned. They lived a perfect life and enjoyed perfect community with God. This perfection is God's standard. Perfect is the way God desires His people and world to be. It's how He created it, and He expects it to mirror His own perfection.

Unfortunately, perfection didn't last long on earth. Adam and Eve decided to trust themselves (lean on their fallible perspectives) instead of trusting

God (whose perspective is infallible). Created beings thought they knew better than their Creator. They disobeyed Him by eating the forbidden fruit, and in doing so, ushered sin into the world like a cancer. Sin not only consumed Adam, Eve, and all their descendants (including us), but it also marred creation—all the animals, plants, weather, etc. The worst consequence of sin is that it seriously deformed the relationship between man and God. No longer could man walk with God unhindered in a state of perfection. Sin diseased the relationship and contaminated it beyond a cure—at least, any cure man could produce on his own.

The ultimate consequence of sin—any and all sin—is death. If Adam and Eve had remained in their perfect state and obeyed God, they would have lived with Him forever. But once they removed themselves from God's protective hand, they opened up inevitable doom—death. Death is the consequence of sin; it's what all sin deserves. But it's not limited to the death we think of when someone ceases breathing. Death in its fullest sense is eternal separation from God. We are eternal beings who will spend eternity either with God or away from Him. Sin broke the relationship between God and man, and that break automatically thrusts us into the throngs of hell.

Think of it this way. One drop of food coloring contaminates an entire pitcher of water, right? The smallest drop causes irreparable damage to the crystal-clear water, and once contaminated, the water has no chance of being made clean (or clear) again. Sin is like food coloring. The tiniest drop of sin (lies, theft, jealousy, lust, pride, etc.) contaminates our entire beings, and there's nothing we can do about it. We might be able to make restitution for our wrongs, but restitution never erases the fact that we have sinned.

Sin (our food coloring) is a big deal because it disqualifies us from being with God. God is perfect—completely pure (crystal-clear water, if you will). Crystal-clear water cannot be mixed with water that's been contaminated with food coloring without being contaminated itself. Thus, our sin separates us from God, making it impossible for us to be in fellowship with Him. The alternative for fellowship with God is fellowship with Satan in hell. Sounds harsh, but it's true (and, by the way, we're accountable to truth whether or not we want to believe it).

All of us are contaminated by sin, and justice from God requires adequate punishment for it—which is death. According to this logic (based on Scripture), the judgment in Judges against the Canaanites is not only justified, but it is completely necessary. God's standard is perfection and people (particularly the Canaanites) failed to uphold it. They were not perfect people; in fact, they reveled in quite a plethora of debasing sins.[10] The punishment for their failure is death and hell, which God has every right to enforce. In fact, true justice *demands* that God enforce punishment for the crimes we commit against Him. A perfect God must uphold justice—He must right all wrongs (i.e. punishing sin); otherwise He's not a God to admire, follow, and want as our Lord.

But wait...there's grace

Calling sin a mistake is like calling an elephant a mite. Sin is far graver than a mere mistake, for its consequences demand a price so high it's completely out of our reach. We can rectify mistakes, but we cannot rectify our sin. God is completely justified in leaving us in our sin and letting us rot in the hell we've chosen to pursue. But part of what makes God so amazing is His grace and mercy. While we deserve death and hell, we don't have to accept it as a foregone conclusion. God gives us grace, and He did the same for the Canaanites.

God wasn't content to leave us in our sin. He loved us too much to watch us wither away in death. He came up with a plan (the gospel) to redeem the world and reconcile us to Himself. In other words, He made a way to clean our contaminated water so we could be with Him. We can't clean our own water any more than we can separate food coloring from a pitcher of water. But God can, and that's exactly what He did.

The culmination of His plan came through Jesus Christ, the member of the Trinity who came to earth, lived a sinless life, died on the cross, was buried, and rose again. This adopted us into God's family, secured us into His glorious future, and made us ambassadors of this plan while we remain on earth. Jesus is God's gavel of justice. Through His sacrifice, our wrongs are righted in God's sight. He bore the consequences of our sin and took our place in death so that we may be restored to God. To put it simply, Jesus became contaminated by our sin so He could pour His righteousness into us. He pours His clear water into our colored water until it overflows with pure water and we stand justified before God.

God's grace through Jesus enforces justice (Jesus accepted the punishment we deserved) and upholds His love for us (we have the choice to accept the gift and be reconciled to Him even though we don't deserve it). We don't have to accept Christ's clean water. We can remain stuck in the muck and mire of our colored water, awaiting impending doom for eternity apart from Him. But even a child knows this isn't ideal! Given the chance to be made pure, clean, innocent, justified, and in right standing with God for all eternity *for our good*—who wouldn't jump at the opportunity?

Although Jesus hadn't yet been born when the Canaanites lived, God still extended a way of salvation to them through His people Israel. God gave the Israelites His law—the way to maintain a pure relationship with Him through obedience and sacrifices. Canaanites had the opportunity to join Israel in obeying God's laws and exercise faith in a Savior who would come one day. They could have accepted God's mercy, repented of their sins, and be restored to God. If they had, justice would have been upheld, and they could have embraced life anew with God as their leader.

Unfortunately, they forfeited their opportunity, and God gives us a record of it. Way back in Genesis, God tells Abraham that his descendants (Israel) would eventually enter and possess a land flowing with milk and honey. (These were good adjectives, I assure you.) However, before arriving, they would be sold into slavery and suffer four hundred years of captivity. Then

He tells Abraham why:

"For the iniquity of the Amorite is not yet complete."[11]

God allowed Israel to suffer four hundred years of captivity so the Canaanites (who were currently in the Promised Land) would have a chance to repent. He didn't want Israel moving in without giving the current residents a chance to see the light. And four hundred years is a long time! Many generations had the opportunity to repent and come to God. But instead, they kept sinning. They relished their cancer-like depravity and let it consume their lives through acts of debauchery and horrendous evils.

The Canaanites perpetually refused to taste the sweet nectar of God's grace, and this drew God to the line of justice. Judgment is often delayed but not forgotten. They marred the world long enough with their sins, so God decides to purge the world of them. Killing the Canaanites was not only necessary (they needed to be gone so Israel could take their rightful place in the land), it was absolutely just (their sin demanded the consequence of death, especially since they refused God's grace).

God is sovereignly omniscient

Another aspect of God that's crucial to our understanding of His justice is His sovereign omniscience. Sovereignty refers to His supreme and unmatched authority; omniscience means that He knows everything. His knowledge is limitless. This helps us understand the Canaanite judgment because it puts us in our place. We do not have unmatched authority, nor do we possess unlimited knowledge. God knew everything about the Canaanites, which means He knew (more than we ever could) the depths of their sin. Only God knows the hearts of man. While we hold out hope for change in people, God knows who's incapable of change and who will continue refusing His grace, no matter how many chances they get. Because He sanctioned the destruction of the Canaanites, we can rightly assume that they held no hope of change or reformation.

Hold onto hope

God's cleansing justice on earth is displayed in part now but will be carried out completely when Christ comes again. In the meantime, we need to redefine our understanding of justice to match His. *First, all of us deserve death because of our sin.* Sin is far more than a mistake that demands a slap on the wrist. It's a consuming plague that kills our souls like advanced cancer destroys a body. Thus, God has every right to leave us to the demise our sin requires. If we experience any good thing on earth, it's solely because of His grace, not our merit.

Second, although we deserve otherwise, God chooses to lavish us with grace. Since God needs to be fully just in order to be fully perfect, sin must be punished. That's why He gives us salvation through Jesus—the ultimate sacrifice who took our place at death's door. Christ received the penalty we deserved. If we accept Him, we stand as perfect in our positions with God. We will never be perfect on earth (dratted sin!) but we are forgiven, and His Spirit works in and through us to make us more Christ-like every day.

Finally, since God is infallible and we are not, we can trust in His sovereign omniscience. Even when bad things happen, we can stand secure, knowing He's in control and is working everything out for His glory and our good.

The Canaanite judgment is difficult to read about, and we'll never have an emotionally satisfying answer for the killings. We may comprehend it on an intellectual or theological level, but it's still never easy to hear about. The good news is that it shouldn't be. We should never be okay with sin and the judgment it entails, because we were created for perfection. But instead of cowering in resentfulness, we should do justice, love kindness, and walk humbly with our God (Micah 6:8). Use your righteous anger for good, and in those times when despair seems overwhelming, echo the cries of the saints who have come before us: "Come, Lord Jesus, come!" He's coming!

--

Judah is God's first agent for ushering Israel into the Promised Land, and what begins as a general account of conquests turns specific when Caleb and his family conquer Debir (1:11).

If you're acquainted with details of Israel's history until this point, you may recognize Caleb's name. Caleb stood with Joshua as the only two of twelve spies who determined the Promised Land was worth pursuing despite its forbearing residents. Though not an Israelite by blood (he was a Kenizzite), Caleb was grafted into Israel as a proselyte who professed faith in God (Numbers 32:12). In response to Caleb and Joshua's faith, God allowed them—and only them—to enter the land. All others from their generation, including Moses, were banned from entering because they lacked faith and disobeyed God.

So here we are. Joshua has died, but Caleb is alive and ready to claim the land he was promised years ago. He has a slight problem, though: he's old. He doesn't have the physical stamina, strength, or energy to fight as he once did, so he comes up with a plan. The man who conquers Debir for him will receive Caleb's daughter, Achsah, as a wife. Barely a moment goes by before Othniel, his younger brother, rises to the challenge and captures Debir for Caleb. Caleb honors his promise and gives Achsah to Othniel in marriage (1:12-13).

Now I know what you're thinking: *Othniel married his niece?* Yep. Sounds downright gross to us, but in that day it was pretty common to marry relatives (not full-blood relatives like brothers and sisters, but uncles and nieces definitely made the cut).

As it turns out, Achsah was quite the catch too. In a culture that treated women as objects to be owned, Caleb raised her with wisdom, respect, and dignity. After marrying Othniel, she had the presence of mind (and courage) to secure springs of water in addition to the land they had inherited (1:14-15). Smart woman! Springs of water in those days were of great value, and Achsah boldly asked for them, providing her family better opportunities for their future.

Achsah rode the wave of optimism that captivated Israel as they kept pursuing their land. She believed God's promise of land and took action in securing a portion of it for her family. Her faith stands in stark contrast to her tribe, Judah, who refused to proceed in battle without the help of their younger brother tribe, Simeon. Achsah plunges forward in faith with great courage; Judah hesitates and puts conditions on their obedience. It's easy to determine whose faith we should emulate!

Caleb's family secures their land as Judah continues their conquests. At this point the author includes an informative note about the Kenites, the descendants of Moses' father-in-law (1:16). Like Caleb and his family, this group of people grafted into the tribe of Judah. This means they voluntary converted to the faith of Israel—making Yahweh their God and identifying themselves as His people. Now that they're a part of Israel, they travel from the city of palms (most likely Tamar or another oasis settlement) and end up in the wilderness of Judah.[12]

As Judah's invasions near an end, they keep their promise to Simeon and help them conquer their land, which includes a city named Hormah (1:17). The victories until this point have been quite easy, and Israel must be feeling pretty good about themselves. Unfortunately, their unbridled success won't last much longer.

In a surprising turn of events, Judah's string of victories screeches to a halt. When they come to the last part of their invasion, they aren't able to secure victory because the Canaanites living in the valley have iron chariots (1:19). Remember, until now, Israel has been a bunch of desert wanderers with barely any military experience to boast of. They haven't even established a land for themselves, much less garnered a full military arsenal. By way of contrast, the nations occupying their land have deep roots and are well versed in warfare, which includes technology that far surpasses what Israel has access to.

But, you may be thinking, *they've been victorious until now. Why doesn't God think of a creative way to beat the iron chariots?* Great question. He definitely could have, but ultimately He didn't because Israel didn't remain faithful to Him. His response to their unfaithfulness is to leave some nations behind to serve as "thorns" in Israel's flesh. (But we'll dive into those details in a minute).

After Judah's momentum ceases because of the insurmountable iron chariots, the other tribes of Israel follow their demise. Benjamin fails to drive out the Jebusites, Manasseh doesn't conquer all the cities they are given, and neither do Ephraim, Zebulun, Asher, Naphtali, or Dan.

The tribe of Joseph makes a particularly embarrassing error as well. In an attempt to be cunning, Joseph sends spies to scout out Bethel, the city they wanted to conquer. The spies find a man and strike a deal with him: they'll let him and his family escape unscathed if he'll show them the entrance to the city. While this may sound like a good idea, it proved humiliating. Joseph secures victory over Bethel, but the man they released moves on and builds another city exactly like the one they just destroyed. All their work proves utterly worthless in the end (1:22-26).

By the end of chapter one, God gives us significant insight into the condition of Israel's conquest (1:27-36). Their land not only contains people who were supposed to be driven out, but its borders are defined by the enemy's occupancy of the land. What a sad tribute about Israel, who has anxiously awaited the Promised Land for years.

The beginning of chapter two explains why Israel failed to conquer the land (and it was more than lacking proper weaponry). God sends an angel to remind Israel of their covenant with Him: He'd give them a prosperous land, and they would follow and obey Him. Well, they failed. Not only did they break the covenant, but they made covenants with the pagans surrounding them! They refused to destroy the idolatrous altars, so in turn, God would allow their enemies to be aggravating thorns in their sides (2:1-5).

SECTION TWO (JUDGES 2:6-3:6)

Section One of the introduction started with strong hope and optimism, but Section Two provides us with what is happening behind the scenes on a spiritual level, and it leaves a sour taste in our mouths.

The beginning of this section brings us back to Joshua's death and reminds us yet again that Israel has no viable leader. All the elders who led with Joshua have died, and a generation rises up "who did not know the Lord, nor yet the work which He had done for Israel" (2:6-10).

Let's pause a moment. How on earth could a whole generation arise who didn't know the Lord? These people had seen God's miracles and heard about even more from their ancestors who lived during the time of Moses. Not only should they have been aware of God, they should have been in a constant state of awestruck wonder! It would be bad enough if they simply decided not to follow Him, but the fact that they didn't even know Him or what He had done for Israel takes their apostasy to a whole new level. (Side note: God always preserves a remnant of faithful believers, but they're sometimes unseen. The generation we're talking about here represents the majority of Israelites, but certainly not every individual.)

Who was at fault for this spiritual catastrophe? While many answers can be theorized, much of the fault lies with the parents of this new generation. As adults, parents, and grandparents, we have the responsibility and divine calling to invest in the lives of our children. If we don't teach them about God and nurture their relationships with Him, how can we expect the next generation to know and follow Him? While God holds the future, He's chosen to use people as His agents. How can we represent Him and expect our children to do the same if we're not constantly training them up in His ways?

The glaring gap of faith in Israel reveals a serious lack of education, the fault lying heavily upon the previous generation. While this new generation could have taught themselves of God and His laws (they did have the

Torah—the first five books of the Old Testament—at this point), lacking instruction from their parents significantly stinted their desire for God. The result? A faithless generation who forfeits the covenantal blessings God extended to them.

CYCLES OF DEGENERATION

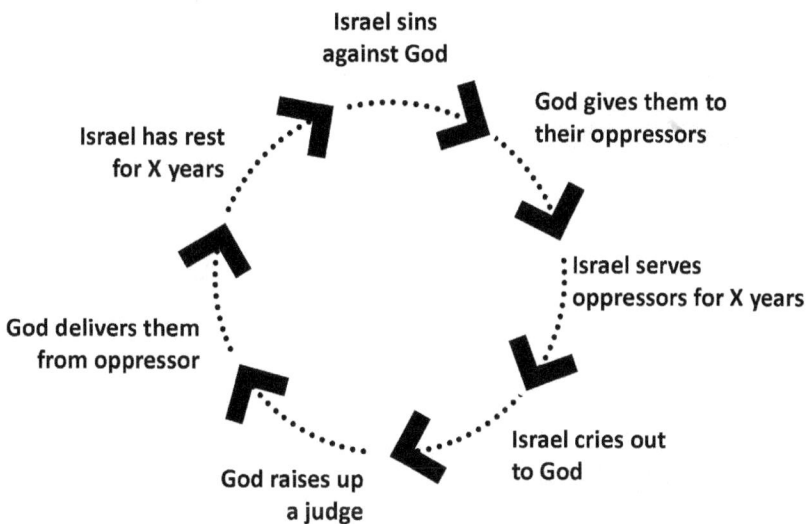

With a shaky spiritual heritage, Israel leaps into a cavern of disobedience and institutes repeated cycles of degeneration in their morality, spirituality, emotional state, and society (see graphic above). First, they sin against God by disobeying Him. They ignore Him and His covenant, choosing to do what they want instead of what He commands: they prostitute themselves with the pagan gods of the nations around them (2:11-13). Israel is supposed to be God's chosen people—a people who remain faithful to Him at all costs. Now they are harlots for idols—"gods" who aren't even gods at all![13]

Second, their behavior causes God's anger to burn against them, which results in Him giving them what they want (2:14-15). If they want to be like other nations, then He'd let them be conquered by them. (Let's see how long their admiration lasts when they're enslaved by them!) The irony makes us cringe: the people who were supposed to inhabit the land quickly become slaves of the previous (and evil) inhabitants. God delivered them from slavery in Egypt only to watch them become slaves again.

Sometimes the worst that can happen to us is getting our way. Apart from God, we have no idea what's best for us. Yet if we continue in stubbornness and reject His guidance, He may just let us have our way. We may enjoy it at first, but we quickly realize it wasn't the wisest choice. After dredging through the fallout of our realized desires, we wish we'd never gotten what we wanted. It's always best for pray for God's will. If it happens to align with what we want, great! If not, we'll learn that adjusting to His plan instead of imposing ours on Him always works best.

Third in the cycle, and not surprisingly, Israel doesn't like the consequences that come with getting their way. Turns out they aren't so fond of their enemy's gods and customs when it means being enslaved to them. So, fourth, they cry out to God—not out of repentance, mind you; but because they are weary of their punishment and want Him to bail them out.

Fifth, God hears Israel's cries and decides to rescue them (He has more patience than I do!). He raises up a judge, who (sixth) in turn delivers Israel from their oppressors (2:16). Israel finally experiences rest in their land, but far too soon begins the cycle again (2:11-23).

This cycle irritates us because Israel is stupid and seems bent on repeating their failure. It's like watching a child thrash his skull against a wall. We want to grab hold of him, turn him around, and yell, "Stop!" But we can't. They have to live with their mistakes, even when it costs them dearly.

As we've seen, one consequence of Israel's degenerating faith is that God leaves some pagan nations to occupy the Promised Land too (3:1). God now provides us with three reasons why: First, He wants to test Israel by teaching them about war (3:2). Again, Israel has no formal military experience. They were slaves in Egypt and then nomad wilderness wanderers. They're hardly a nation more than a people group, and they need to acquire some war skills if they are going to survive.

The nations left to provide this test were the five lords of the Philistines, the Canaanites, the Sidonians, and the Hivites "who lived in Mount Lebanon, from Mount Baal-hermon as far as Lebo-hamath" (3:3). These nations were to give Israel the opportunity to craft their fighting skills and develop military advancements that would help them in the future. But God has a second purpose as well—to test Israel's faith (3:4). He wants to elevate Himself in Israel's mind by comparing Himself to evil people. If Israel employs even the slightest bit of logic, they will clearly recognize who they should follow! He's giving them a chance to make an informed decision: follow God along with peace, joy, and eternal life, or follow the pagan nations, full of sin, despair, and debasing lifestyles.

So Israel lives with the Canaanites, Hittites, Amorites, Perizzites, Hivites, and Jebusites (3:5), faced with an immediate decision in light of their new situation. They need to decide how they are going to respond to God's test. Will they remain separate from the Canaanites, even though they live near them? Or will they intermingle with the Canaanites and fail their test of faith?

Despite having ample opportunity to make the right choice (as the Canaanites did before them), Israel fails the test. Instead of distancing themselves from the pagan nations, they mingle with them—so much so that they let their sons and daughters marry them (3:6). They become in-laws with people God wanted outlawed! And as if that's not horrible enough, they go further: they start serving their gods. They usurp God's rightful position in their hearts by choosing lifeless idols instead. They figuratively slap God in the face and blatantly disregard every act of mercy, grace, and patience He's poured into their lives.

The most aggravating part is that Israel's failure to be faithful forces us to recognize our own. Each of us struggles with a sin that grips us in its tireless claws and refuses to unhand us. We fail over and over, too weak to break free from its grasp. Our sin may be worry, lust, distrust, pride, or a host of others, but it all reveals our lack of faith in God. When we displace God in our hearts, we act as though He's not enough, as if we need something in addition to Him in order to be fully satisfied. What lunacy, since our hearts are restless only until they rest in Him.[14]

Yet, for both Israel and us, God intervenes. Those of us who know Him personally through Jesus know He'll never let us go. He may punish us and let us feel the pain of our poor choices, but His grace is limitless; His mercy abounds. As long as we have breath, He's not finished with us. He's using us as active agents in His plan of redemption in the world (i.e. the gospel).

God gave Israel many opportunities to turn back and run into His outstretched arms. The nations that didn't leave were supposed to remind them of Him by dire contrast (3:1-4). They were supposed to spur on a greater love for God. But the opposite came to pass. Israel drooled after the pagan nations with lust for self-satisfaction rather than self-sacrifice (3:5-6).

We face the same choice as Israel. Will we pursue God and the covenant we have with Him through Jesus, or stoop to degenerating faithlessness that leaves us empty and void of all contentment, peace, and joy?

GROUP STUDY

INTRODUCTION

"You failed."

Those two words carry more weight than we'd like to admit. Failure is burdensome. It weighs on our shoulders, crippling us from moving forward or trying again. The fear of failure is just as disheartening as failure itself, so much so that we often refuse to get up because we don't want to get knocked down again.

DISCUSS

- Share a time in your life when you failed.
- What were the consequences of that failure? Did it hurt someone? Did it cause a significant loss in profits in a work situation? How did it hurt you?

THE WORD

If failing was a sport, the nation of Israel would be the world champions. ***The biggest trophy of their failure would be for their lack of faith***. Despite the occasional good intentions, they failed to follow God. They chose to live *their* way instead of His way, ultimately failing Him, themselves, and the world they were supposed to be reaching for Him.

The book of Judges showcases Israel's failures better than perhaps any other book in the Bible. Read the passage below for a glimpse into their propensity to failure.

Then the sons of Israel did evil in the sight of the Lord and served Baals, and **they forsook the Lord, the God of their fathers, who had brought them out of the land of Egypt, and followed other gods from among the gods of the peoples who were around them, and bowed themselves down to them**; thus they provoked the Lord to anger. So they forsook the Lord and served Baal and the Ashtaroth.

The anger of the Lord burned against Israel, and He gave them into the hands of plunderers who plundered them; and He sold them into the hands of their enemies around them, so that they could no longer stand before their enemies. Wherever they went, the hand of the Lord was against them for evil, as the Lord had spoken and as the Lord had sworn to them, so that they were severely distressed.

Then the Lord raised up judges who delivered them from the hands of those who plundered them. **Yet they did not listen to their judges, for they played the harlot after other gods and bowed themselves down to them. They turned aside quickly from the way in which their fathers had walked in obeying the commandments of the Lord; they did not do as their fathers**.

When the Lord raised up judges for them, the Lord was with the judge and delivered them from the hand of their enemies all the days of the judge; for the Lord was moved to pity by their groaning because of those who oppressed and afflicted them. But it came about when the judge died, that **they would turn back and act more corruptly than their fathers, in following other gods to serve them and bow down to them**; they did not abandon their practices or their stubborn ways. (Judges 2:11-19)

Not only did Israel fail, but they were repeat offenders. They instituted a degenerative cycle of failing that was shameful to them, yet one we can learn from. Let's take a look:

Israel sins
against God

God gives them to
their oppressors

Israel has rest
for X years

Israel serves
oppressors for X years

God delivers them
from oppressor

Israel cries out
to God

God raises up
a judge

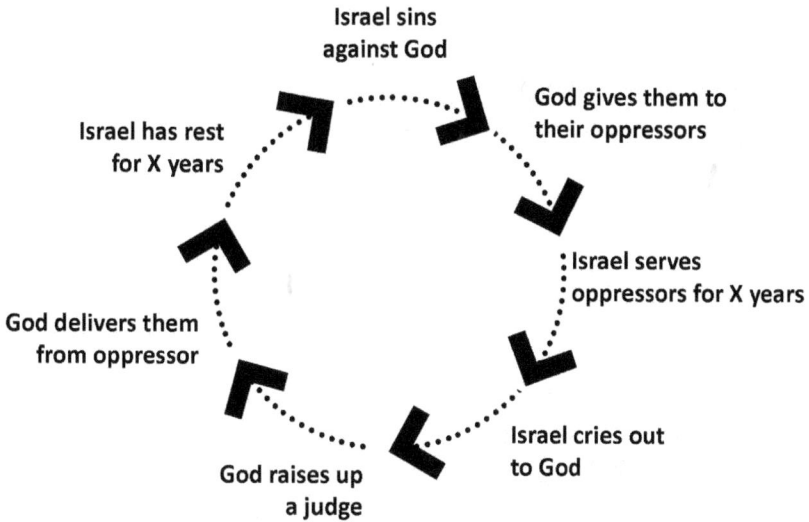

The cycle continued over and over, getting worse as Judges unfolds. What happened between the first and second points in the cycle? What made Israel fail? (The answer lies in the bolded sections of the passage above.)

Discuss/Action

While we can't always avoid failure, we can, like Israel, prevent much of it.

- What do you think Israel could have done to prevent their failure to follow God?
- Was the failure you talked about earlier preventable? How could you have prevented it?
- In what areas of your life are you prone to weakness that might lead to failure?
- What one action step can you take this week to prevent that failure?

Pray

WEEK TWO:
Say Yes

JUDGES 3:7-3:11
PERSONAL STUDY QUESTIONS

1. How does Israel sin against God? (vs. 7)

2. What areas in your life are a constant struggle of sin against God? Refusing to forgive someone? Bitterness? Pride? Adultery—emotional or physical? Racism?

3. Into whose hands does God sell Israel as punishment? (vs. 8)

4. What punishment or consequences are involved in the sin you struggle with most?

5. How long does Israel serve their enemies? (vs. 8)

6. Who is the judge God raises up to deliver Israel? (vs. 9)

7. What happens to Othniel and ensures his victory before he goes to battle? (vs. 10)

8. Does the battle seem complicated or fairly straightforward? (vs. 10)

9. There's beauty in simplicity, and God shines brighter through vessels unmarred with unnecessary gunk. Sin complicates and distracts us from our relationship with God. What are you doing in your life right now to fight the sin you struggle with most? Is it working? Do you need to try something else? If so, what?

10. How long does Israel have rest after their deliverance? (vs. 11)

COMMENTARY

Now that the introduction to Judges is complete, its author records the story of the first major judge of Israel, Othniel.

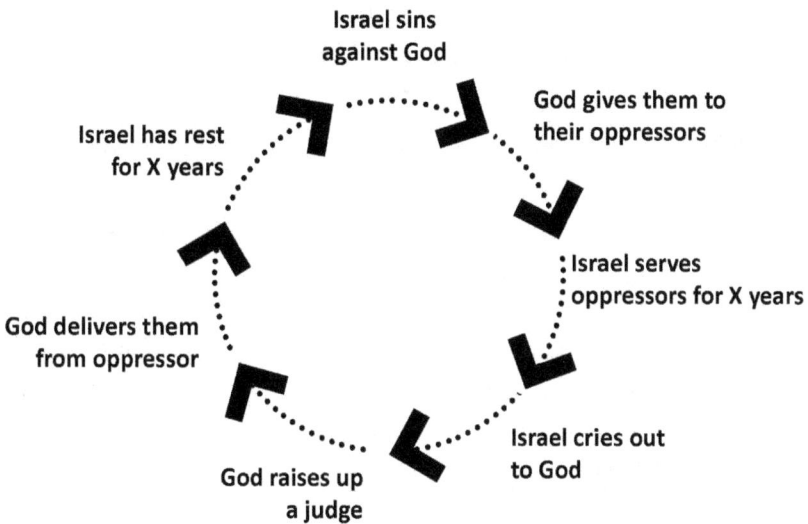

Before Othniel arrives on the scene, God tells us why a judge is needed in the first place: Israel descends into a state of disobedience. They forget the Lord and serve the Baals and the Asheroth[15], two very despicable actions (3:7).

"Forgetting the Lord" is not synonymous with simple forgetfulness (i.e. forgetting where we put our keys). Rather, it's a deliberate action against God Himself. Israel allowed their eyes to wander away from God—the one and only true God—and became more interested in what their neighbors were doing.

The "Baals" refer to one kind of Canaanite god—the god of storms and fertility.[16] The "Asheroth" is a fertility goddess, often represented by a vertical wooden pole.[17] These "gods" were popular among Israel's enemies and soon became popular with Israel too.

Israel's actions here (and elsewhere repeatedly in Judges) remind us of Romans 1:20-25:

> For since the creation of the world His invisible attributes, His eternal power and divine nature, have been clearly seen, being understood through what has been made, so that they are without excuse. For even though they knew God, they did not honor Him as God or give thanks, but they became futile in their speculations, and their foolish heart was darkened. Professing to be wise, they became fools, and exchanged the glory of the incorruptible God for an image in the form of corruptible man...they exchanged the truth of God for a lie, and worshipped and served the creature rather than the Creator.

Israel has access to the God of the universe, but instead of following Him, they choose to lust after man-made idols whose power existed nowhere other than their imaginations. It's no wonder God gets mad.

In response to Israel's idolatry, God sells them to Cushan-rishathaim, king of Mesopotamia, for a period of eight years (3:8). Cushan-rishathaim (we'll call him Cush for short) is an intimidating enemy. First, his name means "dark, doubly wicked," which clearly indicates that he is evil and malevolent in his militant dealings. This probably wasn't his literal name, but his nickname shows the severity of his reign. Second, he is motivated. In verse 8, the author says he came from Mesopotamia (or Aram-naharaim), which was quite far away from Israel (we don't know exactly how far, but it was far). Cush traveled the greatest distance of any oppressor to dominate Israel.[18]

Israel has good reason to fear Cush and want to be rescued from his domineering control. So they cry out to God for help (3:9). It would appear that they didn't cry out to Him until eight years have passed, which begs the question, *What took them so long? Were they that stubborn and unwilling to admit they were wrong?* We're not sure, but it would hardly be surprising.

Regardless of their timeline, Israel does cry out to God, but their cry is not one of repentance. Rather, it mirrors the cry of a little child who gets scolded for stealing a cookie. They have no interest in turning back to God; they only want Him to stop the pain and punishment! So they whine; and God, in His unrelenting mercy, sends a judge to deliver them (3:9).

God's first choice for judge is a man we're already familiar with—Othniel, the son of Kenaz, Caleb's younger brother—from chapter one. While we're not told why God chose him, we can deduce possible reasons from what we know about him and his family.

Othniel feared God

Othniel came from a family who feared and served God. As mentioned before, Caleb was one of the only two spies who trusted God to fulfill His word and weren't intimidated by the pagans living in the Promised Land. Since families were very close during that time, we can assume that Othniel followed in his uncle's footsteps of faith.

It's also interesting to note that the first judge of Israel is a non-Israelite by blood. Othniel and his family have been grafted into Israel (specifically the tribe of Judah) as proselytes because of their faith in God. But no matter how hard they tried, they'd never be of pure Israelite blood. How embarrassing for Israel in a culture all about bloodlines and nationality. Not only did they get themselves into a mess, but now God's not even using one of their own to deliver them! Instead, He uses an "outsider" who displays more faith in Him than any of His bloodline people did.

Othniel obeyed God

If you recall, Othniel received Achsah, Caleb's daughter, as a wife when he conquered Debir. This action—marrying someone within the tribe of Israel, especially someone who feared God—distinguishes Othniel from the rest of Israel. Othniel chose God when the rest of Israel chose idols and allowed their daughters to marry the pagans they failed to drive out.[19]

Othniel remained faithful and pure to God, which helps us understand why God chose him to deliver Israel.

Othniel rose to the challenge

God knew that Othniel would rise to the challenge and say yes to Him. Othniel had already proved his faithfulness to his family by going against Debir when he didn't have to. God knew he would also go against Cush despite his fierce reputation and would subsequently lead Israel for forty years after that. Othniel was willing to do what God asked—willing to say yes to Him despite intimidating circumstances.

Othniel is someone to be commended and admired. Most scholars believe the organizational structure of Judges displays Othniel as the ideal judge. From here on out, it's not just Israel who degenerates in their faith. The judges also begin to deteriorate in morality. Thus, Othniel stands as a fantastic example for Israel (and us) to follow.

After choosing Othniel, God does something wonderful—He allows His Spirit to come upon him as he heads out to battle (3:10).

The Spirit of the Lord

The Holy Spirit served a different role in the Old Testament than He does for followers of Jesus in the New Testament through today. Unlike today, the Holy Spirit didn't reside permanently with people who placed their faith in God. God was present with believers but chose to confine His official presence with them to the Tabernacle and Temple.[20]

Instead of personal and persistent presence, the Holy Spirit came upon people for specific and limited-time purposes. Only four judges are said to have had the Spirit come upon them, and "an evaluation of these texts shows that all involved empowerment for a physical activity."[21] We can think of the Holy Spirit's activity with the judges like a coat—He physically cloaked them with His presence, enabling them to accomplish otherwise-impossible feats.

Though Othniel was a successful warrior once in the past, by the time God calls him to lead Israel as a judge, he is advanced in years.[22] He isn't physically able to lead an army against a fierce king, much less expect to defeat him. But God chooses him, and where He leads, He always provides. Nothing is impossible with Him (Philippians 4:13).

God empowers Othniel to carry out his mission by clothing him with the Holy Spirit. While he gains the physical and perhaps mental stamina to fulfill his calling, Othniel does not receive spiritual benefits (at least directly) with this anointing. He, along with the remaining judges, receive strength, but not salvation or any other spiritual components the Spirit is now often associated with.[23]

Those who accept Christ as their personal Lord and Savior today receive the Holy Spirit as a permanent resident in our lives and hearts. He seals our salvation and indwells us as our ever-present help and guide.[24]

Once endowed by the Holy Spirit, Othniel goes to battle against Cush. This battle account is one of my favorites in all of Scripture, because its simplicity flaunts God's overwhelming presence. The entire battle is restrained to one verse (3:10b):

> When he went out to war, the Lord gave Cushan-rishathaim king
> of Mesopotamia into his hand, so that he prevailed over Cushan-
> rishathaim.

That's it. Blissfully simple, yet profound in power. Othniel does nothing to draw attention to himself; instead, he complies with God's plan and allows Him to lead as He sees fit. The result speaks for itself—a swift and comprehensive victory for Israel.

God delivers Israel from their first terrorizing enemy since Egypt, and they experience sweet rest for forty years (3:11). Othniel continues his leadership prowess throughout the entire four decades, remaining faithful until the very last day of his life.

One of the most admirable goals we can pursue is to live in such a way that God's glory is all that's visible when people look at us. I often pray that God would leave His fingerprint on everyone He brings into my life so they remember Him, not me. Othniel accomplished this, and the stories recorded about him in Scripture leave ample room for God's light, unveiling His majesty in every respect. We'd do well to follow Othniel's example—to live faithfully to God, ready and willing to say yes to Him, even when everyone else seems to be saying no.

GROUP STUDY

INTRODUCTION

Awkward.

That moment when you realize you should take a stand for righteousness when everyone around you is doing the opposite. *Oh, it's just a little flirting; no big deal. Come on, man, another drink won't kill you. Did you hear about what she did last week?*

These situations present us with a choice. We're going to say YES to something—either to the Holy Spirit nudging us in the right direction or the booming voice in our fallen brains, tempting us to concede to what we know is wrong.

Our yesses (whichever direction they go) set us up for either success or failure—spiritually, morally, emotionally, physically, etc. That "flirting" will either stop and lead us closer to Christ or continue and possibly lead to an affair. Another drink may be okay for some, but you know it's not good for you, and that compromise leads to a host of unpleasant scenarios. Gossiping may seem indulgent in the moment, but it leads to schisms in relationships and harms more people than just the object of the conversation.

We each experience opportunities to say yes. *The question is: to whom will we say it?*

DISCUSS

- Share a time when you said yes in a tricky circumstance—for good or for bad.
- What was the outcome?

THE WORD

Othniel, the first major judge, was a yes man...to the *right* thing. When tough circumstances presented themselves to him, he made the right decision, following God instead of his fears, insecurities, or a plethora of other doubts. Read the passage below for a glimpse of his yesses.

> Then from there he went against the inhabitants of Debir (now the name of Debir formerly was Kiriath-sepher). And Caleb said, "The one who attacks Kiriath-sepher and captures it, I will even give him my daughter Achsah for a wife." **Othniel the son of Kenaz, Caleb's younger brother, captured it;** so he gave him his daughter Achsah for a wife. (Judges 1:11-13)

> When the sons of Israel cried to the Lord, the Lord raised up a deliverer for the sons of Israel to deliver them, Othniel the son of Kenaz, Caleb's younger brother. The Spirit of the Lord came upon him, and **he judged Israel. When he went out to war**, the Lord gave Cushan-rishathaim king of Mesopotamia into his hand... (Judges 3:9-10)

Othniel's yesses weren't easy. Look closely at the bolded portions of the text above.

- What was involved in Othniel's decision to step up and say yes?
- What do you think he had to sacrifice in order to say yes to God, both in going to war and then judging Israel (a clearly obstinate people) for forty years?

DISCUSS/ACTION

Othniel's accounts of saying yes to God directly contrast Israel's accounts of saying no to Him. Othniel established a healthy pattern; Israel established one that would lead to their demise over and over again. Our yesses establish momentum—either for good or bad. The further along we go in a particular direction, the more difficult it is to turn the other way.

- In what area of your life do you find it difficult to say yes to God?
- What compromises are you tempted to make when you find yourself in a tricky situation in that area?
- What's one action step you can take this week to say yes to Him instead of the things leading you away from Him?

PRAY

WEEK THREE:
Use What You've Got

JUDGES 3:12-3:31
PERSONAL STUDY QUESTIONS

1. Who does God strengthen against Israel because they did evil in His sight again? (vs. 12)

2. Who does the king partner with to defeat Israel? (vs. 13)

3. How long does Israel serve this enemy? (vs. 14)

4. When we fall into sin, we get "stuck" for a season in life. The length of the season depends on several factors, but it's certainly not a waste of time. We can learn a lot from our times of struggle.

5. Think of a time you strayed from God. How long were you in that season? What did you learn from it?

6. Who does God raise up as judge to deliver Israel? (vs. 15)

7. What is a unique trait about him? (vs. 15)

8. What does he make in preparation to attack the king of Moab? (vs. 16)

9. How does Ehud get the king alone? (vs. 19-20)

10. How does Ehud kill the king? (vs. 21-22)

11. What happens that allows Ehud to escape without being caught? (vs. 23-26)

12. How many Moabites do Ehud and his armies kill that day? (vs. 29)

13. How long does Israel have peace after this victory? (vs. 30)

14. Who judges Israel after Ehud (the first minor judge)? (vs. 31)

15. How does he subdue the Philistines (what does he use)? (vs. 31)

16. We must use what we've got. God's given us everything we need to follow and obey Him, though our tools may look different than others'. What are your strengths? How can you use them to better follow God in your daily life?

COMMENTARY

Ehud

Almost immediately after Othniel dies, Israel slips back into faithlessness. The text doesn't tell us exactly how they messed up this time, but we know that whatever they did was awful because the author repeats it twice in one verse (3:12). Their particular sin was most likely idolatry, but that's not the point. The point is not *how* they turn away from God, but *that* they turn away from Him...again.

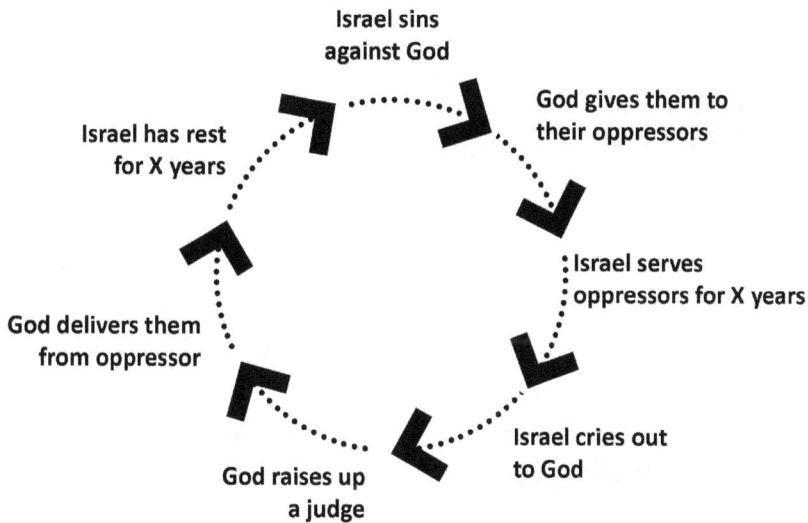

Israel sins
against God

God gives them to
their oppressors

Israel has rest
for X years

Israel serves
oppressors for X years

God delivers them
from oppressor

Israel cries out
to God

God raises up
a judge

Also unmentioned in this passage is the anger of the Lord. But we can rightly assume He's less than thrilled because He strengthens Israel's enemies against them (3:12). He's giving them into the hands of the "lover" they chose over Him.

Whereas in Othniel's account, God "sold" Israel into the hands of their enemies, this time He actually *strengthens* their enemies—empowering them to overcome and oppress. How vast the irony! God's strengthening of Eglon (the bad guy) stands in stark contrast to His strengthening of

Othniel (the good guy) in the previous passage. God refuses to tolerate Israel's sin for another moment, so instead of strengthening them to resist their enemies, He strengthens their enemies to overpower them.

Interestingly enough, this is the only time in the book of Judges that God specifically gives power to Israel's enemies. Other times He "sells" or simply "gives" Israel into their enemies' hands. In this account, He gives power to Eglon, which indicates that Eglon wasn't all that strong before. Unlike Cush, who was a powerful enemy, Eglon is weak. He needs help to subdue Israel, which is exactly what God provides him with. Another embarrassing blow to Israel! First, they're saved by a judge who isn't related to them by blood. Now their own God is raising up a weak enemy to overpower them.

Eglon exercises God's dose of strength wisely by gathering two other people groups to go against Israel with him—Ammon and Amelek. Together they capture the city of palm trees, which is Jericho, and oppress Israel for eighteen years (3:13-14).

Jericho may spark a memory of a children's Sunday school song in your mind: "Joshua fought the battle of Jericho, and the walls came a-tumbling down!" Joshua did, in fact, fight a battle at Jericho, and the walls did come tumbling down. The Jericho battle is the first battle Israel encountered under Joshua's leadership—the very first in their pursuit of the Promised Land (Joshua 6). Israel never rebuilt the city, so the "city of palm trees" would've been a mound of rubble. But the site did keep its military advantages with a good water supply and its dominant location in the Jordan valley.[25]

Israel's faithlessness caused them to fall hard and fast. Within a couple of generations, these undefeatable warriors deteriorate into a crushed, scared people. Instead of reigning conquerors, they're ridiculed captives desperately needing a deliverer.

Before introducing the judge who will come to Israel's rescue, we must take note of the uniqueness of this particular captivity. While numerous evil kings and leaders occupy the pages of Scripture, Eglon is a bad guy who's hard to forget. First, his name means "calf-like." Irony builds when we read verse 17, which states (quite randomly) that he was "a very fat man." Thus, Eglon king of Moab is effectively a "fat cow." If that makes you laugh, good; it's supposed to! Who says God doesn't have a sense of humor?

Israel's captivity is humiliating, but that they are conquered by a "fat cow" raises the level of insult even more. This is a downright embarrassing situation, and one they brought upon themselves. God didn't get through to them with the Cushan-rishathaim captivity, so now He adds a heap of insult to the mix, hoping to get their attention.

After eighteen years of shame, Israel decides they've had enough (3:15). Like before, they cry out to God; but again, this cry isn't one of repentance. It's the cry of a child whining about his punishment—not because he's sorry, but because he doesn't like what he's enduring.

In yet another act of mercy, God answers their cry (3:15). His choice of deliverer is a left-handed Benjamite named Ehud. (Eglon = bad guy; Ehud = good guy). Benjamites descended from Jacob's son Benjamin—the child whose birth took the life of Jacob's favorite wife, Rachel. Benjamin was the youngest brother of the twelve, and though his mother named him Ben-oni ("son of my sorrow") at first, his father changed it to Benjamin ("son of my right hand"). In this name we see more irony since Ehud, a Benjamite, is a *left*-handed man.

This left-handed Benjamite needs a plan. He's going to take on an evil "fat cow" of a man, and apparently isn't fond of the traditional methods of battle, so he makes up his own. He quickly devises a strategy combining his unique left-handedness, bravery, and wit.

First, the weapon. Ehud plans to get up close and personal with Eglon, and he needs to be prepared. The problem is that he doesn't have a weapon. Israel's captors had stripped them of their weapons so they couldn't stage a coup. Pretty smart move for Moab, for it crippled any chance of resistance in Israel.

But Ehud isn't deterred. If he doesn't have a weapon, he'll make one. Using the resources available to him, Ehud forges a double-edged dagger that's about a foot in length (3:16). He then fastens it to his right thigh, presumably with a custom-made sling, hiding it well under his cloak.[26] Eglon's guards would most likely check for weapons, but they'd usually check the left thigh, since that's where right-handed men would hide weapons for a quick draw. By fastening the dagger to his right thigh, Eglon evades the suspicion of the guards and is given opportunity to carry out his mission.

Now that he's got the weapon, he plans the entry. If he's going to conquer Eglon, he needs to get close to him. He decides to take advantage of an upcoming event—the tribute. Israel's captors required them to bring a tribute to Eglon every so often. These tributes were most likely food, some kind of agricultural produce (which doesn't help Eglon's obesity issue!).[27] As Israel's deliverer, Ehud decides to take the tribute himself so he can get close to Eglon (3:17).

With the plan churning in his mind, Ehud arrives and presents the tribute to Eglon (3:17). He manages to do this without raising any flags, then turns to leave with his traveling companions. At this point we're wondering what he's up to, since the man has an unused dagger itching to be used.

But the story takes an interesting turn. Ehud tells the men who helped carry the tribute to go on without him (3:18). Bravely, he turns back to Eglon and tells him he has "a secret message" for him. This piques the fat king's interest, so he commands his attendants to leave them alone (3:19).

Eglon and Ehud make their way up to the cool roof chamber, and Ehud dangles the secret-message carrot in front of Eglon again. Ehud bites this time and forces his mammoth cottage cheese thighs upright so he can hear the message. As he stands, Ehud grabs his foot-long dagger and thrusts it into Eglon's belly (3:20-21). The knife disappears in Eglon's fat belly. His bulging stomach literally swallows the dagger, which subsequently causes him to excrete a bowel movement (3:22).

The dagger that's at least a foot long *disappears* in Eglon's fat belly! His bulging stomach literally swallows the dagger, which subsequently causes him to excrete bowl movement (3:22).

With the mission now complete, Ehud leaves—shutting and locking the doors behind him (3:23). Upon his exit, the guards check on Eglon but find the doors locked. Naturally, they determine that he's busy relieving himself in his cool room (the stench of his excreted bowels prompted this assumption, no doubt!)

So they wait. And wait. And wait some more, to the point of embarrassment. (How long does a man need?) Then they decide to open the doors with a key. What they see stuns them (and probably grosses them out)—Eglon is dead (3:24-25). The fattened-calf man who received tributes has now become a tribute (sacrifice) himself. Oh, the irony!

Ehud now has quite the head start and escapes without hiccup to Seirah (precise location unknown). When he arrives, he blows a trumpet to gather men of Israel to accompany him to war against the Moabites. With confidence he declares, "Pursue them, for the Lord has given your enemies the Moabites into your hands." The men of Israel quickly seize the fords of the Jordan and proceed to kill about ten thousand Moabites, who, the text adds, were "robust and valiant men." They subdue Moab that day and obtain rest for twice as long as Othniel's judgeship—eighty years (3:26-30).

While fascinating, this story raises several questions: *Was Ehud's crazy plan in accordance with God's? Why didn't he just recruit Israel first and fight Moab the traditional way as Othniel did?*

The text doesn't give answers to all our questions, but when we step back and view the story within the context of Judges (and the rest of Scripture), we can produce likely conclusions.

To understand this text properly, we must first say a word about hermeneutics (how to read, interpret, and apply Scripture). Old Testament narratives (including Judges) *describe* stories and events; they don't necessarily *prescribe* or *qualify* the morality of them.

For example, in Genesis 38 (also a historical narrative) we read about a man named Judah, who sleeps with a prostitute. While that's hardly moral, the prostitute turns out to be his widowed daughter-in-law. When caught, Judah repents, though not for sleeping with someone he thought was a harlot. He repents because he didn't do right by his daughter-in-law in the first place. He should have let her marry one of his other sons when her husband died (that was how it worked back then so women could still bear children and have a family if widowed). While it's easy to see the sin from our perspective, the text never condemns Judah for sleeping with a prostitute, but that clearly was *not* the kind of behavior sanctioned by God.

Many narrative texts follow this practice of description, not qualification, which makes stories like Ehud a bit difficult to interpret. But while it may be difficult, it's not impossible.

Let's begin by stepping back to view the book of Judges as a whole. As we've mentioned, one major theme of Judges is degeneration of faith. As the book progresses, Israel's deliberate disobedience and lack of faith get worse and worse, rendering them morally, spiritually, emotionally, and societally void of God and His ways. The judges, too, mirror Israel's steady decline into degeneration. After Othniel, the "ideal" judge, the judges begin declining in morality as well, some subtle, others blatant.

When examining this trend, we're wise to view Ehud's brave plan with caution. While he may not have done anything technically wrong, did he implement wisdom in his plans? The text records no hint of Ehud pausing to ask God what to do or God divinely telling him how best to proceed. Nor does Ehud seem to seek counsel from others around him. He merely thinks up a plan and acts on it with haste. God did raise him up, but there's no mention of the Spirit anointing him or him yielding to God.

Ehud's plan to assassinate Eglon was most likely not the wisest course of action. Had he sought God, he probably would have taken a different path that didn't involve deceit and outlandish scheming. Nevertheless, he uses what's available to him (a dagger, quick wit, and bravery), and God responds by using Ehud's plans to fit His purposes.

God does this often, by the way. Situations like this reveal His sovereignty with crystal clarity. Only God—the supreme and omnipotent King—could use misguided plans for His glory. He can even use blatant evil to accomplish His purposes. Nothing can thwart God's plans, and He's powerful enough to bring beauty and glory from the disarray we make with our lives.[28]

Wherever Ehud's decisions lie on the morality scale, God uses him to deliver Israel from Moab. Israel kills ten thousand valiant Moab warriors and attains freedom for eight decades.

Ehud's account stands in blunt contrast to Othniel's. Othniel didn't need a fancy, risky plan to deliver Israel. He simply trusted God and followed His lead, leaving ample room for God to receive all the glory, honor, and praise for victory. Ehud's approach muddies the waters of honor. Despite merit for risking his life, Ehud ultimately leaves little room for glory to go to God. Sure, God protected him and allowed his plan to unfold. Ehud even attributes glory to Him verbally in his war cry to the Israelites (3:28). But his actions are those of an impulsive thrill-seeker, acting first and thinking second.

Shamgar

Following Ehud's story stands a lone verse that packs a punch. In it we meet Shamgar, the first minor (or noncyclical) judge who delivers Israel. What distinguishes Shamgar immediately from Othniel and Ehud is the lack of details we're privy to—both in his story and the circumstances surrounding the deliverance of Israel.

All we're told is that:

> After him [Ehud] came Shamgar the son of Anath, who struck down
> six hundred Philistines with an oxgoad; and he also saved Israel (3:31).

What's missing? Nearly the entire cycle of events! First, there's no mention of Israel's current state of repeated degeneration. We're not told that Israel did evil in the sight of the Lord, or that they're even in a predicament from which they need saving.

Second, no anger of the Lord is mentioned. God is entirely absent from this account, although from what we've learned from the book so far, the lack of mention does not equate total absence. God sovereignly works behind the scenes, whether we see it or not.

Third, we hear of no particular enemy rising up against Israel. The Philistines are the enemies in this account, but we learn this only after Shamgar has defeated them.

Fourth, we read no mention of Israel crying out to God for help or Him raising up a judge to deliver them. This lack of detail is only natural, we presume, since we're not told what enemy they were facing.

Fifth, the text neglects to mention God raising up Shamgar. Shamgar could very well have hailed himself as deliverer and sought glory in reckless abandon. But careful reading of the brief text makes this rendering unlikely. After all, how many men do you know who could single-handedly slaughter six hundred men with a makeshift weapon? The most likely conclusion is that God did, in fact, raise up Shamgar to deliver Israel—as He did with Othniel and Ehud before him.

Finally, there's no indication of peace between Israel and their oppressors after the battle. For all we know, Shamgar delivers them and they fall right back into captivity.

At this point, it's wise to mention that the book of Judges is not written in chronological order. The stories we read (especially the minor judges) most likely occurred throughout the book and in different locations from where the major judge stories were happening.

Israel not only experienced hardship from enemies because of their disobedience, but they were also dispersed. The Promised Land was originally supposed to be divided among the twelve tribes, but their failure to conquer it left many nations distributed throughout the land. Thus, while Ehud's story takes place mainly in Jericho and the hill country of Ephraim near the Jordan, Shamgar's victory could have occurred anywhere the Philistines were present.

Although many details are missing from the text, God provides us with all the information we need. One interesting feature of Shamgar's story is his identity. Shamgar is not an Israelite by birth. This fact links him to Othniel, who also wasn't an Israelite by blood. Could God be using these two judges to tell us something?

The first major and minor judges God chose are not His own people by blood. During a time when family and blood origin carry great weight, having two judges of non-Israelite birth is unnerving. Israel consistently exuded an air of pride because of their relationship with God (at least, when it was convenient for them), but now they're being rescued by people who are outside the bloodline. That, and these non-Israelite men are exercising faith that "genuine" Israelites incredulously lack!

By using Othniel and Shamgar, God reveals a glimpse into the gospel that we haven't seen much of yet: He wants everyone to be included in His family. His choice of Israel as "His people" was not to promote *exclusivity*, but to use them as agents of *inclusivity*. The plan was always for them to draw other nations to Him.[29] While Israel grossly failed in their part of the plan, God remains faithful and grafts others into His people (in quite prominent roles, no less) to bring about His mission of redeeming all nations, tribes, and tongues.

We'd be remiss to overlook the actual feat of Shamgar in this story. While brief, what he accomplishes is nothing short of remarkable.

Picture the scene: a solitary man finds himself surrounded by a flank of Philistines six hundred strong. Since the Philistines (like every other oppressor at the time) had stripped Israel of their weapons, Shamgar has no sword or shield to engage them with. Looking around, he notices an oxgoad. An oxgoad is "a sharp instrument mounted on the end of a fairly long pole—long enough so that the plowman could jab his oxen in the backside to goad them on so that they would plow faster…at the other end of the oxgoad a metal scraper was attached, which the plowman would use to scrape off the dirt or mud that had stuck to the plow, so that it would function more effectively."[30] Out of options and out of time, he lunges for the oxgoad and begins one of the greatest single-man slaughters in all of history.

Can you imagine being one of the last Philistines? You just watched a chunk of an army legion die at the hand of a single man, and now you're expected to follow suit. I don't think I would've approached Shamgar! And perhaps some didn't. The text leaves room for the possibility that more than six hundred Philistines were once present. There could have been several hundred more, but once they realize Shamgar is not backing down or tiring, they give up and decide to value their lives.

The defeat of six hundred Philistines with an oxgoad is enough to save Israel, at least for a time. Again, we're not sure how long the salvation lasted, but what we do know is that God used Shamgar in an extraordinary way that day. With one man's willingness to risk his life for Israel (a people not even his own by blood) and a makeshift weapon, God delivers His people.

His mercies truly are incomprehensible, aren't they? God rescues an undeserving people in ways that could not help but leave their jaws dropped in awe. While their sense of awe won't last, we have the opportunity to embrace such a response. Will you join me in thanking God for what He accomplished on Israel's behalf? And not just theirs, but for all the amazing ways He's working in *your* life right now? Though we may not see His mercies clearly through the chaos of our lives, take some time and look for them this week. Ask Him to reveal His blessings to you; He's faithful to answer.

GROUP STUDY

INTRODUCTION

When life throws you lemons…make lemonade!

Sometimes life throws us into precarious circumstances. We're backed into a corner with seemingly no way out. We need to take action—to move—but we don't have the resources to do it, at least not to do it well. *We don't have the money to quit our job and pursue our dream; but we know we can't stay here for long. There's no hope for our marriage, but let's give it a Hail Mary anyway. We don't know if we should pursue this investment, but we're not getting a clear answer from heaven either way…*

So we shut our eyes, clinch our fists, offer up a prayer, and move…hoping God will show up and do something amazing.

DISCUSS

- Describe a time in your life when you found yourself in a similar situation—out of good options, out of time, running on fumes, and hoping for the best.
- What was the outcome?

THE WORD

Ehud and Shamgar both faced dire circumstances and didn't just have to *step* out in faith—they jumped off a cliff.

Ehud was chosen by God to deliver Israel from Eglon, an evil king who violently oppressed Israel for eighteen years. Since there were no conceivable military options, he came up with another plan, and a risky one at that. He'd go *alone* to Eglon with a "secret message" and deliver it in the form of a custom-made dagger, killing the king in his own chamber (and losing his dagger in Eglon's ample stomach in the process). Then he had to escape, round up Israel for battle, conquer a kingless army, then continue judging Israel for eighty years.

While not as elaborate a story, Shamgar's situation was no less dire. Read his account below:

> After him [Ehud] came Shamgar the son of Anath, who struck down six hundred Philistines with an oxgoad; and he also saved Israel. (Judges 3:31)

These two men used what they had available to them to leap in faith and pray God would catch them. Ehud had a quick wit and unfathomable bravery; Shamgar made a quick, decisive choice and went all in as well.

- Put yourself in Ehud's position: planning an attack that blurs the line between bravery and reckless stupidity. What do you think went through his mind? What would've gone through yours in that situation?
- What about Shamgar? His claim to fame was most likely a reaction—no time to plan, only time to grab something and go all in. He clearly acted in surrender to God, praying for the best outcome. What would you have done? Fight or flight?

DISCUSS/ACTION

Both Ehud and Shamgar used weapons: Ehud's, a dagger made custom for the job; Shamgar's, an oxgoad grabbed on the spur of the moment. We have weapons too, but sometimes the greatest weapons in our arsenals of faith are unseen. The belt of truth, breastplate of righteousness, shoes of peace, shield of faith, and the helmet of salvation are all weapons that yield far greater results than a dagger and oxgoad (Ephesians 6:10-17).

In addition to growing closer to God, one reason we arm ourselves with His armor in faith is to prepare ourselves for life. We're always "in training," so to speak, as God readies us for obstacles and trials that are sure to come.

- How's your arsenal of faith right now? Are you walking with God, strong and ready for whatever may come? Or are you slipping a bit, growing lethargic in some areas?
- What can you do this week to strengthen and increase the effectiveness of your faith armor?
- How can we pray for you specifically to carry that out?

PRAY

WEEK FOUR:
Seize the Day

JUDGES 4:1-5:31
PERSONAL STUDY QUESTIONS

1. Who does God sell Israel into the hands of this time? (4:2)

2. Who is the commander of the army? (4:2)

3. How long do they oppress Israel? (4:3)

4. Who is judging Israel at the time? (4:4)

5. Where does she judge from? (4:5)

6. When she summons Barak, what does she tell him that God wants him to do? (4:6-7)

7. Sometimes God calls us to take action steps that seem impossible. *Give above the tithe when we're already financially strapped? Invite that friend to come live with us in her time of need—disrupting my space?* Whatever it is, God instructs us to act only when He knows our obedience will increase our faith significantly.

Is He asking you to do something right now? Why are you hesitating? What's the worst that can happen if you obey? I guarantee the *best* that can happen escapes your wildest imagination!

8. Is Barak's response one of brave obedience or doubt? (4:8)

9. What is Barak's punishment for his response? (4:9)

10. What is the outcome of the battle? (4:15-16)

11. Where does Sisera flee? (4:17)

12. Why does he feel safe there? (4:17)

13. What does Jael do once Sisera falls asleep? (4:21)

14. How do you think Barak feels when he finally catches up with Sisera in Jael's tent, expecting to kill Sisera? (4:22)

15. Who sings the song in Chapter 5? (5:1)

16. Who receives the honor and praise at the beginning of the song? (5:1-5)

17. Who is the blessed woman who received glory for the victory? (5:24)

18. How long does Israel enjoy peace? (5:31)

COMMENTARY

We've now been introduced to the first two major judges (Othniel and Ehud) and the first minor judge (Shamgar). Othniel and Shamgar stand as prototypes for their respective judge groups, both being the "ideal" of the major and minor judges. God doesn't write a bad word about them, and while they don't have many details written about their lives, their stories leave ample room for God to receive all honor and glory for delivering Israel.

Ehud earns points for being brave and taking risks for God, though the manner in which he accomplishes his mission is less than admirable. Instead of waiting for God and tuning into what He may desire, Ehud rushes ahead with a plan full of unnecessary risk and deceit. Yet in His grace, God honors it and secures victory for Israel anyway.

Now that Israel has been delivered three times from their enemies, we're inclined to think they'll stay on the right path. But unfortunately, their rediscovered commitment to God lasts only as long as the judges who live to watch over them. When Ehud dies, Israel backslides into apostasy again.[31]

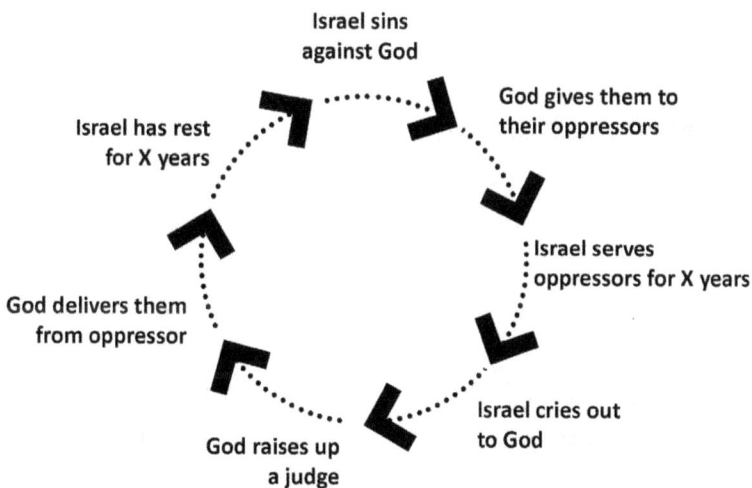

Israel sins against God

God gives them to their oppressors

Israel has rest for X years

Israel serves oppressors for X years

God delivers them from oppressor

Israel cries out to God

God raises up a judge

Chapter 4 begins with the repeated drone of Israel doing "evil in the sight of the Lord" (4:1). One point to note about sin is that "evil never lends itself to originality."[32] Sin is repetitive and grows boring quite rapidly. We may discover a thrill at first, but it never lasts. Contrarily, the more we sin, the more immune we are to its high, which compels us to do it again and again until we're left distraught and utterly hopeless. We can't get enough, so we plunge deeper and deeper into depravity until the ledge of hope seems despairingly high above us.

Sin is an addiction, and we tend to be drawn to the same ones. Israel exemplifies this superbly. They consistently fall into the temptation of idolatry, seeking manmade idols instead of God. Though the specific gods they follow differ as their journey progresses, the sin is the same. With each relapse along the way, the sin becomes worse and worse, yet the people grow deadened to its destructive grip on their lives.

It's easy for us to condemn Israel from our lofty moral perches. But don't let the helium of pride blow you up too far, for the bigger we get, the more prone we are to popping. The atmosphere of our pride squelches the Holy Spirit, and it's only a matter of time before He allows us to fall, giving us the chance to start over with Him keeping us grounded in humility.

Israel's degeneration quickens with each cycle, and the author of Judges pauses now to let us watch as another story of God's unmerited grace unfolds before our eyes.

Like Othniel's account, when Israel does evil in the sight of the Lord He "sells" them into the hands of their enemies. This time Jabin, the king of Canaan, oppresses Israel (4:2). This particular foe is unique in Judges thus far because he isn't a foreign king who travels a distance to overcome Israel. Rather, he is a king living in the land the Israelites are supposed to be occupying outright.[33] In other words, if Israel had obeyed God originally, Jabin and his minions wouldn't exist! Israel would have driven them out according to God's command. But ironically, the king that should have been disposed of long ago now stands as an oppressive force against Israel.

Jabin reigns over Israel for twenty years with his center of operations in Hazor (4:2). Hazor (pronounced "hawt-zor") was located ten miles northwest of the Sea of Galilee.

While Jabin technically reigns, a man named Sisera is in charge of all military operations. Sisera lives in a place called Harosheth-hagoyim (4:2). Scholars aren't certain of the precise location of Harosheth-hagoyim, but it's probably safe to assume it was somewhat near Hazor. We learn another telling fact about Sisera in the next verse, which distinguishes him as the force behind Jabin's reign: he has nine hundred iron chariots at his disposal (4:3).

If iron chariots jar your memory, congrats! You're recalling the mention of iron chariots from the first introduction of Judges. As the account of Judah's conquest comes to an end, we're told that they are unable to complete their mission and drive out the inhabitants of the valley because they have iron chariots.

Again, Israel is not a mighty military force at this time. Just a couple of generations prior, they were slaves in Egypt. They certainly are not vehement foes, capable of brutal slaughters and easy victories—at least, without God's help.

Iron chariots were advanced weapons in that day, which explains why Israel does not possess any. It also explains why they are extremely intimidated by them. To face such a terrifying enemy with the greatest technological advancements would have been daunting, indeed!

To heighten the sense of drama, we must understand that these chariots weren't used as a defense mechanism, but rather for offensive slaughter. On an open plain (which were plentiful around those parts), these chariots would pursue the fleeing enemy. They were, in essence, killing platforms for their drivers.[34] Not only does Israel face an intimidating enemy, but they're facing an enemy with seemingly endless resources that perfect the art of war. Not exactly someone I'd like to cross!

But instead of shaking in their mud-caked sandals, Israel seems to adapt to a life under oppression. While the text reveals they are oppressed severely for twenty years, there's no evidence that they cry out to God until at least that amount of time elapses. So after twenty years of a churning discomfort with Sisera's iron chariots, Israel decides to cry out to the Lord for help (4:3).

In this scene, we're introduced to the next judge of Israel, another one whose identity is rather shocking for those in that culture. (There are two judges in this account, actually, but we'll get there in a minute.) Immediately after seeing Israel under Sisera's thumb, we're told that "Deborah, a prophetess, the wife of Lappidoth, was judging Israel at that time" (4:4).

Her introduction sparks the irony that will carry through this account. Sisera, a foreboding military tyrant, stands juxtaposed to Deborah, a *woman* leader of Israel. As we've read, women were not held in high regard, especially in the pagan cultures surrounding Israel. Israel actually treated women with the most respect and dignity of any people group, but even they belittled women.

A Woman Leader?

An argument that often surfaces at this point casts doubt upon a woman leading Israel. Yes, she actually was leading/judging Israel. Some people believe that she was only fulfilling a judge-type role, not actually serving as an official judge. But that view completely skews the facts set forth in

Scripture. The word "judging" (*shaphat*) referencing Deborah in this passage is the same word used 219 times in the Old Testament. Seventeen of these are used in Judges—all referring to people who are God-sanctioned judges.

Though her judgeship looks a bit different than others (she prophesies and gives counsel to people as opposed to militarily delivering Israel), she nonetheless fits the mold of judge. She is intimately involved in all aspects of Israel's deliverance—morally, spiritually, *and* militarily. She speaks with authority given by God and issues judgments that align with His will. She is also highly involved in the military strategy and support in the battle against Sisera, something women rarely, if ever, took part in.

Israelites accept her as a judge back then, so who are we to question it over two thousand years later? If we're honest, Deborah seems to serve Israel more holistically than any other judge in the book.[35] She undoubtedly was judging Israel, but some argue that she shouldn't have because she was a woman.

While this is neither the time nor place for a full discussion of women's roles in leadership, we'd be remiss to ignore it completely in light of Deborah's role in this passage.

Objections to Women (Deborah) in Leadership

- **She was leading but sinning by doing so.** Many advocates of a hierarchical view of male headship quickly determine that Deborah must have been a conniving, manipulative shrew of a woman who grabbed the reigns of leadership when Israel entered a weakened state. But there's absolutely no evidence in the text that supports such a claim. In fact, the text seems to advocate the exact opposite.

  In this passage, Deborah is portrayed as humble, secure, strong, brave, and willing to obey God regardless of personal risk or cost. She is a God-ordained prophetess. He speaks clearly to her, and she responds by assuming the role of leadership God calls her to.

Deborah lives a life of obedience that contradicts Israel's predisposition to disobedience. So no, she was not sinning by leading Israel as judge.

- **She was leading only because there was not a qualified man around.** This argument is sheer ridiculousness. Not a qualified man? Since when do men have to be qualified in order for God to use them? May I kindly remind you of Moses (a murderer), Jonah (a defiant scaredy-cat), Elijah (a fleeing man who could throw a temper tantrum with the best of two year-olds), David (an adulterer and murderer), Matthew (a despised tax collector), Paul (an accessory to murder), and on and on. Anyone who reads the Bible knows that one of the qualifications of being used by God is *not* being qualified by one's own merit. Otherwise His strengths wouldn't be made perfect in our weaknesses; His glory would not shine through our failures.[36]

- **God used her as a last resort.** Some advocates against the legitimacy of Deborah's leadership also suggest that God chose to use her as a last resort. How sad that some advocate this view. God does transform beauty from ashes by using brokenness to accomplish His purposes. He also works in the grime of devastating circumstances and bad choices to redeem us. But that's not the only way He works.

God is not limited to the confines of our sinful predicaments. His hand is never forced into acting contrarily to His purposes and will; He never *has* to take a particular action because we've stripped Him of options.

God is God. That means He's divinely sovereign and omnipotent. In other words, He can do whatever He wants! If He didn't want women in leadership positions (including Deborah), He could very well have raised up a man. But He didn't, and Deborah isn't the only female breaking the male-dominated mold in biblical history.

Consider Miriam, also a prophetess, who played an important role after the Exodus. Or Abigail, a woman who made the right choice in spite of potentially dire consequences from her husband. Or Mary, the mother of Jesus, who embraced her role in God's plan with a thankful heart even though it cost her dearly. Many others come to mind, but again, this isn't a thorough defense of women in leadership.

Last resorts don't apply to God. He's the *maker* of all "resorts" and can yield our hearts and actions any way He pleases.[37] His sovereignty and our free will merge in ways unknown to our feeble minds, but we can rest assured that Deborah (a God-fearing woman) was used by Him to accomplish His purposes exactly as He ordained them to be carried out. She was not a last resort any more than Samson was (who, by the way, was the absolute worst of the judges; don't worry, we'll get there later).

Attempting to resolve the quandary of women in leadership while strictly adhering to all of Scripture's mandates on the subject is nearly impossible. The more I study the topic, the more convinced I am that it falls within the same category of doctrinal mysteries as the relationship between predestination and free will. Scripture advocates both sides, strongly supporting women in leadership roles while simultaneously exercising caution against it. Ultimately, no easy answer exists. To believe otherwise reveals a handicapped understanding of God's Word, or worse, blatant arrogance derived from bigoted bias.

While we don't have all the answers, we do know that Deborah was judging Israel and did have God's favor and blessing in doing so. God gives her the gift of prophecy, and she exercises it with full authority and humility. She shows no fear in following His lead—obeying even at great personal risk.

The author provides us with several interesting facts about Deborah early on in the text. First, we learn that Deborah is a prophetess (4:4). Prophets were people (both men and women) anointed by God to be His mouthpieces to people. Israel received the majority of prophecies from God, but other nations heard from Him as well (i.e. Jonah/Nineveh). When prophets spoke with God's authority, they were held to insurmountable standards. If ever one of their words did not come to pass, they were to be killed.[38] Thus, their words carried great weight and bore intense responsibility on both speakers and their audience.

Second, we read that Deborah is married (4:4). Her husband's name is Lappidoth, which means "torches." Deborah's name means "honeybee," so that's quite the interesting pair! Nothing more is mentioned of Lappidoth, but knowing Deborah is married tunes us into her life a bit more.

The third fact we learn is the location from which she judges Israel: "under the palm tree of Deborah between Ramah and Bethel in the hill country of Ephraim" (4:5). As you can see in the diagram, this location was actually quite far away from Hazor, revealing the great reach Jabin and Sisera have over Israel.[39]

The last fact we observe in the introduction of Deborah reveals her humility and unpretentious nature: "the sons of Israel

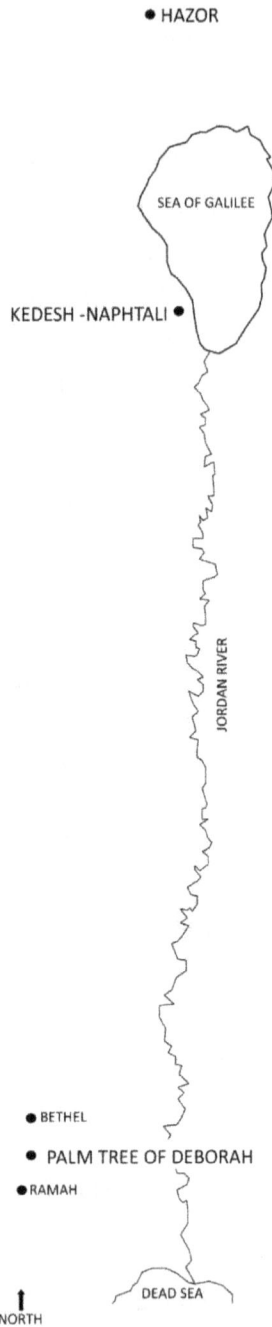

72

came up to her for judgment" (4:5). She is not the type to travel around screaming God's will at the top of her lungs. She doesn't impose her will on people, nor does she seek glory and admonition for her gifts. We meet her exercising her obedience to God in humility and modesty.

What the story reveals next grabs our attention. We've just read that Deborah busies herself judging disputes and giving guidance to fellow Israelites on God's behalf. Her role is typically one of reaction (dealing with what comes to her), not one of offense (seeking situations to reveal God's instruction).

But that changes rapidly with the next verse as we read how she "sent and summoned Barak" (4:6). Contrary to her typical style, Deborah senses a strong word from the Lord, and it makes her proactive. She sends for Barak and has him come to her.

The first facts we learn about Barak ("lightning") are his lineage and location (4:6). He is the son of Abinoam, and resides in Kedesh-naphtali. We're not graced with many details of his family other than the name of his father, who seems absent in the rest of Scripture with the exception of another brief mention in chapter five of Judges. But we do know something about Barak's location. Kedesh-naphtali was located close to Hazor, the central hub of Jabin's authority. How ironic that the man who's close to the enemy does nothing about it, but the woman far away is willing to confront them.

Deborah's word from the Lord is no small command. She tells Barak that God wants him to gather ten thousand men from the tribes of Zebulun and Naphtali for an army, and to march to Mount Tabor with them. Once there, God would draw out Sisera and would secure victory for Israel (4:6-7).

Let's break this down for a moment. Barak arrives at Deborah's call and is struck with news that leaves him feeling punched in the gut. God is calling him to do *what?* How is he supposed to secure ten thousand men and take on Sisera—the militant with nine hundred iron chariots and hordes of soldiers at his disposal?

In the original Hebrew, Deborah phrases God's command to Barak as a question, which seems odd.[40] Some scholars believe Barak already knew what God wanted him to do (from a previous unrecorded encounter) and Deborah is just confirming it.[41] Others (myself included) lean toward Deborah's question being an idiom—a linguistic way to communicate an imperative command. Some translations conveniently remove the question component when translating this verse, emphasizing the idea that Barak is hearing this command for the first time through Deborah.

Nevertheless, God's instruction to Barak seems impossible on the surface. By this time in history, Israel has grown to well over a million people. But Jabin does not reign over Israel in its entirety. Rather, he gains control of tribes and regions closest to him. Thus, Barak securing ten thousand men (men willing to go against quite the intimidating foe, no less) will not be easy.

After gathering the men, he is supposed to march to Mount Tabor and wait for Sisera to be drawn out before them for battle. Mount Tabor was shaped like an ice-cream cone and stood a little over 1800 feet high. This location would have been appealing to Sisera, for the flat plains surrounding it were ideal for his chariots.[42] While awesome for Sisera, it doesn't sound so appealing to Barak!

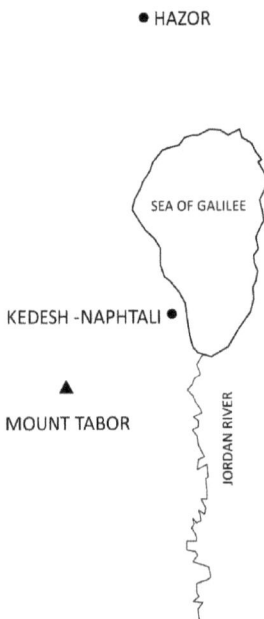

Understandably (from a human standpoint) Barak's reaction is less than astounding. He is a few crayons shy in the bravery box and is looking to put conditions on the call at hand. After hearing God's plan, he tells Deborah, "If you will go with me, then I will go; but if you

HAZOR

SEA OF GALILEE

KEDESH -NAPHTALI

MOUNT TABOR

JORDAN RIVER

will not go with me, I will not go" (4:8). Not exactly a confident leader, is he?

Barak's reaction reminds us of Judah, who earlier asked their brother tribe Simeon to accompany them to battle, even though God had guaranteed victory. Barak, like Judah, is acting like a little scared child, not wanting to move without holding someone's hand. Not only does he hesitate, he also blatantly puts conditions on his obedience. "Fine, I'll go," he reasons with crossed arms, "But I'm not going unless you go with me!" The gender irony rears its head once more. Barak, a man and a warrior, refuses to act in accordance with God, even with guaranteed victory, unless Deborah, a woman, goes with him to symbolically hold his hand.

He certainly does not start his role as delivering judge on a solid note.

Deborah responds according to what God lays on her heart. She promises to go with him but makes one point clear—Barak would not be the one receiving honor for the victory (in addition to God, of course). His hesitancy to obey disqualifies him from receiving full credit for obedience. Rather, the honor will go to a woman (4:9).

Until this point in the story, we're left to believe that the woman will be Deborah, which might make her seem a bit arrogant and smug. "Fine, have it your way. But since you didn't obey and I did, I'll get the glory!" But that's not at all what Deborah means, as the story will reveal.

To his credit, Barak stops arguing and starts obeying. Perhaps in fear of further humiliation (he did just receive a proverbial beat down from Deborah), he sets off on his mission, traveling to Zebulun and Naphtali to gather soldiers. He brings them together at Kedesh before moving on to Mount Tabor—ten thousand men and one very out-of-place woman, Deborah (4:10).

Verse 11 abruptly disrupts flow of the story. While Barak and his troops prep for battle, the author introduces us to a man named Heber. Heber was a Kenite, a group of people originating from Moses' brother-in-law, Hobab.

Several years prior, Moses invited the Kenites to join Israel as helpmeets in their travels. At the time, Israel was ill-equipped for meandering through the wilderness and other terrain—they had just attained freedom as a nation for the first time in four hundred years. The Kenites, on the other hand, were familiar with the terrain and agreed to lend them a hand. They grafted into Israel, particularly with the tribe of Judah, just like Caleb and Othniel. (cf. 1:16).

Heber, the man in our passage, later departs from Judah (reasons uncertain) and moves near the Sea of Galilee.[43] Somehow and also for unknown reasons, Heber makes peace with Jabin, which implies underlying hostility between him and Israel. He makes his home near Kedesh, but not without an air of tension between his family and the Israelites.

That's all we discover about Heber, at least for now.

● KEDESH

LAKE HULEH

● HAZOR

SEA OF GALILEE

KEDESH -NAPHTALI ●

▲
MOUNT TABOR

JORDAN RIVER

The story picks up with a scene of war: Sisera finds out that Barak and his army were posted at Mount Tabor, so he gathers all his chariots and the soldiers who are with him and head out to battle (4:12-13). Lest we forget, "all his chariots" means all nine hundred of his chariots. Sisera's army didn't magically shrink, nor were they ridden with some disease that left them easy targets for Israel. Contrarily, Sisera and his army are as strong as ever, and they have every intention of wiping Barak and his army off the face of the earth.

Now the author takes us behind the scenes with Israel's army. Any bravery Barak gathered before now evades him. He had a difficult time talking about going to battle before; now that it is upon him, he stands overwhelmed and less than thrilled about his previous decision to go. Having God's promise of victory in the past doesn't automatically rid us of fear in the present or future. It didn't for Barak. Trembling at the sight of Sisera's foreboding army, Barak freezes and Deborah steps in yet again.

With the gumption and strength of a coach probing her team for the championship, Deborah tells Barak, "Arise! For this is the day in which the Lord has given Sisera into your hands; behold, the Lord has gone out before you" (4:14). In other words, "Wake up, you dud! God promised you victory over Sisera; now get your behind out there and follow His call to triumph!"

Even though Deborah isn't leading the battle physically, she certainly is leading in the morale department. Leaders are supposed to psych up their troops for battle, but Barak needs a woman (who's not even supposed to be there) to psych him up first. She willingly complies, far more concerned about the Lord's plan coming to fruition than about any bumps in the road.

Do you have a Deborah in your life? They're the kind of people who speak truth and give you the extra doses of cheer you need to get moving. We all get in ruts. We all fall prey to the enemy's lies that we're not good enough or we can't get victory over a battle in our lives. But God says otherwise, friends! He not only tells us about our promised victory in Jesus for all our life battles, but He also uses others to remind, support, and cheer us on to triumph in Him. The only way to lose as Christians is to neglect to play in the game. God supplies us with ample opportunities. Will you seize them? And will you be a Deborah to someone else who needs a proverbial kick to get moving in the direction God calls them to?

Deborah's words break Barak's trance of fear and spur him on to battle. The seedling of faith lingering in his heart sprouts with gusto as he and his army of ten thousand men begin marching down Mount Tabor, valiantly taking on a fierce enemy waiting for them at the bottom.

As promised, God uses Barak and his army to crush Sisera's army with the sword (4:15). Can you imagine being Sisera? You began the battle with laughter in your belly, thinking the "battle" will actually be a rapid slaughter. Sisera didn't need a prep talk like Barak; he was confident and sure of victory. But he soon discovers his error, and is one of few to escape with his life.

Sisera abandons his troops to run for his life as Barak pursues his chariots (4:16). The taste of victory is sweet, and Barak wants to help himself to the full piece of cake. He's not content with simply winning the battle; he wants to annihilate Sisera's army.

At this point, Barak's motivations get blurred. Is Barak pursuing them because he wants to finish the victory thoroughly? Or is he in it for his own gain, hoping to secure the honor of victory even though it had been promised to someone else?

Back then, honor went to the one who killed the enemy's leader, not just the soldiers. Taking down the leader meant crippling the army, like chopping off the head of a snake. Ehud received honor for slaughtering the fat man-cow, Eglon, and secured victory for Israel after. It's likely that Barak wants to do the same. He's not content with a win; he sets his eyes on the coveted honor that God promised to someone else. Maybe he's trying to change God's mind. Perhaps he's trying to redeem himself—he hesitated before, but now that he's in action, he wants to prove he was always the man for the job. Besides, the only woman he could think of gaining the honor is back at Mount Tabor. He's got a huge head start!

Regardless of motivation, Barak seeks to finish the task. He's already experienced humiliation from being chastised by Deborah for delayed disobedience and then needing a pep talk to thaw his frozen posture of fear. Now he's out for blood and won't stop until he gets it. He and his army travel nearly twenty miles northwest to finish off Sisera and the remaining chariots.[44]

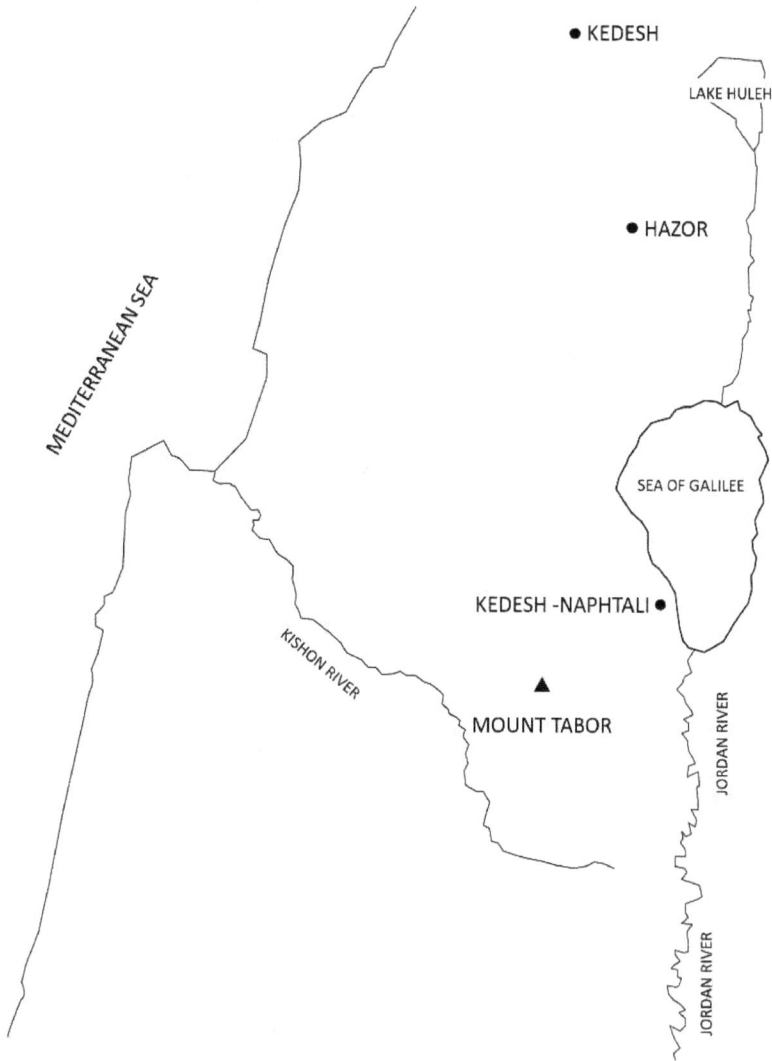

In the midst of the battle, it's likely that God opened the heavens and allowed rain to overflow the Kishon River, located nearby (5:4-5; 19-21). If this is true, the Canaanite chariots would have been sitting ducks! Unable to maneuver their chariots through the muddy ground, "the panic-stricken Canaanites had to cross the swelling Kishon, which swept many of them away, along with their chariots and horses."[45] Those who survived were easy for Barak and his army to overcome. Barak and his men end up killing every last man, chariot riders included (4:16).

Barak's victory is complete in our eyes, but not in his. He won't stop until he receives the honor, which means going after Sisera.

While Barak and his army are thoroughly whooping Sisera's army and chariots, Sisera makes his way to "the tent of Jael the wife of Heber the Kenite" (4:17). The random mention of Heber before doesn't seem so random any more. Sisera travels a great distance to get to Kedesh, over twenty miles northeast of Mount Tabor. That's a long way to run! But he does, and he manages to find Jael's tent.

The text doesn't tell us where Jael's husband, Heber, is, which makes us think he is involved in the battle somewhere. But Sisera knows that Heber and Jael are allies with Jabin and the Canaanites, so he barely hesitates entering her tent when she called to him (4:18).

We learn an interesting fact about Jael right up front: she "went out to meet Sisera" (4:18). Women didn't fight in battles, but we can imagine they were curious about the result of them. What wife wouldn't wait anxiously for her husband to return from battle? In Deborah's song in chapter 5, we receive insight into Sisera's mother and family, who also wait eagerly for the return of their loved ones. Battles devastate families, especially if they happen to be on the losing side. We shouldn't be surprised by Jael's choice to look out for news, but when she sees Sisera, she jumps at the opportunity to get in on the action. She wants more than just a news update.

Seeing Sisera running alone is news in itself. Commanders of armies run after battle only if they're running for their lives. So Jael learns two important facts when she sees Sisera. One, Barak's army has defeated Sisera's; and two, Sisera has managed to escape. With this information, she ushers him into her tent under the guise of care and concern.

Immediately upon entering her tent, Jael covers Sisera with a blanket (4:18). He's exhausted but still trying to maintain authority in the situation. He instructs Jael to give him water to drink and then tells her to stand in the doorway and tell anyone who passes by that she is alone.

Jael obeys as any woman would and goes the extra mile in her obedience. She offers Sisera some milk (which in reality was a chunky, almost cheese-like substance) instead of water, and eases his worries about anyone finding him. The milk pushes him over the edge of exhaustion, and after instructing her to turn away anyone trying to find him, he falls fast asleep (4:19-20, 21b).

What happens next reveals where Jael's loyalty lies. Using the tools available to her (flashback to Ehud and Shamgar who did the same), Jael secures a tent peg and hammer and creeps over to him as quietly as she can, hoping not to wake him. Then, with swift and decisive action, she strikes the peg into Sisera's temple, driving his head into the ground (4:21).

Sisera's humiliation is now complete, revealing Jael's commitment to God and allegiance with His people over her husband's loyalty to Jabin and the Canaanites. In a moment of utter shock, a woman receives the glory for battle, and does so with flair.

It took guts to do what Jael did. Put yourself in her situation. She's a housewife, maybe even a mother. Her life consists of keeping the house tidy, preparing meals, and running the household for her husband and family. She doesn't hold the same political or religious opinions as her husband, but because of her status has no way to voice her opinion or refuse to follow him. Living in the enemy's backyard, she strives to remain faithful to God even though everyone around her is doing the opposite. Crossing her husband carries serious consequences, so she lives in quietness and submission even though it's killing her inside.

Then one day she sees an opportunity, maybe even an opportunity she'd been praying for. Perhaps she prayed for a chance to show her faithfulness to God, to stand up for what she believes. Maybe she prayed vigorously, but over time began to lose hope that God would answer her prayers with a yes. Twenty years is a long time to be in captivity, and her household is aligned with the enemy, making it that much worse!

But then her chance comes. Arduously looking for news, she sees Sisera and invites him in, making the first move. She serves him and plays the submission card well (she's had lots of practice, after all). Somewhere in all this, she realizes that this is her answer to prayer! God has given her the opportunity to get involved and to do so in a huge way. She grabs what's available to her and fulfills God's plan of deliverance—receiving the honor of victory for doing so.

I wish I could say I'd do the same, but if I'm honest, I'd probably be content sitting on the sidelines, watching the plan unfold. It's risky to get involved in the game. To pray for opportunities to be used by God and then seize them when they come can be quite costly.

Jael puts Barak to shame in this area. God gives him ample opportunity to step up with a promise of great victory for His kingdom, but he hesitates twice and puts conditions on his obedience. Jael, on the other hand, is itching to get in the game with no promise of success. When she sees an opening, she takes it without the slightest hesitation.

Who do you tend to align with more, Barak or Jael? God may be calling you to do something that's way out of your comfort zone, and even the thought of it freezes you with fear. While you may not know the outcome, like Jael you too can seize the opportunity and be used by Him to accomplish amazing feats for His glory. Will you grab your tent peg (though preferably without deadly intentions) and get to work? He's waiting and wants nothing more than to bless your obedience.

While the great and mighty Sisera lies dead in a puddle of blood in Jael's tent, Barak continues his pursuit (4:22). He most likely hears reports of the direction of Sisera's flee and goes after him despite the exhaustion that must be creeping its way into his body. Pushing weariness aside, he follows Sisera's trail. He makes his way to Jael's tent, and when she sees him, Jael once again makes the first move by going out of her tent. She greets him and tells him that she knows where Sisera is (4:22).

Jackpot! Barak probably thinks. *All this time and effort will finally pay off!* He'll be able to conclude his victory by killing the commander, ultimately receiving the honor he's had his sights on all along. But his attitude of anticipation when entering the tent quickly sinks into deep disappointment—Sisera is already dead! Deflated, Barak realizes that Deborah's prophecy came true in an unexpected way. The honor does go to a woman—an unknown woman who seized an opportunity that Barak originally forfeited.

Chapter 4 concludes with a confirmation of victory for Israel. God subdues Jabin and allows Israel to overtake his army until he is killed, leaving the army dispersed (4:23-24).

Most of us would be content with the story ending there, but that would rob us of something we often neglect partaking in—celebration!

Chapter 5 recounts a song of celebration most likely written by Deborah, but sung by both her and Barak. It begins on a note of praise, thanking and blessing the Lord for Israel's victory (5:1-5). This is the first mention of gratitude we read about in this book. In all the stories of conquest and triumph Israel experienced thus far, thanksgiving remains absent. How terribly sad! Perhaps if they'd been more appreciative of what God had accomplished, their dedication to Him would have lasted a bit longer.

One aspect of praise is for God raising up leaders in Israel—volunteers who rose to the challenge of going to battle (5:2-3). While the account in chapter 4 concentrates on Barak's lack of initial bravery, we mustn't neglect his ultimate willingness to go, along with the ten thousand men who bravely followed him into dangerous circumstances. These men recognized God at work and joined Him where they could—on the front lines.

Deborah also highlights God's immense strength and sovereignty (5:4-5). The battle, she knows, is not won by mere human effort. Rather, God divinely intervenes on Israel's behalf in the weather as well as their physical abilities. He causes the heavens to pour out water, muddying the land and rendering the daunting chariots useless. This is the same God who struck fear into the hearts of Israel on Mount Sinai, revealing that "the God of Moses, who once revealed His might at Sinai, was still alive and well!"[46]

God is mighty to save, is He not? In addition to being grateful, we'd do well to reflect on God's nature as declared in His Word. Difficult circumstances tend to diminish the power of God in our minds, but God is never surprised or limited by our challenges. Instead of telling God how big our problems are, we should consistently tell our problems how big God is. Proper perspective will follow.

After beginning with praise and thanksgiving, Deborah reflects upon the dire circumstances Israel faced before their deliverance from Jabin (5:6-7). We'd fare well to adopt such a practice on a consistent basis. When life is grand and triumph is secure, we tend to forget where we came from and neglect to remember the intense power of God that brought us out of the pit. Israel repeatedly failed to reflect on their past through a lens of praise, and their repetitive cycle of degeneration is all the incentive we need not to follow suit.

In the days of Shamgar and Jael (remember, these accounts weren't necessarily chronological), the roads within Israel's territories were barren and empty (5:6). People avoided major highways out of fear of enemy attacks. Agriculture was also severely affected by the Canaanites' hostile rule, "the small, unwalled villages of the Israelites being no protection against the forays of their aggressive neighbors."[47]

Israel remains distraught in their oppression until Deborah arises like a mother in Israel. She cares for Israel immensely, particularly about their current status, which is brought on by their blatant idolatry (5:8). Because they prostituted themselves after idols, God delivered them into the hands of their enemies, stripping them of peace and the ability to fend for themselves with courage or weapons of war (5:8).

But hope is never out of reach with God. He is hope! Again, Deborah praises the Lord and thanks Him for raising up people to be His hands and feet in delivering Israel (5:9-11). What a celebration, indeed! Deborah elicits participation in her celebration from everyone and knows that people will be praising God for Israel's deliverance in many generations to come. If only she knew just how long we'd be praising Him with her because of this story!

The next section of the song introduces the tribes who stepped up as volunteers in the Lord's army (5:12-15, 18). Six tribes receive accolades for their participation: Ephraim, Benjamin, Machir (also known as Manasseh),[48] Zebulun, Issachar, and Naphtali. These tribes are not all mentioned in the account of Chapter 4, but since they are included in this song, we are wise to assume participation in the battle—if not as warriors, then of moral support.

The participating tribes are not who Deborah wishes to focus on, however. She's already praised God for those who served Him. Now she takes time to call out those who refused to get involved, those who had ample opportunity to participate in God's mission but forfeited their chance (5:15-17). These tribes include Reuben, Gilead (probably referring to Gad),[49] Dan, and Asher.

Sometimes we erroneously believe that our lack of action will excuse us from consequences. We rationalize that God already has enough people serving in this way or that; surely our absence won't matter. How misinformed we are! When God prompts us to get involved with His plan, He has a specific purpose for our involvement that no one else can fill. He equips each of us with spiritual gifts, talents, passions, and experiences that enable us to provide a unique flair to our contribution in His gospel. If we refuse to participate, we're not only robbing ourselves of His blessing, but we're also robbing the Body of Christ of its full blessing too.

The distinction of tribes between those who served and those who didn't is harsh—shameful for those who failed to get involved. Deborah refuses to allow them off the hook, calling them out by name with an air of regret and disappointment.

Those who stepped out in faith did so at great risk, but their reward is insurmountable. Deborah describes the battle with poetic details that makes us wish we were there to see it (5:19-22)! The fight is heavy amidst the storms of wind and rain, and we can hear the horse's hooves walloping against the murky ground as they drag mud-drenched chariots behind them. What a mighty sight to behold, if only in our minds.

Before moving on to commemorate Jael, Deborah calls out yet one more people group who refused to give aid (5:23). While we don't know the exact identity of the people of Meroz, it's likely that they were located in the area directly affected by the battle, making their lack of participation that much more cowardly.[50] Deborah takes her disappointment with them to a whole new level, indicating that with their lack of participation, they stood against God Himself, not just His people.

When we fail to participate in God's call, we sin against Him personally.[51] Deborah wants to clarify this point before moving to her next point of honoring someone who *did* participate.

Any honor that Jael receives in Chapter 4 is magnified in Chapter 5 (5:24-27). Deborah blesses her repeatedly and without hesitation. She praises her shrewdness in giving Sisera milk instead of water, and using tools she had available to her to end his life. With gruesome detail she describes the nature of his death, very hands-on and nasty for Jael (ladies, can you imagine the mess and stench of all that blood on your living room floor?). But with continued praise Deborah describes an ironic climax to the story—the powerful leader of God's enemy lies dead between the feet of Jael, a lowly woman of no obvious standing or rapport. God's methods certainly cannot be confined to the fallible boxes in our imaginations!

The song's finale gives us a glimpse into Sisera's family, who anxiously awaits the return of their son and hero (5:28-30). Deborah (divinely inspired by the Holy Spirit) takes us into the presence of Sisera's mother, who looks out the window, wondering about the delay in his homecoming. His mother's alertness reminds us of Jael, though the object of their gaze differs. Jael gazes from her tent, looking for an opportunity to be used by God; Sisera's mother looks out waiting for her son to return so he can climb up another rung on the ladder of success.

Even with differing motives, Sisera's mother is struck with worry. Though Sisera is a cruel military leader, she sees him as her son—someone she loves and cares for deeply. Amidst her worry, the princesses attempt to calm her fears with shallow theories of his delay. They suggest that he and his men are merely finding and dividing the spoil, which includes women and material goods. Sisera's mother tries to convince herself of this as well, only to soon realize the truth of his demise.

While we may be tempted to feel pity for Sisera's mother, let us not forget the blatant evil of the man before he became a tent accessory. The "spoil" of women refers to the rape of women. Sympathy sucks right out of us when we realize that, doesn't it? The Canaanites, along with other oppressing leaders, were downright evil in their domination, wreaking irrevocable havoc on those they defeated.

After twenty years of miserable tyranny, God delivers His people from Jabin, causing Deborah to conclude her song with one more praise to God, "Thus let all Your enemies perish, O Lord; but let those who love Him be like the rising of the sun in its might" (5:31). With that, Israel experiences rest from their enemies for forty years—doubling the length of their oppression.

--

You've heard the saying, "God works in mysterious ways." If ever a story revealed the truth in that, it's the story of Deborah and Barak. Nearly every component of this story is topsy-turvy, the opposite of our expectations. We expect Barak to be a man like Othniel—strong, brave, and quick to action. What we discover is quite the opposite, a man who's nervous, afraid, and full of excuses.

We expect Deborah to fulfill a supportive role, acting as cheerleader on the sidelines. What we discover is more—her incredible inner strength, standing behind Barak and acting as his faith surrogate until he jolts from his nervous stupor.

We expect Jael to play the role of charming hostess, especially since her husband is an ally of Sisera. What we witness is a fearless woman ready to take action for God without any guarantee of success or positive outcomes accompanying it.

The difference between the ladies and Barak (other than gender, of course) is Deborah and Jael's willingness to seize the opportunities God placed before them. Deborah judged Israel without fear and led them closer to God with every verdict she decreed. When God changed her routine, she complied immediately and without any complaint. She believed God so much that she poured her faith into Barak as much as she could, hoping her strength would be contagious (which it was).

Jael seized the opportunity to kill the acting oppressor of Israel. Could such an action have serious negative ramifications, especially with her husband? Yes. But she kept God on the rightful throne of her heart, which made the decision easy. She moved quickly and rid Israel's enemy of their leader with every strike of her hammer.

Contrarily, Barak froze in fear and needed jolting twice before moving forward. He hesitated because his comfort was threatened and he clearly had doubts about God's plans. But we should remember that he *did* obey, even if it was a little tardy and perhaps with wrong motivations. God used him, despite his fears and hesitancies, to defeat a mighty enemy.

All three of these characters harnessed seedlings of faith, but only two invested in them consistently. Because Deborah and Jael had their hearts tuned into God, they were able to act immediately when He presented them an opportunity. While Barak did have faith, he spent little time cultivating it, making it difficult for him to respond with bravado when God called him.

God used all three for His glory despite their differing measures of faith. He does the same with us. Just like these three, He gives us opportunities to participate His plan. Our response to those opportunities and the blessings that follow is determined by how much we invest in our faith. We'll hardly seize opportunities (and may miss them entirely) if we neglect our faith and let it grow anemic. On the other hand, if we dedicate our time, energy, and effort to know God and become more like Him daily, we will have the awareness and courage to step out in faith and seize the opportunities He places before us—to His glory and our good.

GROUP STUDY

INTRODUCTION

Order. Certainty. Rhythm.

Life works best when it makes sense, when it follows a pattern we're comfortable with. We don't like when things going awry, when wrenches get thrown into our plans, or when unappealing surprises come our way.

Unfortunately, life never abides by the rules we set for it. Even if it does for a while, it never lasts. Difficulties, disappointments, and unexpected opportunities will ding our lives with their relentless hammers more than once. Acknowledging this is half the battle. The other half is determining how we'll respond when they come.

DISCUSS

- Describe a time in your life when you were surprised, and *not* in a good way—when the world seemed to turn upside down and all your comfort, security, and rhythm of life disappeared.
- What feelings did you wrestle with most during that time?

THE WORD

Despite what we often think (and are told), God does not operate in a cosmic box of rules and rhythms that always makes sense to us. The world tells us that the strong win, and if we do good, good will be done unto us. But God isn't confined to our rules and expectations. He often uses the "foolish things of the world to shame the wise...and the weak things of this world to shame the things which are strong." (1 Corinthians 1:27)

The account of Deborah and Barak in Judges displays this beautifully. Deborah was a woman judge in a male-dominated world, and God used her mightily because of her humility and obedience to Him.

Barak, on the other hand, while chosen to deliver Israel from Jabin and Sisera, forfeited the glory of victory by hesitating and attempting to manipulate the situation for his comfort. Read what happens to him due to his lack of trust, faith and immediate obedience:

> Barak said to her, "If you will go with me, then I will go; but if you will not go with me, I will not go." She said, "I will surely go with you; nevertheless, the honor shall not be yours on the journey that you are about to take, for the Lord will sell Sisera into the hands of a woman." (Judges 4:8-9)

- What was Barak's condition for his obedience?
- What do you think he felt when he heard the glory would go to a *woman*, not to him?
- Who was the woman who gained the glory for the task Barak was supposed to have done? What did she do? (Judges 4:17-21)
- What was the difference between Deborah and Jael's faith/actions compared to Barak's in this story?

DISCUSS/ACTION

God operated well beyond the confines of traditional expectations in this story. Barak (a man and a warrior) was presented with an opportunity to step out in faith but refused to seize it without trying to manipulate the situation to increase his comfort level.

Deborah and Jael, by stark contrast, were considered weak and futile in the world's eyes, yet they responded to opportunities with eagerness and immediate obedience to God, regardless of personal risk or consequence.

- Is God calling you to do something uncomfortable right now? What is it and why is it so uncomfortable?
- What's one step you can take this week that will help you seize any opportunities He gives you to do it?
- This week, will you commit to pray for opportunities to obey—without hesitancy or comfort clauses—so He can gain all the glory and you can move closer to Him in faith?

PRAY

WEEK FIVE:
True Colors

JUDGES 6:1-8:32
PERSONAL STUDY QUESTIONS

1. Who does God allow Israel to become subject to when they disobey again? (6:1)

   • How long are they oppressed?

2. What does the enemy do to Israel that is particularly cruel? (6:2-6)

3. How does the Lord respond initially to Israel's plea of rescue? (6:7-10)

   • How does this differ from the other accounts thus far?

4. Where does the angel of the Lord appear to Gideon? (6:11)

5. What is he doing when he appears to him? (6:11)

6. God has a funny way of showing up unexpectedly in our lives. When we're comfortable in our day-to-day activities and routine, sometimes He turns everything upside-down by prompting us to do something very out of the ordinary.

Has God ever spoken to you this way? Interrupted your comfortable way of life to challenge you to do something unexpected and, frankly, uncomfortable? What was it? How did you respond?

7. What does the angel tell Gideon to do? (6:14)

8. How does Gideon react? (6:15)

9. What "sign" does the angel give Gideon? (6:21)

10. What does Gideon do in response to the sign? (6:24)

11. What does God tell him to do that night? (6:25-26)

12. Does Gideon obey?

    • Why does he take action at night? (6:27)

13. We'd all be rotten liars if we claimed never to be scared, worried, or anxious about living for God. It's hard to trust Him with our kids when they seem to be running away. It's difficult to trust His sovereignty and justice when evil is done to you. It's nearly impossible to forgive when we've been wronged in ways that pierce our hearts. At the root of it all is fear—fear that if we let go, He'll let us down. Gideon's fear is quite understandable.

    What are you afraid of today? What are you refusing to let go of when you know God is calling you to?

14. How do the people of the city respond the next day? (6:28-30)

15. Who stands up for Gideon? (6:31)

    • What does he say?
    • Does it work?

16. What new name does Gideon receive? (6:32)

    • What does it mean?

17. When the Spirit of God comes upon him, who does Gideon call together for battle? (6:34-35)

18. What does Gideon ask for before continuing on to battle? (6:36-39)

19. How does God respond? (6:38-40)

20. Why does God choose to decrease the number of Israel's warriors? (7:2)

21. How do they decrease the number at first? (7:3)

    • How many people leave?
    • How many remain?

22. How does God decrease the number even more? (7:4-6)

    • How many remain?

23. Talk about freaky! It's quite terrifying to be thrown into a situation without sufficient resources and tools to help you out. Your boss just gave you an assignment that's nearly impossible with the resources you've been given to work with. You lost everything when you lost your job—bills are piling up, your kids need money for school and clothes—what are you going to do?

    This may surprise you, but God puts us in impossible situations on purpose so we'll learn to depend on Him rather than erroneously believing we're fine on our own. Only when we have nothing left do we reach out to God with all we have—that's the way He wants it, and in those situations, He shines brightest.

Do you need to let go of something and let God take over? Perhaps there's an area of your life that you need to surrender and turn over control to Him. What is it? How can you go about giving it to Him on a daily basis?

24. What does God say immediately after telling Gideon to go to battle? (7:9-11)

    - Does Gideon take Him up on it? (7:13)
    - What happens? (7:13-15)
    - How does Gideon respond? (7:15)

25. What does Gideon give his men? (7:16)

26. When do Gideon and the men go to the outskirts of the enemy camp? (7:19)

27. What do they do? (7:19-20)

28. How does God secure victory for Israel? (7:22)

29. What happens next? (7:23-24)

    - Who do they capture and kill? (7:25)

30. What complaint does Ephraim bring against Gideon? (8:1)

31. How does Gideon handle it? (8:2-3)

    - How is Gideon's response similar to his father's in 6:31?

32. Who does Gideon approach for supplies for his men? (8:5)

    - How do they respond? (8:6)
    - What does Gideon promise to do for their lack of aid? (8:7)

33. Who does he approach after that? (8:8)

    - How do they respond?
    - What does Gideon promise to do to them? (8:9)

34. Who does Gideon go against next? (8:10)

    - Do they defeat/capture them? (8:11-12)

35. Who does Gideon capture after his victory? (8:14)

    - What information does he gain from him? (8:14)

36. Does Gideon uphold his promises to Succoth and Penuel? (8:16-17)

37. The text reveals the reason behind Gideon's motivation to capture Zebah and Zalmunna. What did they do to Gideon that caused him to lash out with vengeance? (8:19)

38. Who ends up killing Zebah and Zalmunna? (8:21)

39. How does Israel respond to Gideon's battle rampage? (8:22)

40. How does Gideon respond to them at first? (8:23)

41. What does Gideon add to his response that reveals selfish motives? (8:24)

42. Does Israel comply? (8:25)

    - How much does Israel give Gideon? (8:26)
    - What does Gideon do with it? (8:27)

43. What we do with what we've been given reveals a lot about our character. What has God given you? A house? A family? A prominent

position at work? A particular ministry? How are you utilizing those gifts? Are you doing what you can to bring glory to God, or are you using them selfishly?

COMMENTARY

Israel sins
against God

God gives them to
their oppressors

Israel has rest
for X years

Israel serves
oppressors for X years

God delivers them
from oppressor

Israel cries out
to God

God raises up
a judge

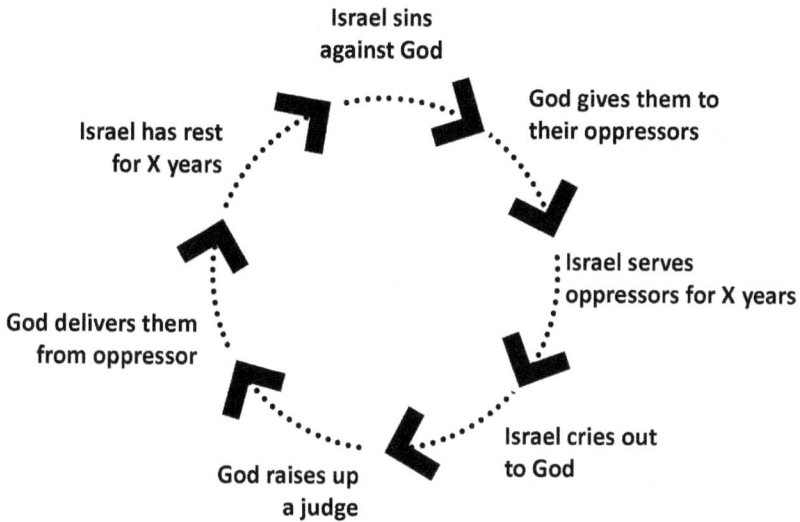

We've now been introduced to three major judgeships—Othniel, Ehud, and Deborah/Barak—and one minor judge—Shamgar. Through each of these, we see Israel floundering deeper in their cycle of degeneration. With Othniel they are sold into the power of Cushan-rishathaim, king of Mesopotamia, for eight years, followed by a period of deliverance and peace for forty years.

Before Ehud comes along, they do evil in God's sight again—rendering them helpless and at the mercy of Eglon and the Moabites. They suffered within the clutches of his grip for eighteen years, then were delivered through a borderline-reckless plan by Ehud. Shamgar follows Ehud's coattails with an impressive victory over six hundred Philistines with an impromptu weapon, delivering Israel once more.

God turns all expectations upside down the next time Israel forsakes Him. He raises up a woman to judge Israel and subsequently allows another woman to gain the victory for the battle Barak led. Israel is freed from the oppression of Jabin and his minion, Sisera, and experiences forty years of peace.

By this point we hope Israel has learned their lesson. After all, they've witnessed four astounding deliverances—all grace since they hardly deserved any rescue. But sadly, as soon as Deborah and Barak are removed from the picture (presumably by death), Israel slips into their cycle of disobedience once again.

Unsurprisingly, Israel does evil in God's sight, which results in God delivering them "into the hands of Midian seven years" (6:1b). This is the shortest length of oppression yet (though Othniel's time comes in a close second at eight years). But from what we can gather from the text, it is a severe oppression.

Midian prevails against Israel with seemingly little effort, leaving Israel running for the hills in fear—literally. The Israelites flee to dens and caves in the mountains to escape Midian's terrorizing oppression (6:2).

Midian's tactic goes above and beyond what is necessary. Instead of simply demanding tribute like Eglon, they wait for Israel to plant crops then camp against them to ravage their produce. However, like Eglon, Midian partners with other people groups in their oppression of Israel. Allying with the Amalekites and sons of the east, Midian strips Israel of every ounce of grain in the fields, as well as other resources like sheep, oxen and donkeys (6:3-4). Living under political oppression is difficult enough; adding the constant destruction of their resources and food takes this oppression to an entirely new level.

Can you imagine living with this much fear? The author tells us that Midian flooded down upon Israel's tents and livestock like swarms of locusts to devastate their lands (6:5). Such imagery reminds us of the eighth plague in Exodus 10. Because Pharaoh stubbornly refuses to let Israel go, God sends numerous plagues to entice him to do so. The eighth plague is locust, which makes me cringe. I'm not a fan of bugs; in fact, I should invest in bug spray because I go through vast amounts every year when spring comes around.

Let's revisit Exodus 10:5-6a for a moment. Moses and Aaron warn Pharaoh about another impending plague, should he still refuse to let Israel go. The plague involves locusts—so many of them that ...

> They shall cover the surface of the land, so that no one will be able to see the land. They will also eat the rest of what has escaped—what is left to you from the hail—and they will eat every tree which sprouts for you out of the field. Then your houses shall be filled and the houses of all your servants and the houses of all the Egyptians, something which neither your fathers nor your grandfathers have seen, from the day that they came upon the earth until this day.[52]

How many ways can we say gross? If I were Pharaoh, I'd say, "Get out of here and take everything with you! No bugs swarming down on me, please!" But that's not how Pharaoh responds, though that's another story.

Through this imagery we tap into how suffocating Midian's reign over Israel is. We think insects are bad, but at least they don't kill you! However, Israel finds themselves surrounded by fierce warriors who *can* kill, and who attack in less subtle yet more taxing ways than immediate death.

Israel has nothing left—no land to call their own, no crops, no valuables (at least not ones that can be revealed publically), and barely enough food to survive. Understandably, "Israel was brought very low because of Midian," and finally, they decide to cry out to God (6:6).

At this point, the typical cycle embarks on a tangent. Instead of simply raising up another judge to deliver Israel as other times, God decides to have some words with them first. He sends a prophet to tell Israel a message. We're not told anything about the prophet, but the message stands impactful enough without the identity of the messenger:

> It was I who brought you up from Egypt and brought you out from the house of slavery. I delivered you from the hands of the

> Egyptians and from the hands of all your oppressors, and
> dispossessed them before you and gave you their land, and I said
> to you, 'I am the Lord your God; you shall not fear the gods of
> the Amorites in whose land you live. But you have not obeyed
> Me' (6:8b-10).

I would not want to be on the receiving end of that rebuke! The
grandparents of the Israelites saw God deliver them from Egypt through the
plagues. Their parents followed Him through the desert and participated in
the claiming of the Promised Land. Despite a few bumps in the road, Israel
had made it. But now that they have, they ignore what God's done in the
past and what He promises for their future. They exchange His goodness
for the emptiness of pagan idols. They disobey His divine order to obey the
lusts of their idolatrous hearts.

While the prophet's chastisement is not directly applicable to us, it certainly
causes us to pause. We're just as guilty as the Israelites for not putting God
first in our lives. When we refuse to dwell on His truth, we get drawn into
lies, and just like Israel, disobedience follows.

God is not happy, and He's not simply going to give Israel what they want
again. (That hasn't worked out very well thus
far). He will deliver them, but not before
giving them a healthy dose of truth—what's
right in *His* eyes, since they've obviously
succumbed to what they think is right in
theirs.

SEA OF GALILEE

MOUNT TABOR

● ORPHAH

JORDAN RIVER

↑
NORTH

After the prophet delivers his message, the
scene changes, and we see an angel of the
Lord descending to sit under the oak of
Ophrah (not Oprah, mind you) (6:11). This
is the first movement of the angel of the Lord
since Chapter 2, when he brought words to
Israel that were similar to the prophet's words

in this chapter.[53] But in this chapter, the angel's involvement will increase significantly. In fact, he will speak directly to the new judge God chooses—something that hasn't happened in the narratives thus far.

Another observation that strikes us as similar is the fact that he appears under a tree. If you recall, Deborah's center of prophetic operations was also located under a tree—the palm tree of Deborah. Trees are apparently great places to gather together! This tree belongs to a man named Joash the Abiezrite. Abiezrites are a family from the tribe of Manasseh, who is one of Joseph's (the coat of many colors guy) sons. This family was allotted land within the territory of Manasseh when Joshua led Israel. Apparently, they succeeded in securing their property, though they're now more akin to slaves living on it than owners, thanks to Midian. On Joash's property within this allotment stands an oak tree as well as a wine press, where we meet our next judge, Gideon.

The first impression we receive of Gideon isn't super impressive. He's in a wine press, which isn't all that strange until we learn what he is doing in the wine press. Instead of pressing wine (which would have been normal), he's beating out wheat (6:11)!

To us buy-food-neatly-packaged-already folk this all sounds quite foreign, so let me explain. When wheat is harvested, it needs to be separated from the chaff that is harvested with it. Usually this process occurred with a threshing-sledge out in an open field so the wind could aid in separating the chaff from the wheat.[54] But since Gideon (and the rest of Israel) cowers in caves away from the Midianites, he improvises by beating out the wheat from the chaff in the more obscure location of a wine press.

Many people focus on Gideon's fear here, claiming he's a pathetic wimp for hiding in a wine press. I find it difficult to agree with that assessment because of the circumstances we have already discussed. This is a terrifying time for Israel! Only a brazen fool would stand in the open, threshing wheat. It'd be a sweeping invitation for the Midianites to ravage the little food they managed to hide. Gideon is doing what he can to survive and employs wisdom and creativity in doing so.

As he goes about his business, he hardly anticipates what he's about to experience next—a theophany.

Suddenly the angel of the Lord appears to Gideon (6:12). The easy exchange of the phrases "angel of the Lord" with "Lord" in this passage insinuates that this individual is, in fact, a theophany as opposed to strictly an angel of the Lord, like Gabriel.[55] A theophany is a visible appearance of God, typically in human form.[56] We cannot see the face of God and live (His glory is far too shocking), so sometimes He takes on the form of humans or natural elements to speak with people.[57]

The Lord appears to Gideon and declares, "The Lord is with you, O valiant warrior" (6:12). While I stand by my assertion that Gideon isn't cowering in fear any more than others in Israel, this statement is still ripe with irony. Gideon may not be a wimp, but nothing about his situation reveals that he's a valiant warrior either.

Without missing a beat, Gideon expresses doubt in the Lord's statement in verse 13:

> Oh my lord, if the Lord is with us, why then has all this
> happened to us? And where are all His miracles which our fathers
> told us about, saying, 'Did not the Lord bring us up from Egypt?'
> but now the Lord has abandoned us and given us into the hand
> of Midian.[58]

With this brief statement, Gideon reveals the fallibility of human perspective apart from God and His Word. First, *God's presence does not unequivocally result in favorable circumstances for us.* If we have accepted Christ as Savior, God is with us all the time. In fact, His Spirit takes up residence in our hearts and lives there permanently![59] However, we all endure times of trial, when we experience less-than-favorable circumstances. Does that mean God has abandoned us? Absolutely not. God remains with us through any and all circumstances (Hebrews 13:5).

Second, *God doesn't always work in the same ways.* As we've seen in the stories of Deborah, Barak, and Jael, God is not a magician limited to a list of mastered tricks. He is sovereign, almighty, and omnipotent—capable of working whenever and however He wants. Gideon mistakenly assumes that God abandoned Israel because He hasn't delivered them from Midian. There were no miracles and no plagues consuming their enemy, so naturally God doesn't care about them anymore. False! What Gideon doesn't yet realize is that this very conversation with the angel is God's way of working to deliver Israel from Midian.

Third, *God isn't a genie who exists solely to make our lives pleasing.* Gideon exercises selective knowledge of the facts with his complaint against God. He focuses on what God did for Israel in the past, not on the covenant still standing between them now. Gideon misses the point entirely. Life isn't about what God does or doesn't do for us. Life is about loving Him, loving others, and living for His glory. Gideon's focus is on what he can get out of the relationship to the utter neglect of the relationship itself.

Lastly, *while we're not always responsible for the circumstances that surround us, we're not always innocent in their making either.* In no way does Gideon acknowledge guilt or responsibility for Israel's current predicament. Even if Gideon was a righteous man and wasn't guilty of idolatry like his brethren (which is doubtful), he would have repented on behalf of Israel. But he doesn't. He remains remarkably silent about Israel's contribution to their circumstances, which is ironic since a prophet just revealed that Israel is completely to blame for their current predicament.

Because Gideon's argument contains zero theological or even logical validity, the Lord ignores him entirely. When Gideon stops talking, God turns toward him and says, "Go in this your strength and deliver Israel from the hand of Midian. Have I not sent you?" (6:14). God is not letting Gideon get distracted. He's making it clear that He is with Gideon and that He is calling him to deliver Israel from Midian.

Why does God tell Gideon to go in his own human strength? It would make more sense for God to promise *His* strength for Gideon, given such a daunting task. While we're not told exactly, it's possible that God is trying to awaken Gideon to his true identity—who he is with God. At the present moment, Gideon exudes no sign of being a mighty warrior or a person capable of leading an army to victory against a foreboding enemy. But as the story unfolds, we see glimpses of his strength, strength that arises when he realizes the power derived from a yielding partnership with God. Nothing is impossible with Him!

But Gideon isn't seeing through God's perspective at the moment, so he offers an excuse—"O Lord, how shall I deliver Israel? Behold, my family is the least in Manasseh, and I am the youngest in my father's house" (6:15). Sounds eerily similar to Moses' objections on Mount Horeb, doesn't it? He also made excuses based on the prevailing order of familial hierarchy. Both men presume God chooses the most prestigious son of the most prestigious family of the most prestigious tribe to deliver Israel. But if Gideon had been paying attention to what's going on around him, he'd realize that none of the judges thus far have been the most suitable or impressive: Othniel, a grafted-in alien; Ehud, a left-handed Benjamite; Shamgar, a proselyte; Deborah, a woman; and Barak, a man struggling to grasp even an ounce of faith.

Once again Gideon reveals his lack of understanding of God. God sees what we don't. While we look at outward appearances, God looks at the heart. His power shines brightest through the powerless vessels He uses. Thankfully, God exercises great patience with Gideon (as He did with Moses) and allows him to be a part of His plan of deliverance.

God responds with another promise of His presence and another guarantee of victory (6:16). He will be with Gideon every step of the way, and Gideon will defeat the enemy as if they were one man. What promises! To be promised God's unwavering presence and complete victory should be enough to jar anyone into a revival of faith. But Gideon's not quite there yet.

Gideon acknowledges what God spoke to him, but now he wants to make sure it actually is God speaking with him. He asks for a sign that proves God's divinity (6:17). Not sure what that sign will be, he begins on a solid note by asking the Lord to remain until he can prepare Him an offering. Gideon prepares a young goat, unleavened bread, and broth (6:18-19). This seems to be quite the substantial offering, given Israel's precarious situation with Midian. Gideon isn't stingy in his offering but gives it freely and obeys the angel's instructions.

The angel of God tells him to put the meat and bread on a rock and pour the broth over it. He extends His staff to touch the meat and bread, fire immediately explodes from the rock. The bread and meat are consumed, and the angel of the Lord vanishes with it (6:20-21). Gideon wanted a miracle, and God certainly delivers!

As soon as Gideon witnesses this "sign" he realizes that he has indeed been speaking with the Lord. Upon this realization, Gideon grows fearful. He thinks he's seen the angel of the Lord face to face, which means sure death according to his estimation (6:22). But God extends peace to him telling him not to fear, for he wouldn't die (6:23). After all, why would God take his life when He just promised to use him to deliver Israel? Gideon isn't thinking clearly, but that's understandable. He did just witness a spectacular miracle.

Upon God's promise of continued life, Gideon does something rather unexpected: he builds an altar to the Lord. He names it "The Lord is Peace," and it remains standing through the time the author wrote the book (6:24).

The same night God speaks to Gideon again (6:25). We're not sure how He chooses to speak to him this time, since the angel has ascended with the offering; but the method isn't nearly as important as the fact that He does speak to him.

God gives Gideon instructions. Gideon is expected to take his

> Father's bull and a second bull seven years old, and pull down the
> altar of Baal which belongs to [his] father, and cut down the
> Asherah that is beside it; and build an altar to the Lord your God
> on the top of this stronghold in an orderly manner, and take a
> second bull and offer a burnt offering with the wood of the
> Asherah which you shall cut down (6:25-26).

Why does God want Gideon to do this? Most likely because of what Gideon had just done—he just built God an altar in an act of worship. But the significance of such an action is rendered mute since a pagan altar still remains on his father's property.[60] God doesn't share glory with anyone or anything else. Worship shared between two objects isn't worship at all. We have only one throne in our hearts. God wants Gideon to purge his family's property from the idolatry that ushered them into the captivity in the first place.

Another issue arises at this point. Israel is crying out to God for deliverance from Midian, but they still have idolatrous altars erected in their land. It's hardly a stretch to conclude that Joash's altars are not the only ones around.[61] How idiotic is Israel for keeping the very idols that prevent them from getting deliverance!

Yet how often do we do the same? We desire God to rescue us or bless us when we're in blatant sin: dating someone who doesn't follow Jesus, not forgiving someone, harnessing bitterness toward a friend, etc. If God has been silent in your life and you're wondering why, begin with a thorough evaluation of your heart. Ask Him to reveal anything standing in the way of your continued growth as His disciple. I promise He will answer! Then you can confess your sin and purge the junk from your heart so you can freely move toward Him again.

Israel misses this step. They don't care at all about following God or remaining faithful to Him; their only concern is getting out of the pit of captivity. They want to feel better, but not at the cost of getting their hearts right with God. Gideon's family owns idolatrous altars, and God refuses to move forward with Israel's deliverance until His leader's own family gets right with Him—at least on the most basic level.

Surprisingly, Gideon obeys God without hesitation. He doesn't ask for another sign or give excuses as to why it isn't a great idea. Rather, he takes ten servants and gets to work. He tears down the altar of Baal and the Asherah (probably a pole representing the goddess of the Phoenicians and Syrians),[62] and offers a burnt sacrifice to God (6:27).

The quirk about his obedience here is the fact that he does all of this under the cloak of darkness. Gideon fears the reaction of his family and the men of the city, so he works at night to avoid (or at least put off) confrontation (6:27). Yes, Gideon is afraid—just as he was when we met him in the winepress and when he realized he was speaking with God. But again, is this fear ultra-cowardly? Is he trembling because he's a pathetic excuse for a man? Or is he a man exercising some wisdom and common sense, considering his circumstances?

Again, I hesitate to write Gideon off as a coward. His fear isn't magnified in his mind—it's quite legitimate and reasonable. Plus, he doesn't let it stand in the way of his obedience. He doesn't even hesitate. He obeys God immediately, which just happens to work out well because it's dark and he has a greater chance of accomplishing his mission without getting stopped by onlookers. Gideon isn't Ehud; but that shouldn't force an automatic label of "wimp" on him, either.

If Gideon wished to avoid confrontation, he is disappointed. Early the next morning, people notice that something is terribly awry—their altars are torn town and a new one had been built! They inquire about it and someone informs them that it's Gideon's fault (6:28-29).

The men of the city approach Joash, Gideon's father, and demand Gideon be given to them so they can kill him (6:30). They're enraged and are looking for blood, which further reveals their complete lack of concern for God and His covenant with them. Not only are they defending their idolatrous altars and images, they're also demanding the death of the one who tore them down! This crosses another line in their theological depravity and reveals just how deadened their hearts have become to truth.

Joash's response will reveal what's in his heart. If he agrees with the men, he's just as pagan as they are—perhaps more so since it will cost him the life of his son. If he disagrees with them, he runs the risk of ridicule and other punishment but would be condoned for a righteous act amidst a demoralized society.

His response is refreshing and unexpected. He appeals to reason and logic (since proper theology is clearly not an option with their skewed mindsets), stating:

> Will you contend for Baal, or will you deliver him? Whoever will plead for him shall be put to death by morning. If he is god, let him contend for himself, because someone has torn down his altar (6:31).

Looking them in the eyes, Joash calls out their lack of faith in their own idols. If Baal really is as mighty and capable as they are claiming, can't he defend his own honor? Why would he need mere mortals to avenge his glory? Using this logic, Joash tells the men to let Baal contend for himself. If Baal is as they say, he can resolve the situation to his liking if he wants.

Hard to argue with that; and they don't. Imaginably with beady eyes and clinched fists, the men head off and leave Gideon alone.

In addition to a calm resolution, Joash renames his son Jerubbaal, meaning "let Baal contend against him" (6:32). Names were of utmost significance in that day, and this new name will follow Gideon the rest of his life.

This scene dims and another comes to light. The author gives us an aerial view of the land, informing us that "all the Midianites and the Amalekites and the sons of the east assembled themselves; and they crossed over and camped in the valley of Jezreel" (6:33). Midian and their allies begin another conquest of the crops against Israel. But God has other plans.

Just like with Othniel, the Spirit of the Lord comes upon Gideon, and he blows a trumpet to call together all the Abiezrites (his father's family) to follow him. He proceeds to send messengers throughout the rest of his tribe (Manasseh) as well as other tribes including Asher, Zebulun, and Naphtali (6:35). Zebulun and Naphtali rise to the call just as they did when Deborah and Barak summoned them for battle. Asher failed to rise up previously but does so now—perhaps to redeem themselves?

Regardless, Gideon stands with 32,000 people at his side. Not quite innumerable like the Midianites and their horde, but certainly enough to make a dent!

But Gideon isn't quite ready to move forward yet. As the men are gathering to him, Gideon's bravado wavers as his appetite for additional confirmation grows. He turns to God and asks:

> If You will deliver Israel through me, as You have spoken, behold, I will put a fleece of wool on the threshing floor. If there is dew on the fleece only, and it is dry on all the ground, then I will know that You will deliver Israel through me, as You have spoken (6:36b-37).

A quick reading of this text might lead us to think that Gideon is testing God to discover what His will is. This perspective, however, is easily refuted by Gideon's first sentence: "If You will deliver Israel through me, *as You have spoken*," (emphasis mine). Gideon *knows* what God said. He knows that God plans to deliver Israel through him. Thus, Gideon already knows what God's will is; he's not trying to discover it by testing Him.

The most agreeable interpretation of this passage is that Gideon is desiring further confirmation of God's will—due to fear, doubt, or a disguised urge for control.

As we know, back then idolatry ran rampant. People worshipped several "deities," and in this particular case it is Baal (the god of the land, in control of crops and such) and Asherah (the generic goddess worshipped by the Syrians and Phoenicians). The term "worship" doesn't adequately describe the relationship between people and these idols, though. It was more like manipulation—people would offer sacrifices and partake in rituals to manipulate the idols into doing what they wanted. For instance, a baby sacrifice (yes, this happened quite frequently) could be used in exchange for good weather and thus, good crops. This expression of "worship" at its heart was nothing more than manipulation to get what they wanted.

Such manipulation could have been the result of fear—"we're terrified of not getting enough food through our crops!" or the desire to be in control—"this idol has to do what we want if we give it something in return." Nevertheless, it boils down to a compulsive need to be in control—to be the one dictating the circumstances, not leaving it up to fate or the powers that be.

The test of fleece reflects Gideon's attempt to manipulate or control God, a practice he'd grown accustomed to by worshiping pagan idols. Since he knows what God wants, he wants to force God's hand of confirmation once again. He doesn't want to move forward until he feels secure enough to do so. Gideon's desire is to be in control; and having God in his back pocket would do the trick.

In an amazing act of patience, God goes along with Gideon's little test. Per his request, God allows the fleece to be dripping wet with dew while the ground around it is bone dry in the morning.

At this point, Gideon would be wise to shut up and move forward with the plan. But why make things simple? Instead, he calls to God again, saying

> Do not let Your anger burn against me that I may speak once more; please let me make a test once more with the fleece, let it now be dry only on the fleece, and let there be dew on all the

ground (6:39).

Seriously, Gideon? Reading this second request makes us squirm. Gideon's focus is 100 percent on himself. He's completely ignoring what God has done for him until this point—appearing to him via a theophany, giving him a miraculous sign of confirmation, protecting him from the men of the city, and raising up several thousand people to go to war with him. Instead of dwelling on those acts of confirmation, Gideon focuses on his feelings of insecurity and of wanting to be in control. He wants to feel confident before moving forward, which is understandable, except he's going about it in all the wrong ways.

Confidence comes from God, not ourselves. No matter how hard we try, we will never be in control of our lives. It's impossible. We may be able to control our actions and our responses to the circumstances surrounding us, but we can never control what happens to us. Gideon is trusting himself and trying to use God as his magic genie instead of submitting to God and relishing in His absolute sovereignty. No wonder he's struggling!

In another act of unfathomable patience, God obliges Gideon's second fleece request (6:40). When Gideon wakes up the next morning, the fleece is dry amidst drenched ground. Gideon may be feeling pretty confident now. Perhaps the second fleece test helped him feel more in control of the situation. If only it would last…

But God knows what's happening in Gideon's heart. He knows that Gideon is using Him to gain confidence instead of stepping out in obedience and trusting Him to keep His word. Yet He still extends grace and patience.

MEDITERRANEAN SEA

SEA OF GALILEE

KISHON RIVER

● ORPHAH

JEZREEL VALLEY

HILL OF MOREH ▲

SPRING OF HAROD

JORDAN RIVER

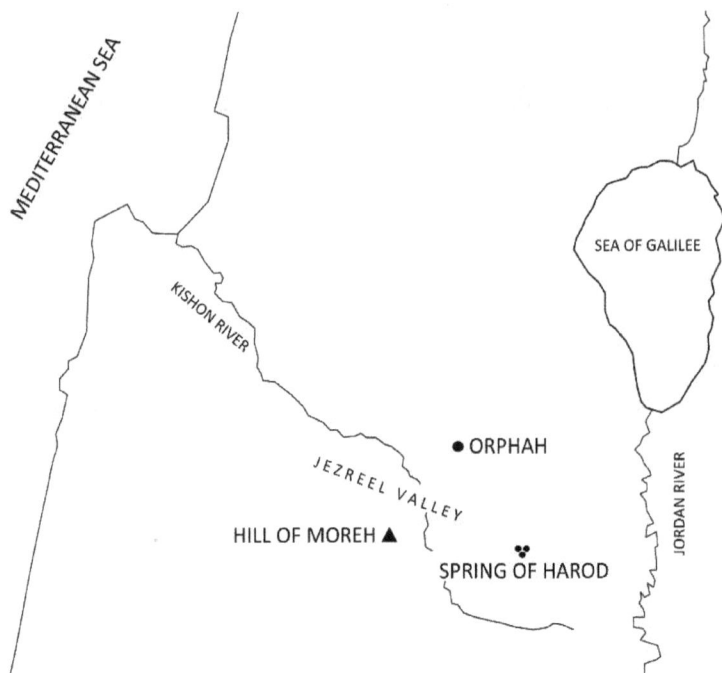

Gideon puts on his warrior face and wakes up early the next morning to camp near the spring of Harod, which is just south (though at a higher elevation) of where Midian is camped (7:1). If the fleece tests and a new day boosted Gideon's confidence at all, God is about to rip it right out from underneath him.

As they are getting settled in their camp, God tells Gideon that they have too many men to go up against Midian (7:2). That doesn't make sense! Midian and their allies have so many warriors they seem innumerable; how could God think 32,000 Israelites are too many?

The reason is simple: Israel has a slim chance of victory on their own with 32,000 men. God wants to eliminate any chance of victory so everyone—including Gideon—knows that it is He who delivers Israel, not themselves (7:2). God wants to abolish any chance of Israel getting arrogant and falsely believing they secured victory for themselves, so He slashes the number of their warriors.

God tells Gideon to dismiss any man who is afraid (7:3). Apparently lots of them are—22,000, to be exact! More than 60 percent of their force walks away, leaving only 10,000. Can you imagine the beads of sweat forming on Gideon's brow? *What is God thinking? I suppose 10,000 will have to work.*

Not so fast, Gideon.

After the 22,000 leave, God tells Gideon they still have too many (7:4). So He gives him more instructions: bring the men down to the water for God to test them. (Who's doing the testing now, Gideon?) The men who lower their faces to the water to drink would be dismissed; the ones who used their hands as cups to drink would remain.

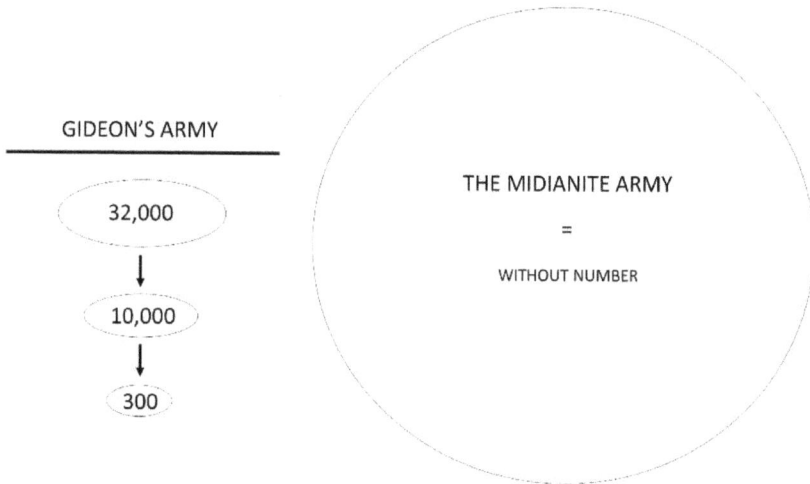

GIDEON'S ARMY

32,000

↓

10,000

↓

300

THE MIDIANITE ARMY

=

WITHOUT NUMBER

To Gideon's great dismay, only 300 men drink from their hands (7:6). God slashes Israel's army from 32,000 to 300 in two swift moves. A puny group of 300 men will go against an army of innumerable soldiers. This ought to go well.

But God doesn't leave Gideon to drown in his thoughts. He promises victory again, ensuring Gideon that He will deliver the Midianites into his hands (7:7). The 300 men gather provisions and trumpets from those who are leaving, and then they settle back into their camp above the Midianites, who are camped in the valley (7:8).

Talk about a long day! What began as promising quickly turns incomprehensible, and God doesn't leave time for Gideon to dwell on it. That very night, He tells Gideon to rise and go down against the Midian camp (7:9-11). But He includes an accessory to His instruction:

> But if you are afraid to go down, go with Purah your servant down to the camp, and you will hear what they say; and afterward your hands will be strengthened that you may go down against the camp (7:10-11).

God precipitates Gideon's hesitation and pulls the rug of excuses right out from under him. Knowing Gideon still isn't ready, God tells him to sneak down to the Midian camp and listen to what they have to say.

When the request is in his favor, Gideon doesn't hesitate to take God up on His offer. With his servant Purah, Gideon heads down to the camp under the cloak of nightfall (7:11). (Gideon seems to prefer working the late shift.) At this point, the author reminds us yet again how intimidating Midian is as an enemy:

> Now the Midianites and the Amalekites and all the sons of the east were lying in the valley as numerous as locusts; and their camels were without number, as numerous as the sand on the seashore (7:12).

Those images come roaring back—"as numerous as locusts," "without number," "as numerous as the sand on the seashore." And here we have Gideon slinking his way down to the camp with his anemic 300-man force waiting close by. Can't say I'd volunteer to be in that position!

When he and Purah reach the edge of the camp, they overhear a man chatting with his comrade about a dream (7:13). He dreamt that a loaf of barley bread was rolling down into the Midianite camp and it squashed the tent—turning it all upside down. His friend quickly responds, "This is nothing less than the sword of Gideon the son of Joash, a man of Israel; God has given Midian and all the camp into his hand" (7:14).

God's sovereignty gleams without filter with this encounter! Eavesdropping, Gideon learns that not only have the Midianites heard of him, but they also are fearful of him. The fear has completely changed sides—consuming the oppressor, not just the oppressed! They know that God will give them into the hand of Gideon, and this dream confirms it.

The irony bubbles to the surface and overflows with this plot twist. Somehow the Midianites heard what God has been telling Gideon over and over again—that He will defeat Midian via the hand of Gideon. God has been driving fear into the enemy the whole time! How sad that God's promises are immediately believed by His enemies, but seriously doubted by the man He divinely calls to lead His people. Gideon's faith is put to shame by faithless pagans. He doesn't know God any more than he knows the idols he's been "worshipping" all his life.

Another truth we learn from the Midianite soldier's dream is that God's work isn't limited to linear and obvious motions. He revels in working behind the scenes, and when we look back on our lives, we can attest to this truth (hindsight is often 20/20). His sovereignty reaches every aspect of our lives, and He's constantly working in and around us to accomplish His purposes. While we may never see the extent of the work of His hand, it's most certainly happening![63] Gideon never believes that, and with his obsession of feeling in control, how could he? Only when we surrender to God and trust Him can we begin to see Him working and then fulfill the role He's calling us to.

Upon hearing this Midianite chat, Gideon responds as he should—he worships (7:15). Right on the outskirts of the camp, he bows down in worship. While worship is a terrific response, it's depressing that it takes Gideon this long to get there. What's even more disheartening is the determining factor of his worship: confirmation of God's plan—from a Midianite! It isn't enough that God tells Gideon His plans directly; Gideon must hear it from the mouth of his enemy in order to believe it.

This confirms Gideon's devious motivations behind the earlier fleece tests. Gideon simply isn't taking God at His Word. He knows what God said and knows it is God Who is saying it, but he isn't content until he hears confirmation from a human's mouth. Oh, what little faith! God's word isn't enough for Gideon, and we can only imagine how much it robs him of further blessings later on.

It's easy to judge Gideon with creased brows of condemnation. But we can't escape the truth that we follow in his footsteps every day. While we may put on a good show, we're guilty of not taking God at His Word too. We harbor bitterness against others who have wronged us when God tells us to forgive. We withhold our tithes and offerings when God tells us to give. We ignore those hurting around us when He wants us to extend grace and love. All of us fail to take God at His Word—masking our failure with waves of rationalization to ease our guilt. Let's use Gideon's story to stop these patterns and fuel our fight against lethargy in our faith!

After bowing in worship to God, Gideon gets up and heads back to the Israelite camp. Immediately upon his return, he declares, "Arise, for the Lord has given the camp of Midian into your hands" (7:15b). It's battle time!

Before heading out, Gideon divides his troops into three divisions of one hundred men (7:16). Instead of swords and shields, he equips each of them with trumpets and torches inside empty pitchers. I wonder if the men at this point are thinking back to stories of old, like when Joshua conquered Jericho. God chose a unique military tactic with them as well. He commanded them to walk around a city several times before priests blew trumpets and the people raised their voices with a loud shout. The fortified walls of the city came crashing down and Israel was victorious!

Such stories must have crossed the minds of some of the men as they stood with strange instruments, preparing to go against an enormous army.

Perhaps some thought their moment had come—they would be able to participate in God's story of deliverance just like their forefathers. How exciting!

Keeping the men focused, Gideon instructs them to watch him and do as he does. The plan sounds fine until we get to the chant. When he blows the trumpet, all the men are to do likewise and yell, "For the Lord and for Gideon" (7:17-18). If they'd limited their shouts to the first three words, that would have been great. But why would Gideon add his name to the credits? Did he not just bow in worship—giving us much relief that he finally understands his place with God? How can he turn and immediately seek credit for himself just moments later?[64] Oh, Gideon.

Without missing a beat (and most likely without realizing his error), Gideon takes one troop of men and heads to surround the outskirts of the Midianite camp. They arrive at the beginning of the middle watch, which would have been around 10 p.m. (7:19).[65] The timing reveals God's sovereignty yet again, for the changing of the guard occurring at this point signifies a weakness in defense (the new guards weren't fully positioned yet).

When everyone reaches their positions, Gideon and the men blow their trumpets with their right hands and break their pitchers revealing the torches in their left hands. Amidst the trumpet sounds they yell, "A sword for the Lord and for Gideon" (7:20b). The men add the word "sword" here to Gideon's earlier instructions, suggesting wisdom on their part. They add the word to make the Midianites believe they are fully armed.[66]

As they carry out the plan, the Midianites are consumed with chaos (7:21-22). Being awakened from a dead sleep, they panic and begin killing each other. In their confusion, they turn against one another, leaving the Israelites without a need to fight (at least initially).

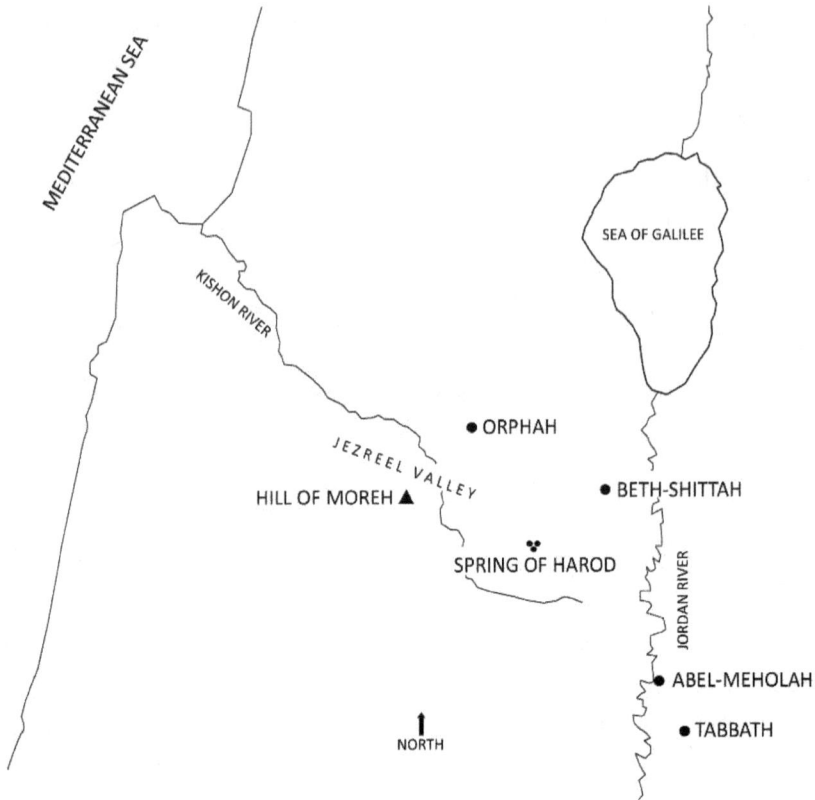

With a serious percentage of Midianite blood spilled, survivors begin to run (7:22). Spurred on by dread, they run to the southeast. Some reach Beth-shittah near Zererah—about ten miles away, some reach Abel-meholah—about fifteen miles away, while others reach Tabbath—about twenty miles.[67] That's quite a distance, though I suppose it didn't seem like much, considering they are running for their lives.

Now that the main thrust of the Midianite army is crushed, Israel calls in reinforcements to finish the job (7:24). They summon people from Naphtali, Asher, and Manasseh to pursue the fleeing Midianites. Gideon also sends messengers throughout the hill country of Ephraim to cover the waters of the Jordan, to keep the Midianites from escaping. This reminds us of Ehud's account, for he also called men from the hill country of Ephraim to seize the fords of the Jordan River so the Moabites couldn't cross over to safety.

In the process of this mobilization of forces, the Ephraimites capture two leaders (chieftains or princes[68]) of the Midianites, Oreb and Zeeb. They kill Oreb at the rock of Oreb and Zeeb at the wine press of Zeeb (7:25). Careful readers sense the irony of these death locations. The rock reminds us of the rock that Gideon placed his offering on for the angel earlier in his story. Poetic justice is now complete with a Midianite leader dying on a rock—once symbolizing an offering to the Lord. The wine press of Zeeb takes us back to where we first met Gideon, in a wine press! How far God has taken Gideon—from a serious doubter hiding in a wine press to a "valiant warrior" (the very first name the angel attributes to him) who leads an army that kills the enemy leader in such a wine press.

Chapter 7 concludes the hunt and massacre of Midian, and we all expect the bloodshed (and story) to end there. Not all the Midianites have been killed, but they're certainly not in a position to oppress Israel anymore. But Gideon experiences a shift sometime between the initial attack and now. He almost becomes a different person. A timid, doubtful, and uncertain man now becomes a heartless warrior consumed with revenge.

Chapter 8 begins with a complaint. The men of Ephraim are upset with Gideon for not calling them to join the fight against Midian initially (8:1). Basically, they're throwing a temper tantrum for not getting included at the onset. But Gideon will have none of it. Not backing down, Gideon exudes the negotiating shrewdness of his father back when Gideon was in trouble for taking down the idols:

> What have I done now in comparison with you? Is not the gleaning of the grapes of Ephraim better than the vintage of Abiezer? God has given the leaders of Midian, Oreb and Zeeb into your hands; and what was I able to do in comparison with you? (8:2-3a)

Gideon definitely inherited the smooth-talking, quick-witted genes from his daddy. He showers Ephraim with compliments, dramatically emphasizing their feat of capturing and killing the Midianite leaders—which far outweighs any of Gideon's own accomplishments. His tactic works. A very appeased Ephraim dismisses their charges and leaves Gideon alone (8:3).

Along with being politically brilliant, Gideon also reveals his transformation. Such a strategic tactic doesn't surface from a heart that's timid and insecure like he was before. Rather, Gideon is confident, not seeming the least bit concerned about receiving honor for this battle. His mind is on something else entirely.

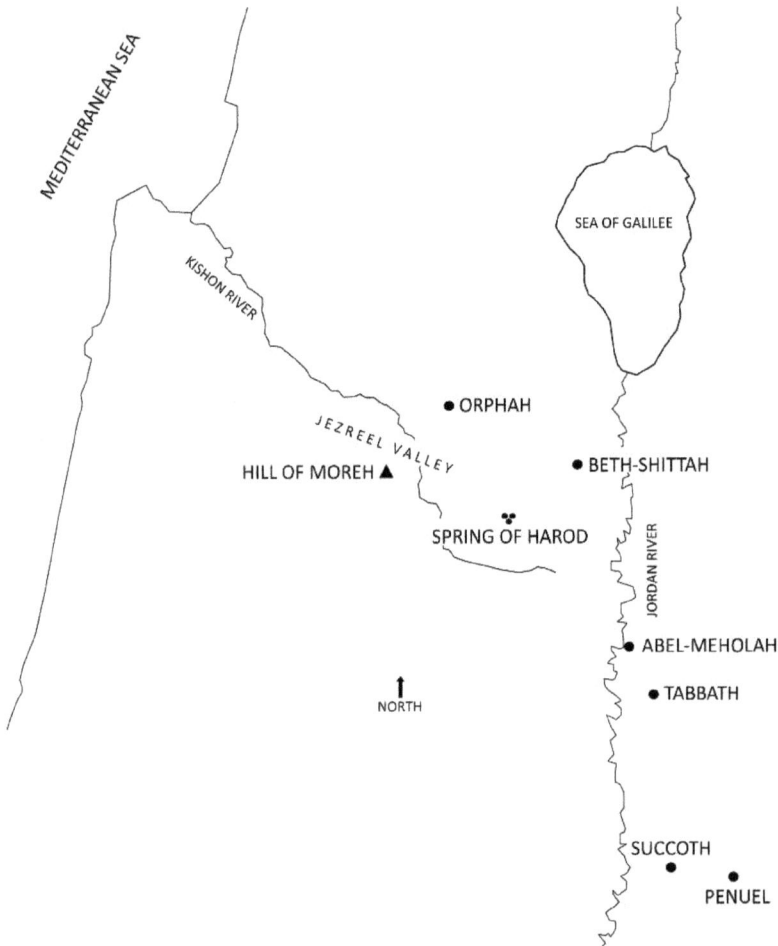

When finished with Ephraim, Gideon takes his 300 men to cross over the Jordan. By this point they are exhausted, but they press on (8:4).

They arrive at a town called Succoth and ask the people to give them bread to nourish them as they pursue the Midianite kings Zebah and Zalmunna (8:5). At this point, it's unclear why Gideon continues his pursuit of Midian, specifically their kings. Their leaders and army have been killed and dispersed, no longer threatening Israel with oppression. So why does Gideon continue? God is silent, so we're left to guess Gideon's motivation. Is it to finish what he began for God? Or to finish to his own satisfaction? Or another reason yet unseen?

After hearing about such a remarkable victory, we'd think the leaders of Succoth would give Gideon and his men whatever they want. But that's not what happens at all. Rather, they respond:

> Are the hands of Zebah and Zalmunna already in your hands,
> that we should give bread to your army? (8:6)

In other words, "We refuse to get involved (even in something as small as food) until we know for sure that Israel is victorious. Come back with Zebah and Zalmunna in captivity, and you can have all you want!" Not exactly the morale Gideon and his men are looking for, and they respond equivalently (8:7). Perhaps driven from lack of sleep and exhaustion (or just unbridled anger), Gideon tells the leaders of Succoth that *when* God gives Zebah and Zalmunna into his hands, he will thrash Succoth's leaders with wilderness thorns and briers. Ouch!

While Succoth isn't excused for their lack of support, Gideon's response hardly seems justifiable. He should have trusted God to execute proper punishment on Succoth, not taken it into his own hands with a promise of harsh retribution. God's continued silence in this account suggests Gideon may be operating outside His initial plan of deliverance, pursuing a personal agenda from this point on.[69]

Moving on from Succoth, Gideon and his sapped entourage make it to the city of Penuel (8:8). Gideon repeats his request of provisions, and Penuel responds like Succoth—they will not give the men provisions. Upon a second rejection, Gideon lashes out with a greater threat than before (8:9). Once he secured Zebah and Zalmunna, he would return and tear down the tower of Penuel. Towers served an important function of defense in those days, so tearing it down held greater significance than merely the destruction of real estate.

Tapping into their dwindling reserves of adrenaline, Gideon and his men press on. They learn that Zebah and Zalmunna are camping in Karkor with the remnant of their armies—15,000 men. We learn from verse 10 that 120,000 Midianite soldiers have been killed. So while 15,000 men is still an intimidating number, it's not nearly as scary as the previous total of 135,000!

Gideon's group attacks the camp when they're unsuspecting (following their early strategy the night before) and manages to disperse them (8:11). The Midianites flee with their kings, but Gideon and his men capture them and rout the entire army (8:12).

Having sealed the victory, Gideon is free to return home with his head held high. But he isn't about the let Succoth and Penuel escape without punishment for their former unpatriotic actions. On his way back, he captures a young man from Succoth and forces him to tell him the names of the princes and elders of Succoth, seventy-seven men in total (8:14). When he arrives in the town, he parades Zebah and Zalmunna in front of them, showing off the prize they doubted he could attain. He then proceeds to fulfill his threat—thrashing the princes and elders of Succoth with thorns and briers from the wilderness (8:15-16).

Penuel came next, but with added vengeance. Instead of merely tearing down the tower (which would have been punishment enough), Gideon kills all the men of the city (8:17). If there was ever a doubt about Gideon's motivations before, now there's not. He is clearly out of line and possibly out of control. Refusing to give supplies is bad, but not punishable by death. Gideon and his men murder the men of the city—their fellow countrymen—ironically acting to punish the town's unpatriotic actions. Murdering one's own people doesn't seem very patriotic either, Gideon!

After finishing off the men of Penuel, Gideon turns to Zebah and Zalmunna. He asks them a question, "What kind of men were they whom you killed at Tabor?" (8:18). Since the author never mentions Tabor before in conjunction with Gideon, we're left uncertain as to what Gideon is referring to. We can responsibly assume that Zebah and Zalmunna were involved in a killing or massacre at Tabor—a mountain in Galilee that borders the tribes of Issachar, Zebulun, and Naphtali.[70]

The kings' response gives us further insight. They tell Gideon that the men they killed "were like you, each one resembling the son of a king" (8:18). Quite a statement from two kings! Their response also confirms the transformation of Gideon. Gideon's change was so drastic, it must have been physically noticeable. Now he exudes an air of authority and power that evaded him entirely before.

Gideon's next statement reveals the reason he strove to capture Zebah and Zalmunna. The men they killed were his brothers, and he tells the kings, "if only you had let them live, I would not kill you" (8:19). Now we're certain Gideon is out for personal revenge, not a holy crusade for God and His people.

Revenge played a crucial role in the transformation Gideon experienced. When he realized he was winning against Midian during the initial battle, he capitalized on the momentum and decided to fuel the anger smoldering his heart since the news that his brothers were killed. When the Midianites subdued Israel, Gideon's anger was confined to a seething brew. But now that the tables have turned with Israel's victory, Gideon unleashes the revenge that's been stewing in his heart for so long.

We expect Gideon to kill the kings, but he surprises us again. He turns to his eldest son, Jether, and tells him to kill them instead (8:20). Gideon tries to include his son in the victory, perhaps to solidify his position and give him an opportunity for honor (at least in his mind).[71] But Jether doesn't draw his sword. Due to his youth, he is afraid and freezes (8:20).

Zebah and Zalmunna seize the opportunity to get a word in and say, "Rise up yourself, and fall on us; for as the man, so is his strength" (8:21). These two kings are nothing if not resolute! They show no fear in their impending death, challenging Gideon to rise up and kill them himself if he is the man he portrays himself to be.

With patience now a barren wasteland, Gideon kills the kings and takes the crescent ornaments that adorned their camels' necks, which signify royalty and high standing (8:21).

With the deaths of Zebah and Zalmunna, the deliverance from Midian comes to a concrete end. Although the second act of the battle story leaves much to be desired, we now expect the final cycle remarks that have concluded previous stories; namely, that the enemy is subdued and Israel experiences peace for a certain number of years.

Unfortunately, the story continues and does so in a manner that mirrors the degenerative state of Israel. When Gideon secures victory over the Midianites, the men of Israel approach him with a proposition. They want Gideon and his sons to rule over them (8:22).

Has Israel learned nothing? God is the One who delivered them from the hands of Midian; He simply used Gideon to do so. Also, God is the One who is supposed to reign over Israel as King, not a mere mortal—especially one with such significant faults. It's as if God is completely irrelevant to Israel, so much so that He doesn't even cross their minds. They seek to worship what they can see (keeping in line with their idolatry), except this time, he has a face and a name: Gideon.

The first sentence of Gideon's response makes us cheer with hopeful expectations. He quickly says, "I will not rule over you, nor shall my son rule over you; the Lord shall rule over you" (8:23). Yay, Gideon! Great answer. God is the One who should rule over Israel and who should have the attention of their hearts.

If only Gideon had kept his mouth shut.

The next part of Gideon's response eradicates any hope previously grasped. "'I would request of you, that each of you give me an earring from his spoil.' (For they had gold earrings, because they were Ishmaelites)" (8:24). While this doesn't seem all bad at first, what he does with the earrings makes us cringe:

> The weight of the gold earrings that he requested was 1,700 shekels of gold, besides the crescent ornaments and the pendants and the purple robes which were on the kings of Midian, and besides the neck bands that were on their camels' necks. Gideon made it into an ephod, and placed it in his city, Ophrah, and all Israel played the harlot with it there, so that it became a snare to Gideon and his household (8:26-27).

Fail. Total, utter failure, Gideon. First, he collects an offering for himself, not God. Then he has the audacity to use the "offering" to construct the very item God detests—an idol. Gideon's story ends where it began, though on a far more devastating note. His first act with God was to tear down the idols of his household and to replace them with an altar for the Lord. Now, as an accomplished warrior and leader of Israel, Gideon constructs an idol similar to what he tore down at the beginning of his rise to valiancy.

The ephod he constructs is unclear in purpose, though it probably was intended to "figuratively represent not only the garment that clothed a sacred image but also the image over which the garment was draped."[72] Just like Gideon's fleece tests, his ephod represented his desire to control God. He intends to use his idol to manipulate the God who delivered Israel from Midian.

Gideon never trusts in the Lord; or if he did, he did for only a moment before the first battle. This blatant act of idolatry symbolizes a slap in the face to God and completely dethrones Him from the hearts of the people He just saved.

It's enough to make us cry…and it gets worse.

Having effectively led Israel back into the idolatry God fought so hard to eliminate, Gideon assumes a position as makeshift king in Israel. Midian is subdued and the land is at peace (at least politically) for forty years until

Gideon's death (8:28). Gideon moves back home to Ophrah and acts like a king of foreign nations instead of the righteous and mighty leader God desired him to be (8:29).

Taking many wives, Gideon increases his family to include seventy sons (8:30). This type of behavior was typical in those days, even among Israeli kings later on. As if his wives weren't enough, Gideon takes concubines as well, one of them bearing a son named Abimelech (8:31). After forty years reigning as Israel's "king," Gideon dies and is buried in the tomb of his father, Joash, in Ophrah (8:32).

--

Thus comes the end of Gideon, the valiant warrior. Gideon reveals his true colors of selfishness and an obsession with control through a lifetime of decisions that place him, not God, on the throne of his heart.

Though barely visible, Gideon's teeny bud of faith pushes upward. He recognizes God's call on his life and obeys Him despite numerous delays and hesitancies. Even though he doesn't finish strong (quite the opposite, actually), God does use him to deliver Israel from the domineering hand of Midian. Imagine how different the story would have been if Gideon had unleashed his faith by trusting God as King instead of trying to manipulate the circumstances so he could be king himself!

Despite Gideon's blunders, we cannot miss God in this story. His mercy, patience, grace, and love leave us amazed. The world has yet to realize the fullness of God in His uninhibited love for us. Such a revelation would probably leave us dead from shock. We remain so blind to God and His love for us, even though He explicitly describes it in His Word. Israel doesn't see God's love for them either (nor do they even want to see it), but we have an opportunity to seek and embrace God's love for us through Jesus Christ every day. May we learn from Israel and Gideon's mistakes— making God our King and savoring His love instead of brazenly rejecting Him as they did.

GROUP STUDY

INTRODUCTION

"Circumstances do not make the man, they reveal him." James Allen

Integrity and character take lifetimes to build and only moments to shatter. Our true colors shine brightest in daunting circumstances, and we've all experienced moments when we don't shine as brightly as we'd like.

DISCUSS

- Describe a time in your life when your true colors were revealed, and they weren't as pleasant as you hoped they'd be.
- What were the circumstances?
- What did you learn about yourself?

THE WORD

Gideon was a man with great skills, but a less-than-shining character. He led his army with confidence and dealt cunningly with those who would cause potential problems (Judges 8:1-3). But ultimately, Gideon chose to look out for himself, making decisions through the lens of self-preservation instead of self-sacrifice for God's glory.

Though God used him to accomplish much regardless of character flaws, Gideon's true colors emerged after delivering Israel from the fierce grip of Midian. What started as hopeful leadership quickly turned putrid when his actions refused to reflect his words. Read the passage below:

> The men of Israel said to Gideon, "Rule over us, both you and your son, also your son's son, for you have delivered us from the

hand of Midian." But Gideon said to them, "I will not rule over you, nor shall my son rule over you; the Lord shall rule over you." Yet Gideon said to them, "I would request of you, that each of you give me an earring from his spoil." (For they had gold earrings, because they were Ishmaelites.). They said, "We will surely give them."…Gideon made it into an ephod, and placed it in his city, Ophrah, and all Israel played the harlot with it there, so that it became a snare to Gideon and his household. (Judges 8:22-25a, 27)

- How did Gideon start strong in this passage?
- How did he immediately compromise his integrity as a leader—as *God's chosen* leader?
- What do you think was the turning point for him? What would you have been tempted to do in such a situation?

DISCUSS/ACTION

When push came to shove, Gideon desired his own glory rather than God's. After obtaining victory in the battle over Midian, Gideon pursued his desires (revenge for his brothers) over God's desires and timing. He then proceeded to live as a king to the people, which resulted in the cycle of idolatry being ignited yet again (before he died, unlike previous judges).

D.A. Carson once said, "It is always a wretched bastardization of our goals when we want to win glory for ourselves instead of for Him." In these times our true colors shine…

- Is there an area of your life right now in which you're seeking (or accepting) glory for something that doesn't belong to you? Or perhaps letting people think something of you that isn't true behind closed doors?

- What steps do you need to take to repent of that? With God? With others?
- What are some practical ways to divert the glory of your future successes and accomplishments to God—merging your true colors with those others perceive in you?

PRAY

WEEK SIX:
Sins of our Fathers

JUDGES 8:33-9:57
PERSONAL STUDY QUESTIONS

1. When does Israel fall back into sin again? (8:33)

2. In addition to forgetting God, who else does Israel treat badly? (8:35)

3. It's amazing how short our memories are sometimes. We do something kind for a friend, and she conveniently forgets when we need help later on. Or someone betrays us, which immediately erases years of confidence and trust.

   Exercising wisdom and discernment in relationships is difficult, especially when we've been wronged. But God requires that we be at peace with all men (Romans 12:18). We are created for relationships, and we thrive only when we're in them.

   Is there someone you need to reconcile with? What must happen in order for reconciliation to be achieved? What can you do this week to make it possible?

4. Who are Abimelech's parents? (8:31, 9:1)

5. Who does Abimelech go and speak to in Shechem? (9:1)

6. What does Abimelech want to be? (9:2-3)

7. What does Abimelech do with the money the Shechem leaders gives him? (9:4)

8. What does Abimelech do to his brothers? (9:5)

9. How do the men of Shechem respond to Abimelech's actions? (9:6)

10. The lone survivor of the brothers, Jotham, stands up for justice against Abimelech. In your own words, summarize what he says to them: (9:7-20)

11. What is his point? (9:16-20)

12. What does Jotham do when he finishes his speech? (9:21)

13. How long does Abimelech rule over Israel? (9:22)

14. Why does God cause schism between Abimelech and Shechem? (9:24)

15. What does Shechem do to Abimelech and his men? (9:25)

16. Who does Shechem put their trust in behind Abimelech's back? (9:26)

17. What position does Gaal desire in Shechem? (9:29)

18. Who grows angry with Gaal and sends messengers to Abimelech? (9:30-31)

19. What advice does he give Abimelech through the messengers? (9:32-33)

20. Does Abimelech listen to him? (9:34)

21. Who wins the battle—Gaal or Abimelech? (9:40-41)

22. Who does Abimelech turn his violent attention to next? (9:42-45)

23. What does Abimelech do when he hears that all the leaders of Shechem are gathered in the tower? (9:48-49)

24. Who does Abimelech go after next? (9:50)

25. As Abimelech and his worthless men begin reenacting their previous strategy, who puts an end to his evil plans? (9:53)

    • How does she do so? (9:53)

26. How does Abimelech die? (9:54)

27. How do the men of Israel respond to Abimelech's death? (9:55)

28. Does God execute justice in the end? (9:56-57)

COMMENTARY

As the book of Judges progresses, the judges mirror the degeneration of the people they deliver. Ehud moves impulsively and recklessly in his victory over Eglon. Barak's fear and hesitancy to obey God strips him of the glory he so desperately seeks. Gideon accomplishes victory despite multiple arguments, excuses, and demands of confirmation. Victory proves insufficient for him even when he gets it. Instead of being satisfied, he seeks personal revenge and then accepts the people's honor, which belonged only to God.

While we always hope for the best, the story following Gideon hardly shocks us. Since Gideon usurps God's position as king in Israel and hardly advocates faithfulness, it's no wonder his children follow in his footsteps.

Abimelech's story is one of blatant disregard for God. (Even the best rationalizers can't figure him as a God-feaer.) There's some silver lining in this, though—he is not a real judge. He was never called by God to be a judge, so his lack of faithfulness makes sense (though isn't excusable). He never pretended to care about God, nor does he seek to acknowledge God's existence. All Abimelech cares about is himself, and his life is a potent display of what happens when that's the road we choose to take. But we'll get there soon enough.

Gideon barely takes his last breath before Israel decides to play the harlot with the Baals again (8:33). Since Gideon initiated this behavior by creating the ephod and idols, Israel's behavior isn't surprising. The author gives slightly more detail to their idolatry this time around, though. Instead of merely stating that Israel did evil in the sight of the Lord, the author tells us:

> The sons of Israel again played the harlot with the Baals, and made Baal-berith their god. Thus the sons of Israel did not remember the Lord their God, who had delivered them from the

hands of all their enemies on every side, nor did they show
kindness to the household of Jerubbaal (that is, Gideon) in
accord with all the good that he had done to Israel (8:33-35).

Baal-berith means "baal or lord *of the covenant,*" which is highly ironic,
considering Israel is supposed to be in a covenant with God, not Baal.[73]
Israel willingly rejects God and all He has done for them, including their
deliverance from every enemy imaginable (8:34). I don't know what the
Israelites are telling their children about their history and heritage, but they
certainly aren't passing on the amazing stories of God's rescue and
sovereign protection over them!

If falling away from God isn't terrible enough, Israel also turns against
Gideon's family and begins treating them harshly (8:35). While Gideon
didn't lead them into an upstanding and committed relationship with God,
he did deliver and protect them from their enemies (with God's help, of
course) for forty years. Thus, the fact that Israel turns against Gideon
reveals the increasing depravity of their hearts—they're not even standing
by their physical deliverer and protector! When Gideon dies, it once again
becomes every man for himself, and they begin their newfound "freedom"
by following their own leader.

We're reintroduced to Abimelech at the start of Chapter 9. Abimelech ("my
father is king")[74] is the illegitimate son of Gideon with a concubine who
resided in Shechem (8:31). Shechem is located just south of Ophrah, where
Gideon's family still resides. With Gideon dead, his sons are presumably
still ruling, though not with the full support of Israel. Perhaps Abimelech
notices the people's weariness of Gideon and his family, so he decides to
capitalize on it.

Knowing his less-than-upstanding identity as a concubine's son won't get
him far in life, he decides to go to his mother's city and promote himself to
them. Speaking to his mother's relatives he says:

Speak, now, in the hearing of all the leaders of Shechem, "Which is better for you, that seventy men, all the sons of Jerubbaal, rule over you, or that one man rule over you?" Also remember that I am your bone and your flesh (9:2).

Abimelech inherited the smarts of his father and grandfather. He begins his search for power in a place he knows he'll be welcomed (with his mother's relatives). Once there, he uses shrewd manipulation to get their attention, reasoning that it's better for one man to rule over them as opposed to seventy of Gideon's sons. He also casually reminds them that, unlike the seventy, he is related to them by blood. Surely they'll support him over the rest of his brothers!

His mother's relatives bite the bait. This situation reminds us of politics today—if we can get someone elected to a leadership position, we'll have him in our back pockets to accomplish our agendas! Abimelech's family gets consumed with the prospect of power, so they appear before the leaders of Shechem with Abimelech's proposal (9:3). Having his family as his greatest advocate confirms Abimelech's shrewdness. Appearing to the leaders of Shechem as his own advocate would get him laughed out of the room. But since he's convinced his family to support him, he can stand by with false humility and allow them to do the bidding for him.

The leaders of Shechem receive the proposal with open arms, especially since he's a blood relative (9:3). To solidify the deal, they give Abimelech seventy pieces of silver (conveniently corresponding to the number of Abimelech's brothers), which are taken from the temple (or house) of Baal-berith (9:4). You'd think they'd do a bit of checking into Abimelech before making him a leader. Though not privy to background checks like we're used to, they certainly could have investigated a bit! But no, they want power and Abimelech promises exactly that. Cheers to ill-thought decisions, gentlemen!

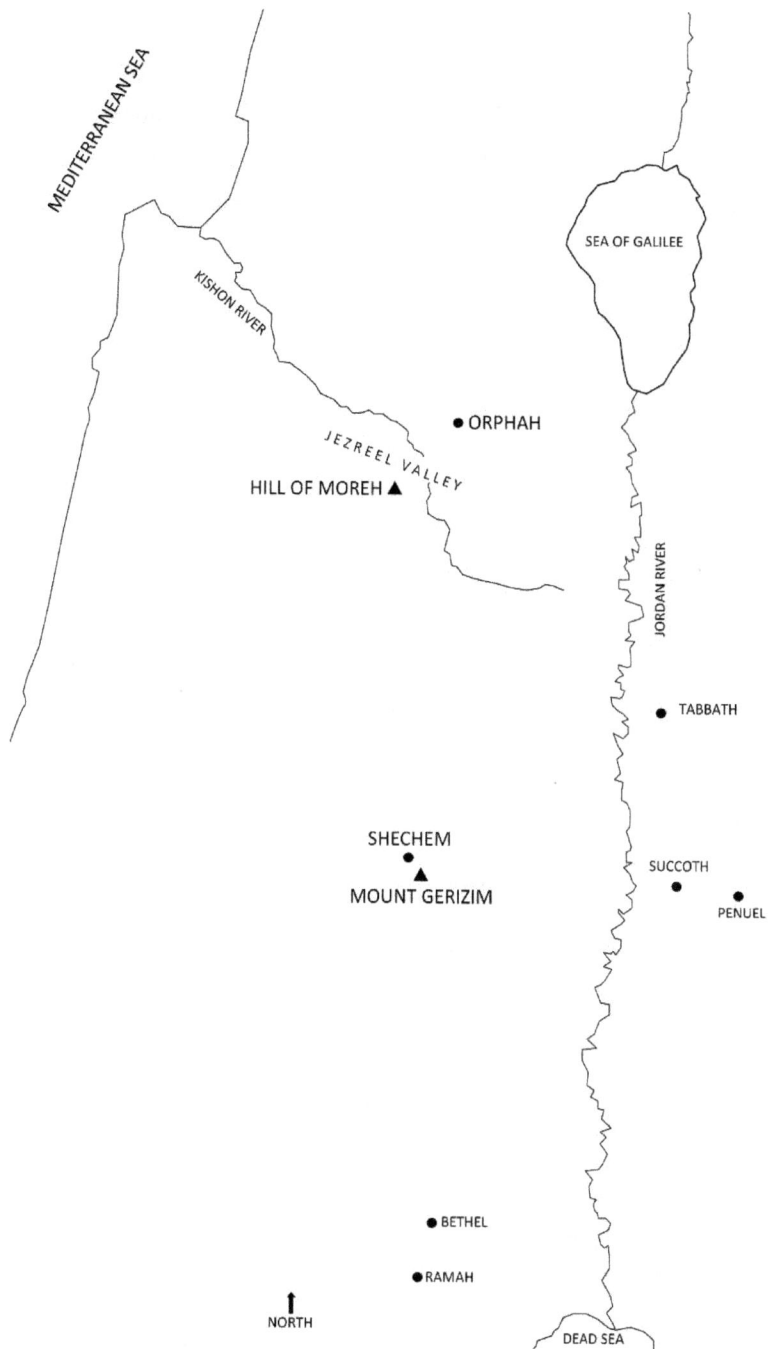

MEDITERRANEAN SEA

KISHON RIVER

SEA OF GALILEE

● ORPHAH

JEZREEL VALLEY

HILL OF MOREH ▲

JORDAN RIVER

● TABBATH

SHECHEM
●
▲
MOUNT GERIZIM

SUCCOTH
●

● PENUEL

● BETHEL

● RAMAH

↑
NORTH

DEAD SEA

139

Abimelech's first acts as leader are appalling. As soon as he receives the money, he hires a bunch of "worthless and reckless fellows" to follow him and act as his minions (9:4). This move completely undermines his competence as a leader. Natural and respected leaders gain a following simply by being themselves. Abimelech gains a following through bribery, and it's the worst sort of following one could have.

Their first task as Abimelech's monkeys is to help him kill his brothers (9:5). Perhaps fueled by jealousy and/or the desire to lead without competition, Abimelech and his horde travel to Ophrah and kill sixty-nine of his brothers upon a single stone. This stone was likely one used to slaughter animal sacrifices, making Abimelech's actions that much more grotesque and one that sinks our hearts.[75] How do you get so consumed with jealousy and selfish pursuits that you murder sixty-nine men? And not just strangers, but your own flesh and blood! Abimelech abuses his newly acquired power in the worst way, and the sickening part is that he doesn't think twice about it. He eliminates the competition permanently, and the fact that they were blood brothers is inconsequential to him.

The lack of strong defenses on behalf of the brothers tells us they weren't concerned about attacks.[76] After all, the land has experienced peace for forty years; who would expect such a gruesome slaughter? They're shocked at Abimelech's eruption. Each of them probably gawked in horror as their brothers' screams were silenced before them, knowing they were next.

Only one brother escapes the massacre, and in the chaos he runs to hide himself (9:5). When Abimelech finishes murdering his brothers, the men of Shechem and Beth-Millo assemble together to make Abimelech king. The inaugural ceremony takes place by the oak of the pillar which is in Shechem (9:6). Oh, that's just grand, Shechem. Officially make him your leader *after* he reveals his heart of ice. Not exactly a leader I'd want to follow!

Abimelech now takes the place of his father as makeshift king, and does so through an incredulous shed of blood. Shechem is just as guilty as Abimelech, however. Not only have they refused to defend the innocent brothers, but they actually praise and reward Abimelech for his treacherous act. Both parties are guilty and can't escape the blood on their hands.

When Jotham, the sole survivor of Gideon's sons, discovers what happened to his brothers, he takes action (9:7). He makes his way up Mount Gerizim to deliver his famous discourse. It's highly ironic that Mount Gerizim is his choice of location, for "the mountain was traditionally associated with the blessing of God; now it would be the site of a curse that would tear the nation's social fabric in pieces."[77]

Standing in a strategic acoustic location where his voice can be heard, Jotham shouts a parable to the men of Shechem:

> Once the trees went forth to anoint a king over them, and they said to the olive tree, "Reign over us!" But the olive tree said to them, "Shall I leave my fatness with which God and men are honored, and go to wave over the trees?" Then the trees said to the fig tree, "You come, reign over us!" But the fig tree said to them, "Shall I leave my sweetness and my good fruit, and go to wave over the trees?" Then the trees said to the vine, "You come, reign over us!" But the vine said to them, "Shall I leave my new wine, which cheers God and men, and go to wave over the trees?" Finally all the trees said to the bramble, "You come, reign over us!" The bramble said to the trees, "If in truth you are anointing me as king over you, come and take refuge in my shade; but if not, may fire come out from the bramble and consume the cedars of Lebanon" (9:8-15).

The parable reveals Abimelech and Shechem's treachery against Gideon's family. Since no one else seems to have a heart warmer than the climate of Antarctica, Jotham will exercise his on their behalf. The bramble (a worthless shrub) aptly represents Abimelech, who is hardly qualified for any kind of leadership position, much less a makeshift king. Jotham proclaims that if Shechem and Abimelech have dealt with integrity in making Abimelech king at the expense of Gideon's family, then rejoice. But since that's clearly not the case, Jotham says:

> But if not, let fire come out from Abimelech and consume the
> men of Shechem and Beth-millo; and let fire come out from the
> men of Shechem and Beth-millo and consume Abimelech (9:20).

Jotham curses Abimelech and the men of Shechem for their colossal sin against Gideon's family. The curse also foreshadows their impending doom, for their actions do not rest easy with the sovereign and almighty God, either. As soon as Jotham finishes his declaration against Abimelech and his entourage, he flees to Beer (south of the Dead Sea) and remains there to avoid further encounters with Abimelech (9:21).

Even though Abimelech is not a legitimate judge, he still reigns over a segment of Israel for three years (9:22). At the end of these years, God decides He's had enough. He sends an evil spirit between Abimelech and the men of Shechem, causing Shechem to deal treacherously with Abimelech.

We should not become distracted by the fact that God sends "an evil spirit" to disrupt the relationship between Abimelech and Shechem (9:23). The phrase "evil spirit" (*ruah raa* in Hebrew) appears several times throughout the Old Testament, and suggests a "calamitous spirit," or one that causes "negative and destructive effects on the object."[78] God is not evil; nor is He the source of evil. But He does allow evil to occur in this life (a byproduct of freewill and fallibility), and in this case, He uses it to draw out the inevitable friction between "self-seeking opportunists and those capable of treacherous murder."[79]

Conflict between Abimelech and Shechem is unavoidable because both seek success and preservation above anything else. Hostile callousness leaves no room for selfless peace. By sending an evil spirit to them, God simply hurries the inevitable friction along.

If we're still struggling to understand the whole "evil spirit" phenomena, the author even gives us the reason God did it:

> So that the violence done to the seventy sons of Jerubbaal might come, and their blood might be laid on Abimelech their brother, who killed them, and on the men of Shechem, who strengthened his hands to kill his brothers (9:24).

God is just; and He keeps evil on a leash (as we discovered in week one). After three years, He sets a plan in motion for Abimelech to fall in a way that punishes Shechem for their role in egregious acts as well.

Shechem is the first party to flare up in their dissention. For unmentioned reasons, they set ambushes against Abimelech and his men on the tops of mountains, robbing all who might pass by (9:25). Abimelech is informed of their betrayal but doesn't take action, at least not yet.

Meanwhile, a man named Gaal visits Shechem with family members and gains the trust of the men there (9:26). We have no information about Gaal other than the fact that he's the son of Ebed (also an unknown individual). But he somehow manages to sweet-talk the men of Shechem into trusting him, much like Abimelech had done three years prior.

Shechem's new relationship with Gaal is celebrated by a festival in the house of their god (9:27). The wine begins flowing, which makes their tongues loose, and soon they are cursing Abimelech. Gaal capitalizes on their vulnerable state and says:

> Who is Abimelech, and who is Shechem, that we should serve him? Is he not the son of Jerubbaal, and is Zebul not his lieutenant? Serve the men of Hamor the father of Shechem; but why should we serve him? Would, therefore, that this people were under my authority! Then I would remove Abimelech (9:28-29).

Look who wants the power now? Directly contrasting Abimelech's previous proposal, which focused on his *Shechem* heritage, Gaal turns the crowd's attention to the other side of Abimelech's lineage—Jerubbaal (Gideon). "Gideon wasn't from Shechem, so he clearly can't be trusted," reasons Gaal (even though he isn't from Shechem either). Since Gideon's blood flows through Abimelech's veins, Gaal entices Shechem to serve the men of Hamor before serving Abimelech. Hamor means "donkey," and the expression "men of Hamor" may be equivalent "to the 'sons of the treaty,' since the sacrifice of a [donkey] was an essential feature in the ratification of a treaty amongst the Amorites."[80]

Gaal has Shechem's undivided attention and then injects his motive for speaking against Abimelech—he wants to be their king and leader! If Shechem would make him their leader, he promises to rid them of Abimelech, something they have been thinking about for a while anyway. In a final dose of intoxicated bravery (or stupidity), he calls to Abimelech, who is not present in the room, "Increase your army and come out!" (9:29). This man is ready for a fight, and the men of Shechem seem to be backing his plans.

Unbeknownst to them (or absent from their concern), Abimelech's lieutenant and the leader of the city, Zebul, is listening (9:30). Seething with anger, he sends messengers to Abimelech to inform him that Gaal and his relatives are stirring up the city against him (9:31). He then suggests a plan: Abimelech and his men should lie in wait in the fields outside the city. When morning dawns, they should rush upon the city and kill Gaal and whoever comes out to fight against him (9:32-33). Apparently blood is the only type of communication these people understand.

Abimelech agrees with Zebul (his position as leader is being threatened, after all), and he does as Zebul suggests (9:34). In the morning, Abimelech and his men wait in the fields of Shechem and divide into four companies.

When Gaal wakes up and stands at the city gate, he sees the people and mentions it to Zebul (9:35-36). Feigning ignorance, Zebul assures Gaal it's only the shadows of the mountains moving as the sun rises. As minutes draw on, Gaal once again speaks up and tells Zebul that it's a company of men, not mere shadows. Knowing it's too late, Zebul challenges Gaal: "Where is your boasting now with which you said, 'Who is Abimelech that we should serve him?' Is this not the people whom you despised? Go out now and fight with them!" (9:38).

In a hurried frenzy, Gaal charges out with the leaders of Shechem on his heels to fight Abimelech (9:39). No doubt all the partying the night before does not bode well for them early this morning. Abimelech and his men seize a rather effortless victory over Gaal and the men following him (9:40).

Abimelech chooses not to enter the city, opting to remain in Arumah (near Shechem) instead (9:41). Zebul gets busy ejecting Gaal and his relatives from Shechem's city limits. They are no longer welcome within the walls of the city, which is quite understandable, considering the havoc they caused.

Now that the culprits of destruction have left, we're tempted to think Abimelech and Shechem will reach peace (or at least an understanding) again. The battle has been fought; surely they will move on. Not so much. God isn't yet finished punishing them for the blood they shed.

The next day the people of Shechem leave the city walls to go to the fields (9:42). This was not unusual; for fields were not located within the city walls. Thus, farmers and other workers would need to travel outside the walls so they could tend to their fields and livelihood. Abimelech learns that the people are returning to their typical daily routines and concocts a plan of his own (9:43). This time he takes his people and divides them into three units. He has them wait in the field, and when he notices the people coming out of the city, they all emerge from their hiding places to slaughter them.

What did these poor farmers and merchants ever do to you, Abimelech? But as we've seen, Abimelech's heart is calloused and hard. He cares more for revenge and self-imposed vindication than the lives of others. Some leader. As if this isn't awful enough, Abimelech and his band of worthless vagrants leave their positions in the fields and head for the city gate (9:44).

Once there, they continue their attack on the people of Shechem, slaying many more. Though it takes all day, they capture the city and murder the people within it. Out of sheer spite, they also "razed the city and sowed it with salt," rendering it worthless (9:45).

The leaders hear what is happening and head toward the tower of Shechem for safety (9:46). Can't really blame them! Can you imagine hearing (and perhaps witnessing) the slaughter of an entire city? Can you hear the screams? Mothers heave infants to their bosoms, franticly trying to hide them from Abimelech and his maniacal horde. Children who laughed just moments before meet death in their next breath. Blood pelts the ground like rain in a thunderstorm as bodies spasm after life evades them. The scene is gruesome. Abimelech and his men act as crazed extensions of Satan himself—out for blood and with no intention of stopping until their definition of vengeance is secured.

Abimelech discovers that the nobles of the city are now hiding in the tower (9:47). Instead of going straight for it, Abimelech tells his men to follow him and do as he does reminding us of Gideon's instructions to his men in 7:17 (9:48). These are the first recorded words of Abimelech since his proposal back in 9:2. He and his cronies travel to nearby Mount Zalmon to slice branches from trees. Once everyone holds one, they follow Abimelech to the foot of the tower of Shechem and lay them against the inner chamber (9:49). We can see where this is headed. Someone ignites the branches with fire, and the tower burns. Inside, one thousand people choke from the smoke seeping under the doors. Part of Jotham's curse is fulfilled with this horrific act. He decreed fire to "come out of Abimelech and consume the men of Shechem," (9:20) and that's precisely what happens.

Placing our agendas above God's comes at a heavy cost. Abimelech and Shechem put themselves above all else, and liters of blood and myriads of lives are taken unnecessarily. Our idolatry may not result in the death of thousands of people, but the consequences are dire nonetheless. When we usurp God's position with our own idols (fame, position, reputation, relationships, etc.) we sacrifice the blessings He yearns to pour into our lives. We also, perhaps unknowingly, hemorrhage our relationships with God and with others, incurring faith-crippling consequences like relational friction, bitterness, arrogance, loneliness, distrust, and anxiety. Just like Abimelech and Shechem, we move further away from God when we cater to our sin, inviting havoc and evil into our lives as well.

The consequences are far from over in the story of Abimelech, however. Filled with rage like his father before him, Abimelech continues his thirst for blood against the citizens of Thebez (9:50). This city is unmentioned until this point, but its strategic reference here leads us to believe that it stands in relatively close proximity to Shechem, and thus, within the realm of Abimelech's self-imposed rule. For some reason, Abimelech is not pleased with them, so he decides to do something about it.

Abimelech and his men camp against and capture Thebez. In a last-ditch effort of defense, the people of Thebez head for the city tower (9:51). Whether they've heard of Shechem's recent tower demise is uncertain. But it also doesn't matter at this point. The tower is their last chance for survival. They stuff themselves in and hope for the best.

Once inside, Abimelech must have thought they were an easy target, just like before. He gathers his men around it, planning once again to burn it with fire (9:52). Perhaps in his haste or arrogance, he neglects to pay attention to what is happening above him. If he had, he may have lived.

Above him in the tower stands a woman holding an upper millstone in her hands (9:53). This millstone would have been quite heavy, made of basalt or sandstone.[81] It served as a grinder, a chore usually undertaken by slaves in prominent households, or wives in smaller ones. This was a humiliating task for a man, but was a recurring domestic task for a woman.[82]

Using the tool available to her (like Ehud, Shamgar, and Jael), the woman hurls the millstone toward Abimelech. It finds its target and crushes his skull. I would have loved to watch the woman's reaction. I probably would've been like, "No way! It actually worked!" as I jumped up and down like a schoolgirl in line for ice cream. Perhaps this woman was wiser, more self-controlled. I envision a smile curling her lips as her fellow citizens rally around her with praise. "Hooray!" And from the men, "Why didn't I think of that?"

Stunned but not yet unconscious, Abimelech looks up to see the culprit of his demise. Noticing it's a woman, he calls his armor bearer and tells him to kill him with a sword "so that it will not be said of me, 'A woman slew him.'" The young man complies and kills the dying man (9:54).

How humiliating for Abimelech, a man sure of his competence and propensity for victory. After easy defeats over Gaal and Shechem, he haughtily believed Thebez will fall without much effort. To be defeated by them—worse, by a woman with a millstone—completely defies reason and brings him to the lowest point imaginable before death. This brings Jael's story to mind, for the great and mighty Sisera never dreamed of meeting his end by the hand of a woman either.

Adding insult to his death (though he never knew it), all his men leave for their homes when Abimelech dies (9:55). This retreat in light of sure victory tells us they never were loyal to Abimelech to begin with—only to the funds, lifestyle, and/or popularity an alliance with him secured.

While Jotham's curse came to fruition quite literally with Shechem, it doesn't come through with "fire" in Abimelech's downfall (though fire is involved). But his downfall comes just the same. The actions of both Abimelech and the men of Shechem are now repaid. Justice is complete.

> Thus God repaid the wickedness of Abimelech, which he had done to his father in killing his seventy brothers. Also God returned all the wickedness of the men of Shechem on their heads, and the curse of Jotham the son of Jerubbaal came upon them (9:56-57).

God exacts justice on everyone for every sin. He's perfect, and not taking action against the sins of the world would defy His nature. Fortunately, through Jesus Christ, our sins are cleansed, and He enables us to stand before Him blameless and upright. But unlike Abimelech and Shechem, we must repent, and repentance involves a complete transformation. It's not enough to be sorry or regret our actions. We must match our sorrow with actions that mirror God's perfect heart, not our deformed ones. Even though we still struggle with sin after accepting Christ, He's moving us toward holiness. But we must persevere!

God's mercies and unfathomable love are available for anyone who will receive them. Israel continually refused to accept His grace and lovingkindness by prostituting themselves to idols. But once again, we have the opportunity to learn from their mistakes. We don't have to stand condemned and enslaved to the sin that claws at our hearts. We can be free through the blood of Christ. Will you accept it?

Abimelech refused God and made his own agenda the priority of his life, following in his father's footsteps. While we cannot change where we come from (or who our parents are) we certainly can refuse to follow their paths. The past need not be repeated if we proactively change our course. Abimelech never broke the generational sin of his father. In fact, he made it much worse. But we don't have to follow in his footsteps or the footsteps of our parents (if they're unpleasant). With God's help, we can conquer generational sin and set up new heritages for our children and future generations.

GROUP STUDY

INTRODUCTION

The apple doesn't fall far from the tree.

Most of us are far more like our parents than we'd like to admit. We inherit personalities, quirks, passions, talents, and skills from them—sometimes much to our chagrin. "Generational sin" is a term used to describe negative behavioral patterns passed down from generation to generation. Some of us recognize our negative tendencies and choose to rise above them. Others remain ignorant—either willingly or unknowingly—and continue in the rut our parents paved for us.

While we can't escape our heritage, we can determine how far we fall from the tree.

DISCUSS

- What habits, behavioral patterns, personality quirks, or talents have you received from your parents?
- What negative characteristics do you notice in your parents? Do you see those characteristics in yourself? Give an example.

THE WORD

As mentioned last week, while Gideon was used by God to deliver Israel from Midian, he also lacked integrity and came to the end of his life on a poor note—contributing to the reestablishment of Baal worship via his ephod.

His illegitimate son, Abimelech, inherited Gideon's sordid character and led Israel deeper into their cycle of degeneration. He usurped his family's rule, killed all but one of his brothers, and subsequently launched into a vengeful tirade against multiple peoples and cities.

One particular skill Abimelech inherited from his father and grandfather was his ability to steer people into doing what he wanted. Compare the following accounts of Gideon and Abimelech:

> Then the men of Ephraim said to him [Gideon], "What is this thing you have done to us, not calling us when you went to fight against Midian?" And they contended with him vigorously. But he said to them, "What have I done now in comparison with you? Is not the gleaning of the grapes of Ephraim better than the vintage of Abiezer? God has given the leaders of Midian, Oreb and Zeb into your hands; and what was I able to do in comparison with you?" Then their anger toward him subsided when he said that. (Judges 8:1-3)

> And Abimelech the son of Jerubbaal went to Shechem to his mother's relatives, and spoke to them and to the whole clan of the household of his mother's father, saying, "Speak, now, in the hearing of all the leaders of Shechem, 'Which is better for you, that seventy men, all the sons of Jerubbaal, rule over you, or that one man rule over you?' Also remember that I am your bone and your flesh." And his mother's relatives...were inclined to follow Abimelech, for they said, "He is our relative." (Judges 9:1-3)

- What similarities do you notice between Gideon (Jerubbaal) and Abimelech?
- The differences between the two lie primarily in the motivations behind their actions. What do you think were their motivations in these two accounts?
- Was Abimelech using his inherited skills and tendencies for good or for bad?

151

DISCUSS/ACTION

While we are products of our parents to an extent, we can choose how to use what we inherit from them. Abimelech inherited Gideon's skill of influential communication but used it for selfish purposes, which resulted in Israel's demise.

- What can you do to overcome the negative characteristics you've inherited from your parents? How can you use your skills in positive ways instead of negative ones?
- What are some practical steps you can take this week to deliberately use what you've inherited from your parents for good?

PRAY

WEEK SEVEN:
Empty Vows

Judges 10:1-12:7
PERSONAL STUDY QUESTIONS

1. Who arises after Abimelech to judge Israel? (10:1)

2. How long does he judge Israel? (10:2)

3. Who arises to judge Israel after him? (10:3)

4. How long is his judgeship? (10:3)

5. How many sons does he have? (10:4)

6. What gods does Israel serve after he dies? (10:6)

7. Who does God sell Israel into the hands of when they turn away from Him this time? (10:7)

8. How long do these enemies afflict Israel? (10:8)

9. How does Israel respond to their affliction? (10:10)

10. How does God respond to their plea? (10:11-14)

11. What does Israel do to indicate genuine repentance this time? (10:16)

    Genuine repentance (not just shallow remorse) requires action—persistent, consistent action that mirrors God's ways, not our own. Most times when we get caught in sin, we want to change, but we give up after only a couple of attempts. God wants us to persevere, and He makes it possible through His Holy Spirit, who dwells within us. Nothing is too difficult for Him, and we can overcome any sin if we persistently yield to Him and place Him on the throne of our hearts.

    Do you need to repent of a sin in your life right now? What will repentance require of you? How can you take action in your repentance in your daily life?

12. Does Israel wait for God to choose a leader for them? (10:18)

13. What strong characteristic is mentioned about Jephthah? (11:1)

14. What distinctive flaw compromises his status as a legitimate son? (11:1)

15. Who drives Jephthah out of his father's household? (11:2)

16. Who gathers around Jephthah when he flees to Tob? (11:3)

17. Who comes to Jephthah when the sons of Ammon rise to fight against Israel? (11:5)

18. Why did they come to him? (11:8)

19. What do they offer Jephthah in exchange for his military help and leadership? (11:10)

20. Once Jephthah is inaugurated as leader, what does he do? (11:12)

21. How does the king of Ammon respond to him? (11:13)

22. After recounting a diatribe of Israel's history, what's the point Jephthah tries to communicate to the king? (11:23-27)

23. How does the king of Ammon respond? (11:28)

24. What significant action takes place as Jephthah prepares to rally troops? (11:29)

25. What does Jephthah vow to God? (11:30-31)

26. Nearly every person on the face of the earth has tried to make an exchange with God: "Oh, God, if you'll do *this* for me I promise to do *that* forever and ever!" Have you ever made a rash vow to God? How did it turn out? Did He give you your request? Have you upheld your end of the bargain?

27. Who's victorious in the battle? (11:32)

28. Who comes out to greet Jephthah when he returns home? (11:34)

29. How does Jephthah react? (11:35)

30. What does his daughter ask for when Jephthah tells her of his vow? (11:37)

31. Does Jephthah carry out his vow? (11:39)

32. What custom took place in Israel in honor of his daughter? (11:40)

33. Who comes complaining to Jephthah after the victory? (12:1)

34. What happens as a result of the feud? (12:4-6)

35. How long does Jephthah judge Israel? (12:7)

36. Who arises to judge Israel after Jephthah? (12:8)

37. Who did he give his sons and daughters in marriage to? (12:9)

38. How long does he judge Israel? (12:9)

39. Who judges Israel after him? (12:11)

40. How long does he judge Israel? (12:11)

41. Who is the next (and final) minor judge of Israel? (12:13)

42. What do his sons and grandsons do? (12:14)

43. How long does he judge Israel? (12:14)

COMMENTARY

Abimelech's reign (and life) have now come to an end, and he leaves Israel no better than when he began (just like his dad). Everyone is doing right in their own eyes, and no one is seeking after the Lord. The cycle continues in a downward spiral, and by this point we're not optimistic about anything changing.

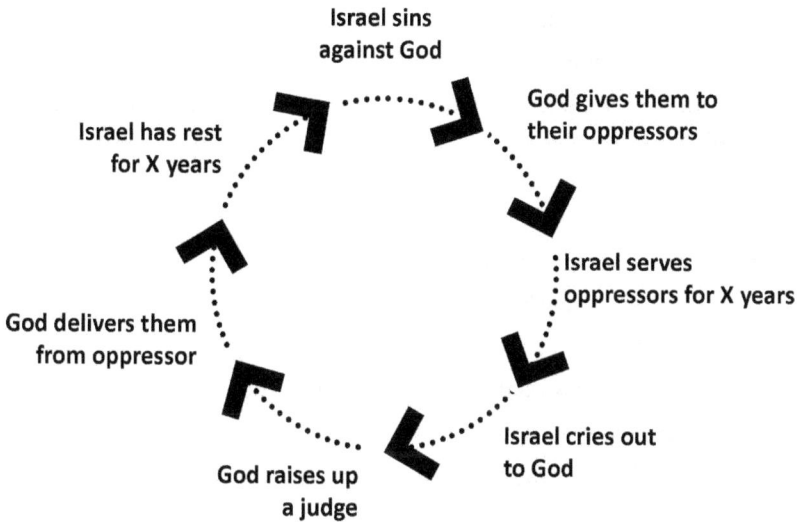

Before getting into the next major judge story, the author pauses the narration to mention two minor judges, which is the first reference to this group since Shamgar in 3:31. After Abimelech dies, the second minor judge, Tola, rises up to save Israel (10:1). As with most minor judges, we're not told much about Tola other than his heritage (he is the son of Puah, who is the son of Dodo, who is a man of the tribe of Issachar), and his location (living in Shamir in the hill country of Ephraim). We also learn that he judges Israel for twenty-three years before dying and being buried in his hometown, Shamir (10:2).

After such great detail in the stories of Deborah, Barak, Gideon, and Abimelech, we're left a little deflated when reading this account. It seems dry and void of an interesting plot. But, as with the rest of Scripture, when we put on our observation caps, we can dig into the details and get a more complete picture of Tola's judgeship.

First, while there is no explicit mention of Israel sinning against God, we can reasonably assume that this is the case, since they weren't following Him under Abimelech's self-imposed rule. Second, the author neglects to mention who Tola saves Israel from. Nor do we know how long they have been oppressed under the mysterious enemy's hand. These details would be nice, but at this point, they're hardly necessary for us to grasp the situation. Israel continues playing the harlot after idols, triggering God's withdrawal of protection. After enduring oppression for a certain time period, they cry out to Him and He raises up another leader to deliver them.

What we do know is that Tola is from the tribe of Issachar, who are the descendants of Issachar, the fifth son of Leah, Jacob's first wife (Genesis 29:21-26; 30:18). But what's peculiar about Tola is his current location. Shamir is located within the hill country of Ephraim, which is not Issachar's territory.[83] Issachar isn't mentioned in the introduction as one of the tribes who failed to claim the land allotted to them, but clearly, "some of the clans of Issachar had given up on occupying their own allotment and had moved to another site, one they could easily occupy."[84]

Issachar isn't living up to their potential and hasn't secured their allotted land. While that should be a distressing fact, in light of Israel's relentless idolatry, it's merely a side note. Tola rises from his hometown to save and judge Israel (or at least the areas directly surrounding him) for a total of twenty-three years.

Along with other details already mentioned, the author neglects to shed light on the morality of Tola's rule. We have no idea if he led Israel closer to God or away from Him, but since the judges decline with every new account, it's safe to assume Tola probably didn't drive Israel back to a right standing with God.

After leading twenty-three years, Tola dies and is buried in Shamir—again, a mismatched burial site for the tribe he belonged to.

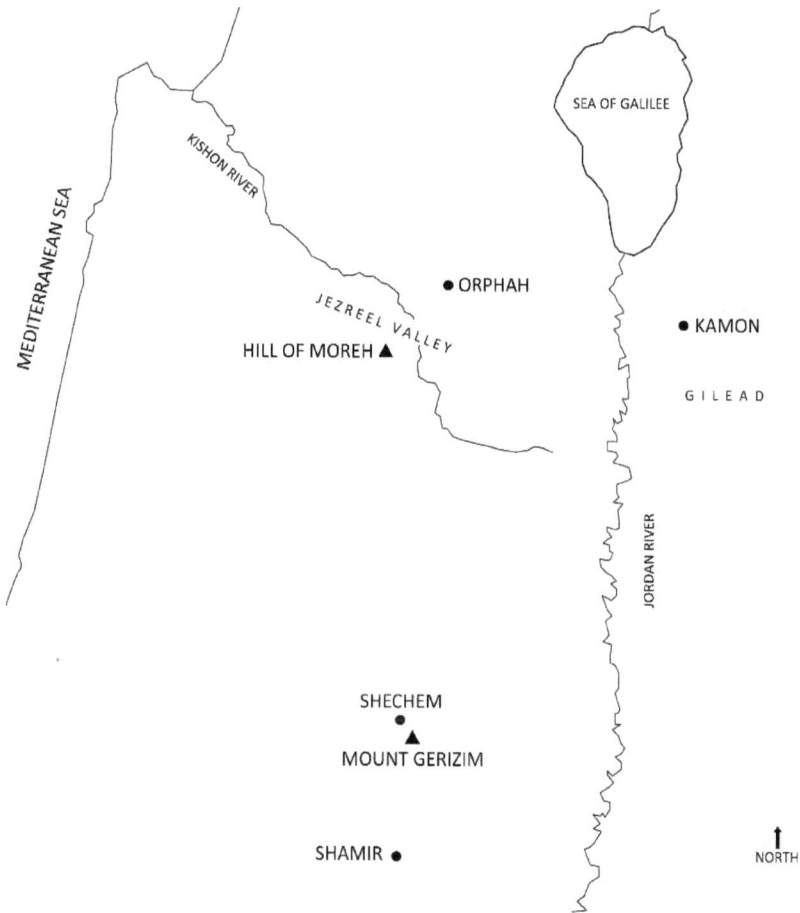

Israel presumably falls back into idolatry when Tola dies (assuming they ceased in some capacity under his rule), leaving room for another judge to arise. Jair takes the judgeship after Tola and judges Israel for about the same length of time as his predecessor, minus one year (10:3). We learn that Jair is a Gileadite who (naturally) hails from the region of Gilead. Gilead was located east of the Jordan River and, during the time of Moses, boasted "good forests, rich grazing lands, and abundant moisture."[85] When Israel began occupying the Promised Land, the tribes of Reuben, Gad, and half the tribe of Manasseh were allocated portions of the land of Gilead.

Unlike Tola, Jair seems to be located within his tribe's allotted territory. But that's where the good news ends. Similarly to Gideon, Jair makes his judgeship like a kingship—a title and position reserved for God as Israel's true leader. We glimpse his motivations by what the author reveals about his family:

> He had thirty sons who rode on thirty donkeys, and they had thirty cities in the land of Gilead that are called Havvoth-jair to this day (10:4).

Since bearing thirty sons would be quite impossible for one woman (especially back then, when lifespans were shorter), Jair must have had several wives and/or concubines. This practice mirrors the pagan cultures surrounding Israel, one that should not have been adopted by God's people.[86] In addition to having multiple wives, Jair also has his sons ride on donkeys (a symbol of royalty) and occupy thirty cities in the land. He may not have reigned as an official king over Israel, but his actions certainly reveal such aspirations.

When twenty-two years of judging Israel are complete, Jair dies and is buried in Kamon (10:5). Kamon is mentioned only here in all of Scripture, but "has been identified with some ruins about one mile northwest of the modern village Qumen."[87]

With two more judges gone, Israel once again descends into the full cycle of depravity. This time, however, the specific names of multiple idols are listed along with their apostasy. They forsake the true and living God for:

> The Baals and the Ashtaroth, the gods of Aram, the gods of Sidon, the gods of Moab, the gods of the sons of Ammon, and the gods of the Philistines (10:6).

Israel is no longer content serving one idol; now their cravings are satisfied only by pantheism. God gets angry once again and sells Israel into the hands of the Philistines and the sons of Ammon (10:7).

I can't imagine being God; can you? Would you not be tempted to erase Israel from the face of the earth and simply start over as He did with Noah several hundred years prior? I know every drop of patience would be squeezed dry from my bitter heart by now, yet God deals kindly with Israel. Even in giving them over to their enemies, He's being kind by paying attention to them at all! He'd be completely justified to wipe His hands of them; yet He continues pouring out grace through waves of patience and kindness.

The Philistines and sons of Ammon afflict and crush Israel for eighteen years (10:8). Interestingly enough, the particular geographical focus of this oppression is in the land of Gilead, where Jair lived and reigned. But tyranny seeps through the porous borders of Gilead, extending to the tribes of Judah, Benjamin, and Ephraim—leaving everyone greatly distressed in its wake (10:9).

Such distress causes Israel to cry out to God once again. But unlike previous cries, Israel actually admits to error:

> Then the sons of Israel cried out to the Lord, saying, "We have sinned against You, for indeed, we have forsaken our God and served the Baals" (10:10).

Quite the confession from a bunch that doesn't seem to care one iota about God! Despite the admission, God doesn't let them off the hook. Instead, He reminds them how He delivered them from the Egyptians through the exodus, and also the Amorites, sons of Ammon, the Philistines, the Sidonians, the Amalekites and the Maonites (10:11-13). In spite of all His faithfulness, Israel forsook Him and served other gods. Therefore, He concludes, He will not deliver them again. Instead God suggests they "go and cry out to the gods which [they] have chosen; let them deliver [Israel] in the time of [their] distress" (10:14).

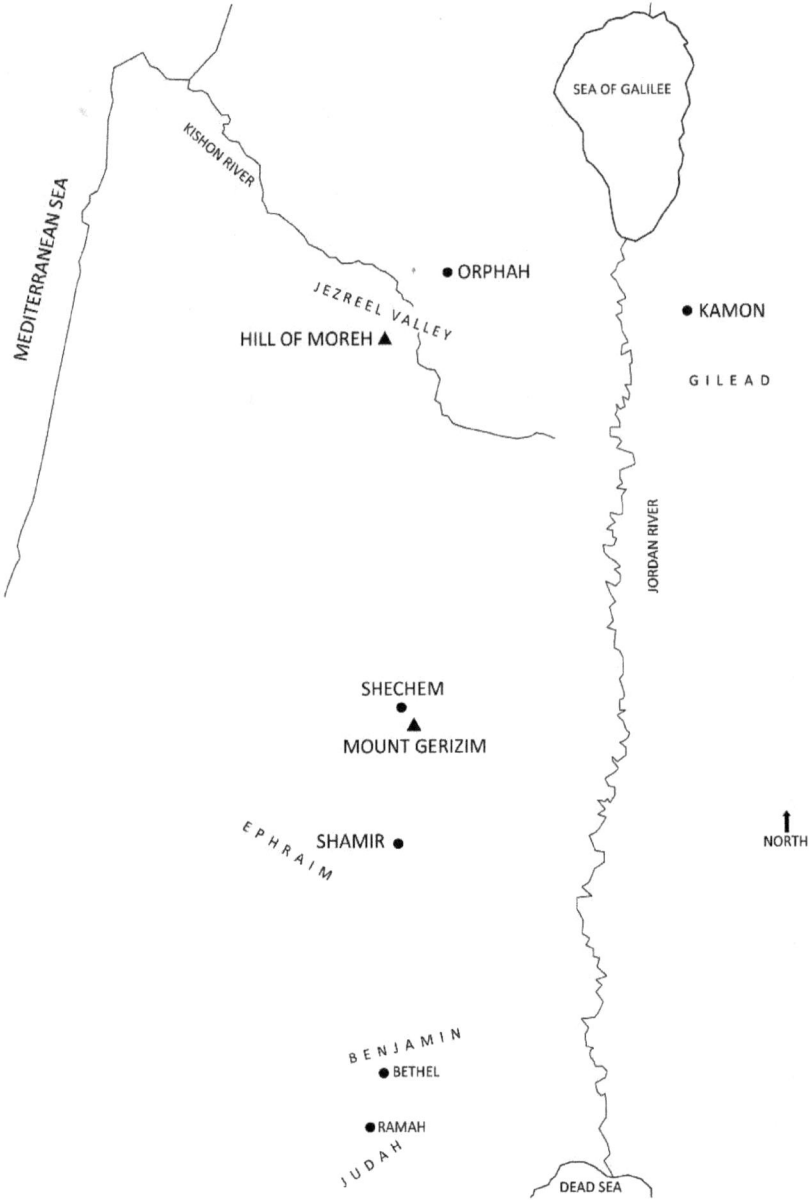

Is that a hint of sarcasm we detect from God? I believe so. He's tired of dealing with Israel and their shallow cries for help. If they want help, they should ask it from the idols they chose to believe in. God's response here reminds us of Gideon's father's response to the men who wanted to kill

Gideon for tearing down the town idols. Both argue the same point: if the gods you're serving are real and who you say they are, let them contend for themselves. Let them save you!

Massage this point for a moment. Anything that replaces God on the throne of your heart is an idol, be it a relationship, job, kids, a portfolio, fitness, etc. Can any of those things save you? No, they are all fallible and can be taken away.

Through these judges God asks, "Why cry to Me when you have put your faith in something else? Why do you put your faith in something else in the first place? Why do you trust the created rather than the Creator, who alone is sovereign and can save you?"

The sons of Israel hear these questions, yet they persist in their pleas and admit once again that they have sinned. They petition God to do whatever He wants to them, as long as He delivers them from their enemies (10:15). All they care about is feeling better and becoming free from the oppression. Though they verbalize repentance, will they exude a posture of it in their hearts?

Israel begins their repentance on a positive note. Repentance isn't only apologizing for sin; it's turning 180 degrees in the opposite direction (words *and* action). Words without action isn't repentance, and Israel does respond by acting on their words this time. They "put away the foreign gods from among them and served the Lord" (10:16a). They appear to be genuine, and their actions get the attention of God, who "could bear the misery of Israel no longer" (10:16b).

But before we get to God's action plan, Israel and God's conversation gets interrupted. The author informs us that the sons of Ammon camp in Gilead against the Israelites (10:17). In defense, Israel rises up and camps in Mizpah. Wait, Israel! Why not finish your conversation with God? Surely He'll guide you in your next steps. You've gotten His attention and elicited His pity; see it through!

But they don't. Like so many times before, Israel proves easily distracted. Facing their enemies, they turn their focus to the most *urgent* problem they have, not the most *important* one (fixing their relationship with God). Who would lead the fight for them against their enemies (10:18)? What man would rise up for the challenge? The elders promise that such a man will surely become head over all the land of Gilead.

Israel's most pressing, unseen, and crippling problem is that they've closed their conversation with God. They care not about His plan or seeking after Him at this point. They simply move forward with their own plans, which suggests they never cared about God's in the first place. They, like Gideon before them, sought only to use God to accomplish their agendas—in this case, their deliverance from the sons of Ammon and their allies.

Israel looks to a man instead of to God, which unravels the repentance they began so strongly with before. Also against them, they don't have abounding options for military leaders. But there is someone they can turn to. A man named Jephthah is a valiant warrior and lives in the land of Tob (11:1,3).[88] Valiant warriors within Israel's borders are rare, so he seems to be a great option. But there's a slight problem: Jephthah is the son of a harlot. His father's name was Gilead, who committed infidelity against his wife by visiting a harlot and fathering a son with her.

Gilead brought Jephthah into his home and raised him with his other sons, but when the boys grew up, the full-blooded brothers rise against Jephthah (11:2). They have no interest in sharing their inheritance with him, so they drive him out. Leaving the region of Gilead, Jephthah heads to the land of Tob, where a bunch of worthless individuals begin following him (11:3). Unlike Abimelech's gang who got paid, these men follow Jephthah voluntarily. Perhaps they notice his skill and decide that allying with this man could prove fruitful later on. Or maybe they're bored and looking for an adventure. Regardless, they join with Jephthah as his dedicated band of outlaws.

Jephthah and his men manage to make a name for themselves as warriors in

Tob. We're not sure who they fought to accrue such a title, but they create a fierce reputation nonetheless. The shunned half-brother becomes a brave warrior. He didn't let his past dictate his future, that's for sure!

When the sons of Ammon begin attacking Israel, the elders of Gilead make their way to Tob to offer Jephthah a proposition (11:4-5). They ask him to become their chief (i.e. commander, not absolute leader) in fighting against the sons of Ammon (11:6). This offer, by the way, is not their first offer to the *legitimate* citizens of Gilead. Before, they offered a full title of leadership to the one who would stand up and fight for them. But for Jephthah, they decrease their offer, hoping he won't notice. It wouldn't do to have a half-breed be *completely* over them, after all.

Quite the gall these gents have, especially when considering their role in Jephthah's exile in the first place. While they may not have directly contributed to Jephthah's exile by his brothers, they certainly never stood up for him. Now, when their lives are at stake and they're out of options, they seem eager to get him on their side (though with reservations about giving him full authority).

But Jephthah develops critical thinking skills in his outcast state. He's not about to help the people who rejected him simply because they ask. So he takes the opportunity to make them sweat a bit...

> Did you not hate me and drive me from my father's house? So
> why have you come to me now when you are in trouble? (11:7)

At this point, Jephthah is interested in far more than a title; he wants reinstatement as a full citizen of Gilead.[89] Knowing the elders (some perhaps his relatives) have no way to justify their previous actions, he wants them to increase their offer, which they do. (11:8). Instead of just making him a chief, they now make him head over all the land of Gilead.

Listening to their increased offer, Jephthah decides to bring God into it. He asks for confirmation: would they really make him head over Gilead *if the*

Lord delivers the sons of Ammon into his hand (11:9)? By including the name of God into his argument, he heightens the accountability and throws them up against a wall. Jephthah is binding them to their promises before God (10:15), even though they've already begun failing their previous promises of worship by taking matters into their own hands.

Because the elders are out of options, they agree to his terms. They respond as he hopes, "The Lord is witness between us; surely we will do as you have said" (11:10). The deal is sealed (even if with serious lack of exuberance) and Jephthah goes with the elders to the town of Mizpah (11:11).

Once there, the people make him head and chief via an impromptu inaugural ceremony (11:11). While this ceremony includes the Lord's name (as Jephthah did in verse 9), it's doubtful that God sanctioned it. Neither Jephthah nor the elders seek God's will and favor in this arrangement. They didn't seek His plan before appealing to Jephthah, nor do they abide by any kind of ordained method for his inauguration. Rather, their concern is having their actions appear legitimate to everyone around them. They use God as a tool to confirm what they want to do; they do not seek after Him and conform to what He wants to do.[90]

God is silent in this whole affair, which piques the reader's interest. What will happen? Will He thwart their plans or go along with them as He did for Ehud? We have been told that He "could bear the misery of Israel no longer" (10:16), so we suppose He'll secure victory for His backsliding people.

Officially in position as head and chief, Jephthah sends messengers to the king of Ammon, hoping to resolve the conflict amicably (11:12). Using a level head and reason (much like Gideon's father), he asks the king why he is coming to fight against Israel. Introducing logic to the situation will hopefully deflate the intense emotions that typically surround war. His exercise of logic worked with the elders of Gilead (though begrudgingly), so hopefully it'll work here too!

The king responds with his reason for attack:

> Because Israel took away my land when they came up from Egypt, from the Arnon as far as the Jabbok and the Jordan; therefore, return them peaceably now (11:13).

In the king's eyes, Israel stole his land and he wants it back. This explanation, along with the majority of the stories in this book, pulses with God's sovereignty. The king is accusing Israel of something that supposedly happened several generations prior. Why would he act in retribution now unless God had turned his heart to do so? We don't know what prompted the king's thirst for battle (or if he is just looking for an excuse to fight), but whatever the reason, we see God channeling hearts to accompany His will for Israel despite their faithlessness.

When Jephthah hears the king's answer, he's less than amused and subsequently returns a hefty discourse of historical facts for the king to chew on (11:14-27). He informs the king (quite rightly) that Israel did not take away the land of Moab from the sons of Ammon. This assertion paralyzes the king's argument and "undercuts the Ammonite claim right from the beginning. Israel cannot give back to Ammon that which was never Ammon's."[91]

The land in question actually belonged to the Amorites, not the Ammonites (which makes the king of the Ammon seem rather inept). Several hundred years prior when Israel asked the Amorite king for permission to pass through their land, he refused and proceeded to fight Israel—giving Israel cause to fight back and win, which they did. Now the land belonged to them, fair and square. Israel did fight for the land in question and win it in accordance with the rules of war, but it was the land of the Amorites, not the Ammonites.[92]

Even after crushing the king's defense, Jephthah continues his argument. The crux of his case rests in the claim that God gave Israel the land (regardless of original owner), so it's rightfully theirs (11:23-24). Just as other "gods" help pagan nations accrue land (that remains theirs after battle), so Israel's God secured the land for them. Jephthah also contends that if they had such a problem with it, they should have voiced their concerns long before now. With all these arguments, Jephthah exudes competence and wisdom as Israel's new leader.

While his logic seems valid and he displays a great deal of articulation, Jephthah is as theologically ignorant as the king. The major flaw with his premise (thus revealing the perspective of his heart) is that he equates God with the idols that other nations serve.

> He "identifies faith in Yahweh with the *practices* of the surrounding national cults rather than the *ideals* of biblical faith. He localizes Yahweh as though he is just like Chemosh, Milcom, Baal, and so on (i.e., gods can only exercise their power in their particular localized areas)."[93]

To Jephthah, God is like the gods of the pagans surrounding Israel. He may be strong and may have granted victory to Israel, but it's nothing more than a cosmic accident, since other gods can defeat Israel too. This perspective advocates that all gods (including Yahweh) are on an equal playing field, battling out their wills against each other. How insulting to the true and sovereign God who holds the universe (humans and lifeless idols included) in His hands.

While this theological error most likely evades the king's notice, what catches his attention is Jephthah's assertion that Chemosh is the Ammonite king's god. Chemosh is actually the god of the Moabites! Jephthah seems to be getting nations and their gods confused, as the king did with Ammon and Amorite history. The deity of the Ammonites is Milcom, not Chemosh.[94] This mistake most likely strips Jephthah's argument of any validity in the king's eyes.

Though Jephthah's reply is hardly without flaw, he does leave the king without a logical reason to continue his fight. The land rightfully and undoubtedly belongs to Israel, leaving Ammon with no ammunition to question it. But the king ignores him and proceeds anyway, probably fueled by anger or embarrassment for being shut down so thoroughly by Jephthah (11:28). He needs to defend his honor somehow; nothing like a horrific battle to give him the chance!

Since battle is inevitable, Jephthah prepares for it. Before he does anything, though, the Spirit of the Lord comes upon him (11:29). He decides to empower their plan after all! This is the third time His Spirit is said to come upon a judge, the others being Othniel and Gideon. This particular anointing displays His grace. At no time does Israel ask for God's help in selecting a leader, nor do they even ask Him to affirm Jephthah once they choose him. They simply act as though they're the ones in control. But God goes along with their selfish plans, having already determined to save Israel from Ammon.

God chooses to use Jephthah, but not because His hands are tied by Israel's actions. He goes along with their plans, knowing they will unfold exactly as *He* plans, not as *they* plan. As Solomon writes in Proverbs 16:9, "The mind of man plans his way, but the Lord directs his steps."

As discussed previously with other judges, the Spirit's presence upon Jephthah isn't indicative of his theological soundness or moral uprightness. Rather, the Spirit aids in physical tasks. In this case, the Spirit helps Jephthah in two ways: gathering troops to fight against Ammon and then defeating them

But before heading out to battle, Jephthah makes the biggest mistake of his life. In a fit of rashness, he prays:

> If You will indeed give the sons of Ammon into my hand, then it shall be that whatever comes out of the doors of my house to meet me when I return in peace from the sons of Ammon, it shall be the Lord's, and I will offer it up as a burnt offering (11:30-31).

What a stupid prayer, Jephthah! God isn't like the other "gods," able to be manipulated according to man's craftiness. But Jephthah has already revealed his ignorance when it comes to Yahweh, and his motive is clear: he is trying to manipulate God into doing what he wants. He's clueless as to God's Spirit on his life (which is quite sad) and feels the need to secure his plans by getting God on his side. If only he realized that God was already on his side! (Or better yet, that he was already on God's side!)

After the vow, Jephthah goes out to battle and thoroughly annihilates the sons of Ammon (11:32). Israel destroys twenty cities in a wide span within Ammonite territory (11:33). Victory is sweet, straightforward, and uncomplicated as Othniel's was, and it would've happened that way without the vow! But alas, the sweetness of victory would soon be poisoned by the bile of death.

On his journey back home, Jephthah is most likely euphoric and riding the high of adrenaline. No doubt he just accomplished the greatest victory he'd ever known; now he's ready to celebrate with his loved ones. But as he nears his house in Mizpah, he's met first by his daughter—his only child—playing tambourines and dancing, having heard the news of victory (11:34). His exhilarated demeanor mutilates into self-disgust. His only daughter! How could *she* be the first one to come greet him? Why couldn't it have been an animal, as he thought it would be?[95]

The text tells us she is his only child: she "was his one and only child; besides her he had no son or daughter" (11:34). Family life was probably difficult for Jephthah and his band of outlaws, which may explain why he has only one child. We're not told if his wife (assuming he was even married) is still alive, or anything about his family situation.

His family stands in stark contrast to Gideon and Jair's. Both prior judges have several dozen children, which indicates a harem of wives and concubines. Jephthah, on the other hand, has only one child, weakening his position as king-like figure. Though it's doubtful he cares much about such a title now. His dearly beloved daughter would soon die because of his foolhardy and rash vow.

Jephthah responds to the sight of his daughter by ripping his clothes and crying out, "Alas, my daughter! You have brought me very low, and you are among those who trouble me;" (as if it's her fault), "for I have given my word to the Lord, and I cannot take it back" (11:35). The scene is appalling: a father kneels down and tears clothes from his adrenaline-laced body, shaken to the core by the consequences of his own words. His daughter must die as a sacrifice because of his treacherous vow—the kind of sacrifice normally reserved for animals (like what Abimelech did to his brothers).

Now imagine being his daughter. Instead of being embraced and hoisted up by daddy to soar in victorious circles overhead, she learns that she will die, and not even for a good reason! Her whole life lies ahead of her, but she'll never live it. Because of one impulsive vow made by her father, her life will come to an end.

As readers, this makes our blood boil. What moron makes such a rash vow, especially since he had no way of knowing who would come out the door first? That, and victory was already in his hands. If only he'd paused and sought after God, the vow would never have been made.

Jephthah fears overwhelming harm if he does not fulfill his vow, which confirms yet again his ill-sufficient view of Yahweh. Jephthah thinks of God as a distant and cold entity—an enforcer who seeks to make life miserable for all who don't abide by His rules. In other words, he's willing to sacrifice his daughter's life because he's afraid of what will happen if he doesn't. But what, Jephthah, could possibly be worse than killing your own daughter?

Nevertheless, there might be hope. Biblically astute readers are aware of a clause God gives in Leviticus 27:2-3 for vows made in haste:

> When a man makes a difficult vow, he shall be valued according
> to your valuation of persons belonging to the Lord. If your

valuation is of the male from twenty years even to sixty years old,
then your valuation shall be fifty shekels of silver, after the shekel
of the sanctuary.

There's a way out! If Jephthah or his friends (or anyone within proximity)
knows of this law, there's hope! By giving fifty shekels of silver to the Lord,
the vow will be void, and his daughter can live. But in a sickening
revelation, we see that no one seems to know about the law. Jephthah and
Israel's ignorance about Leviticus 27 reflects their ignorance of God in
general. For someone who thinks he knows so much, Jephthah knows
scarce little, and his daughter is about to pay the ultimate price for it.

His daughter isn't aware of the Law, either, which makes her response to
Jephthah all the more incredulous. In humility and obedience, she tells her
father that she will go along with the repercussions of his vow (11:36). Yes,
she will lay down her life so he can fulfill his vow to the Lord. She's more
willing to obey at the cost of her life than Israel is to obey God who wants
only to give them life!

A sweet, humble girl is about to be killed for nothing. It's the most
devastating waste of life we can imagine. If only Jephthah had given three
seconds' thought to the vow before he uttered it. If only he had realized the
same kind of intimate relationship with God, his Heavenly Father, as his
daughter did with him. If only the Gileadites had sought after God before
taking action in the first place. None of this would have happened! But
since no one can live under the weight of "if only," his daughter makes one
request before the vow is fulfilled. She desires to go away with her friends
for two months to mourn the life she would never live (11:37).

He grants her request and at the end of two months, he kills her (11:39).
No one knew of the law in Leviticus 27; no one offered another solution.
She dies, and her death is transformed into an annual custom. Every year
"the daughters of Israel went...to commemorate the daughter of Jephthah
the Gileadite four days of the year" (11:40).

Ironic that Jephthah doesn't get an annual commemoration for his victory, but his daughter does for willingly upholding his irrational vow. Though his victory seems like a lifetime ago now. The very hands that butchered countless Ammonites now bear the bloodguilt of his very daughter.

But the story isn't over. While Jephthah is still mourning the loss of his only child, a fellow tribe rises to attack him with unfounded accusations (12:1). Who else would it be but Ephraim, who also poured complaints into Gideon's ear in chapter 8? Their accusations are the same as before: Why did Jephthah fight the sons of Ammon without them? Their anger seems to have escalated, for they utter a threat against Jephthah, which they never did to Gideon. They intend to burn his house down on him for not including them in battle.

Sounds a bit extreme for being overlooked in a fight! People tend to overreact when they are threatened in some way. In this instance, it seems that Ephraim's pride is threatened. Israel won a victory over the sons of Ammon without their help. It's scarcely a blameworthy action, but they attack Jephthah with pent-up hatred nonetheless.

Unlike Gideon, Jephthah doesn't exercise political savvy when dealing with Ephraim:

> I and my people were at great strife with the sons of Ammon; when I called you, you did not deliver me from their hand. When I saw that you would not deliver me, I took my life in my hands and crossed over against the sons of Ammon, and the Lord gave them into my hand. Why then have you come up to me this day to fight against me (12:2-3)?

Apparently Jephthah *had* called out to Ephraim for help, but for whatever reason (perhaps one mirroring Succoth and Penuel's in chapter 8), Ephraim refused. Jephthah decided he didn't have time for political nonsense, and he wasn't going to appease their childish behavior. So he moved ahead without them. Now that victory is complete, Ephraim comes out with fists flying, trying to twist the truth to make Jephthah look bad.

Well, Jephthah's patience has burnt out. He's coming off an emotional roller coaster and now is irate. His anger over his daughter's death (and himself for his stupid vow) now has a new target: Ephraim. He gathers the men of Gilead to fight them, hungry to unleash his rage (12:4).

Utilizing a familiar battle tactic, the Gileadites capture the fords of the Jordan River on the opposite side of Ephraim. When any Ephraimite fugitives attempt to cross over, the men ask their identity. If they claimed not to be an Ephraimite, they forced them to pronounce the word "Shibboleth." (For some reason, Ephraimites could not properly pronounce "Shibboleth;" it came out sounding like "Sibboleth.") If a man failed the test, the Gileadites would seize and murder him (12:5-6).

Just when we think the mindless killing has come to an end, Jephthah and his men slaughter an additional 42,000 men. And not just any men—Israelite men! While Ephraim left much to be desired in finesse and maturity, they were allies. They were brothers! But in his anger, Jephthah acts rashly again—murdering a significant percentage of an Israelite tribe. His depression over the destruction of his own family ironically leads to the destruction of the family of Israel.

Following the Ephraim massacre, Jephthah judges Israel for six years before dying and being buried in one of the cities of Gilead (12:7).

--

Like most judges before him, Jephthah's life and actions mirror Israel's state of spirituality—declining rapidly in cycles of degeneration. They're withering away morally, emotionally, politically, and spiritually, all because they refuse to keep God as the priority. With every judge cycle their hearts calcify, hardening to any sensitivity to God or His Spirit in their lives.

Our hearts are vulnerable to the same fate every time we supplant God as priority in our lives. It may begin slowly and barely detectable. We may take a new position at work, lured by a glamorous salary without first seeking God and His will. Longer hours mean more time away from family, multiplying the tension already present.

Or perhaps we allow our children's poor behavior to slide because we're exhausted. It's just one time. But soon that one time becomes two times, which swiftly becomes a dozen times. Pretty soon the kids are running our households, and we're no longer leading them at all, much less in a way that points them to Christ.

Regardless of venue, displacing God with our desires (position, comfort, ease, image, etc.) inevitably leads to our own cycles of degeneration. When we move away from God, we begin dredging a path that gets deeper with every step we take. Jephthah's plan began with ignorance and resulted in murder. Like him, we quickly walk into a pit that's impossible to escape on our own. The thought of correcting the issues seems overwhelming, so we sink back into the muck. We can continue only so long before the rationalizations become our grid of thinking. Lies become the truth we believe, and we become content in the sludge that threatens to sink us.

Israel knew God and His ways when Moses and Joshua led them. They knew right from wrong and established safeguards to keep them on the right path. But soon they got distracted, allured by the lifestyles of the pagan nations surrounding them. After living in the trench of idolatry so long, leaving seemed too difficult, so they did the bare minimum to survive—they called out to God for deliverance. As soon as He did, they dove right back into their pits and kept digging. Before long, their entire worldviews were corrupted by the nations they sought to emulate. They were so corrupt that they could no longer distinguish truth from the lies they'd been telling themselves.

Paul Miller correctly notes that "when the covenant relationship between God and His people is neglected, the faculty of moral judgment atrophies. It not only becomes impossible to do right, it becomes impossible to *know* what is right." That's what happened to Israel, and that's what can happen to us if we enthrone anything but Jesus in our hearts.

The book of Judges may be difficult to read; looking in a magnified mirror with harsh lighting is never flattering. But the pill that's so hard to swallow is one that can save our lives. Put God first, friends. Each story thus far has revealed the dire consequences when we don't, and we're not finished yet.

--

Ibzan, Elon, and Abdon

Jephthah's account is bookended by five of the six minor judge accounts. Preceding his story are Tola and Jair; following him are Ibzan, Elon, and Abdon—the last of the minor judge accounts.

Ibzan follows Jephthah as Israel's leader (12:8). He is from Bethlehem (*not* the same Bethlehem where Jesus was born).[96] We don't know much about him, since this is the only time he is mentioned in the Old Testament. But we are given some facts about him:

> He had thirty sons, and thirty daughters whom he gave in marriage outside the family, and he brought in thirty daughters from outside for his sons. And he judged Israel seven years (12:9).

First is the noteworthy size of his family. Like Gideon and Jair, Ibzan prioritizes a position of power, revealed by the substantial number of his offspring. Following the practices of pagan nations around him, he takes several wives and concubines (most likely), which gives his family influence as self-professed royalty.

This fact alone reveals his lack of regard for God. He should have been concerned about making God Israel's king, not filling the role himself. But what he does in his children's lives confirms his selfish motivations (as if there were ever any doubt).

He gives his daughters—all thirty of them—in marriage to people outside his family/clan. While uncertain, the reference to "outside" people likely refers to people outside Israel entirely, especially when referring back to chapter 3:5-6.[97] This is a very big no-no. Technically, Israelites are permitted to marry outside their nationality, but they had strict rules for doing so. Anyone brought into Israel from outside had to become a proselyte—a convert to Judaism—in order to keep Israel on the right track spiritually.

But even with those restrictions, God didn't want Israel intermarrying with the people they were supposed to destroy in the Promised Land.[98] Had they obeyed God and driven them out originally, they would have had no problem (can't marry people who aren't there!). But since they failed, intermarriage became a very real temptation and opportunity to turn away from Him.[99]

In addition to breaking God's command by intermarrying, Ibzan is also guilty of adopting pagan practices. In the ancient world, those of royalty or high status would give their daughters in marriage to strategic people in order to secure treaties with their families/cities/etc.[100] This would, in turn, elevate their status and secure their authority and power. Solomon practiced this, and it lowered the quality of his reign and shattered his relationship with God.

> Now King Solomon loved many foreign women along with the daughter of Pharaoh: Moabite, Ammonite, Edomite, Sidonian, and Hittite women, from the nations concerning which the Lord had said to the sons of Israel, "You shall not associate with them, nor shall they associate with you, for they will surely turn your heart away after their gods." Solomon held fast to these in love. He had seven hundred wives, princesses, and three hundred concubines, and his wives turned his heart away. For when Solomon was old, his wives turned his heart away after other gods; and his heart was not wholly devoted to the Lord his God (1 Kings 11:1-4).

While Ibzan doesn't acquire nearly the harem Solomon did, his microcosm of Solomon still has consequences. Instead of defeating Israel's enemies, he makes treaties with them through his children's marriages!

Giving his daughters to "outside" people is only part of the equation, though. Ibzan also brings "outside" women in for his thirty sons. This is another political move and leaves his family (and tribe) more vulnerable to outside influences that don't honor God. At this point in the book, it's doubtful there's much to protect theologically within Israel, since they've all seemed to abandon God. But they're not even trying to maintain the appearance of propriety anymore (as they attempted with Jephthah and his ordination). They, along with their judges, are participating in the very practices God wants to rid them of.

Ibzan judges Israel for seven years, just one longer than Jephthah. After him arises Elon, a Zebulunite (12:11). Zebulun is a tribe that derived from the man Zebulun, Jacob's sixth son with his wife, Leah. They're a smaller tribe, but as we've seen, God raises up leaders without prejudice. All we know of Elon is his tribal heritage and the fact that he judges Israel for ten years. After that, he dies and is buried at Aijalon in the land of Zebulun (12:12).

The final minor judge is named Abdon, and he is the son of Hillel the Pirathonite (12:13). Pirathon is a town in the tribal territory of Ephraim.[101] Abdon joins the likes of Gideon, Jair, and Ibzan before him, having forty sons and thirty grandsons (12:14). His motivation for having so many offspring most likely mirrors his predecessors—an attempt to gain fame and a king-like status among the people.

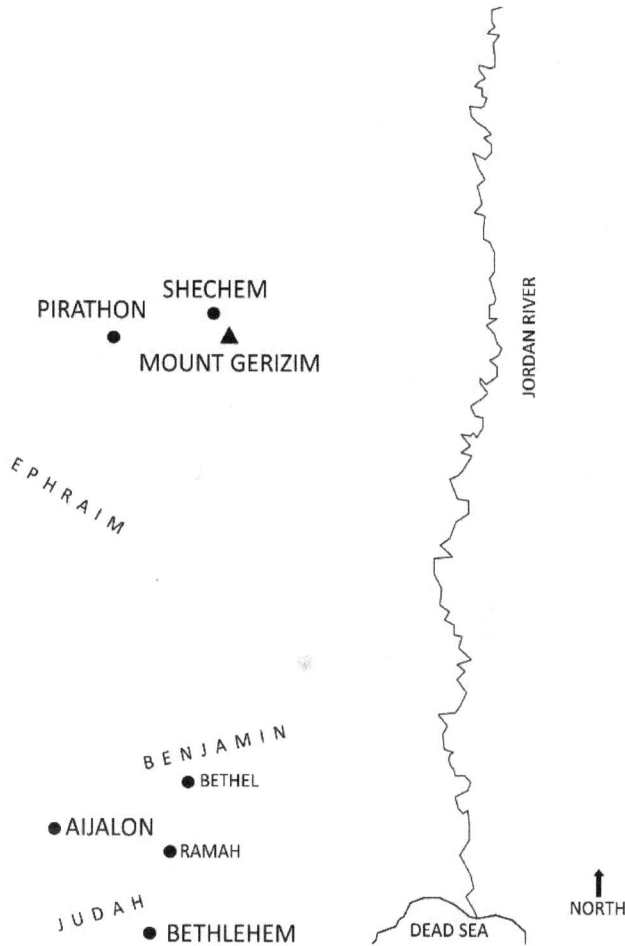

To substantiate this point, all his sons and grandsons ride on donkeys, which, again, is a symbol of royalty (12:14).[102] Abdon has no interest in leading Israel closer to God unless he receives king-like status in the process. His only concern is for himself and making his family a fortress in Israel—betraying the position of judge in the process. He judges Israel for eight years before dying and being buried in Pirathon (12:15).

What's lacking in all these last minor judge accounts is mention of Israel's sin or cry for help, God's action in raising up a judge, the judges delivering Israel through them, or having peace during their reign. We can reasonably assume that Israel sins (it *is* the thread weaving through the book). But we don't know if they fell into enemy hands and needed deliverance. Nor are we told that God chose these men to judge Israel. He most likely did, since there's no indication they were self-appointed judges like Abimelech. But they're hardly redeeming the judgeship position to the status God originally desired it to be.

Israel sins against God → God gives them to their oppressors → Israel serves oppressors for X years → Israel cries out to God → God raises up a judge → God delivers them from oppressor → Israel has rest for X years

Any peace experienced by Israel during this time would be restricted to politics, for they certainly aren't at peace with God on a corporate level. God preserves a remnant of faithful followers, but we see no evidence of their existence from the sky-high view the author reveals to us.[103] All we see is the spiraling depravity of Israel, and it's leaving us with pits of distress in our stomachs.

Tola, Jair, Jephthah, Ibzan, Elon, and Abdon (along with the other judges) show us the magnitude of what God can accomplish despite using broken and sorely misguided vessels. Even though we get distracted by the drama and depravity of these men and their decisions, we cannot neglect the fact that God used what little faith they had to achieve major feats.

Jephthah's faith was meager, but he did stand up and take action when called upon. He could've left his countrymen to face Ammon on their own—a situation that would've ended in certain annihilation. But he didn't. Even if his reasons weren't all that sound, he stepped up and God used that movement to ignite a campaign to deliver His people from the sons of Ammon.

God uses what we give Him to accomplish His purposes for His glory and our good. It's obviously preferable to give Him our all and our best, but His sovereignty is not confined to the expanse of faith we display. He can redeem any situation. Though, we should learn from Jephthah and try not to make life needlessly complicated.

--

With the minor judges and Jephthah in our rearview mirror, we're left musing on some weighty truths.

God's love for us is real and incomprehensible.

Love is a word often abused and belittled in our culture. We love pizza; we love our spouses. We love our jobs; we love our new lipstick. It's little wonder we have a warped view of God's definition of love.

God defines love in a way that makes us squirm: love isn't an emotion. It isn't butterflies you get when your gaze locks on a pretty girl. It's not infatuation that carries you through the first couple years of marriage then violently disappears. Love is a sacrificial choice to put someone before yourself. It's a *decision* combined with *action* that lasts throughout eternity.

That sounds great in theory, but when it's confined to bringing breakfast to your spouse in bed, it misses the point entirely. God loves us far beyond material blessings of comfort, though those are undoubtedly agreeable. His love extends to the death of His Son. A Father, willing to send His own Son to a horrific death on a jagged wooden beam so we can live, knows a kind of love we're rarely privy to. But though we may not often experience that degree of love, we're called to embrace it and make it our own through Christ—first to God, then to others.

That's why reading stories of Israel in the time of the judges is so mind-blowing. God *loves* them despite having every reason not to. He merges His decision to love with action: giving, extending grace, rescuing, and restoring an obstinate people who don't even pretend to love Him back. That's love. While it's nice when love is reciprocated, true love doesn't require any in return.

The more we meditate on that, the more unfathomable it is. God's love crosses every threshold we erect between ourselves and Him, and He continues giving even when we don't deserve it. As long as we have breath, He's not done with us. He loves us and gives everything to call us His own.

Jephthah, the minor judges, and Israel neglect this overwhelming love either by ignorance or conscious choice. Both result in the same—they forfeit genuine life that could've easily been theirs had they only accepted God's gift of love.

Ignorance is dangerous.

The phrase "ignorance is bliss" is stupid and treacherous. Ignorance is perilous, and the more ignorant we are, the greater chance we have of missing out on the life God offers us.

Jephthah's ignorance of political, historical, and theological facts leaves him in a vulnerable position and ultimately costs him the life of his daughter. If blessings ever arise from ignorance, it's sheer grace from God. We're held accountable to His truth whether we know it or not.[104] Get in His Word and get close to people who know it and are moving closer to Christ. While knowledge doesn't guarantee wisdom or obedience, neither can happen without it.

There's only one throne of priority in our hearts.

Because we're not yet with Jesus face to face, we're always going to struggle with the throne of priority in our hearts. The "throne of priority" simply refers to the primary person, position, action, or aspiration we focus on and strive for.

If we profess Jesus as Lord and Savior, the throne belongs to God, and He should always be seated on it. Unfortunately, like Jephthah and the minor judges, our personal (and selfish) aspirations beat God to the seat. Instead of submitting to Him and increasing His presence in our lives, we elevate ourselves by giving our desires more attention than His. This usurps His rightful position as King in our lives and transports us into a misguided perspective of life and faith.

When we don't abide in Christ and keep Him enthroned in our hearts, we fall prey to the sin that grips us in its relentless chains. We descend into ignorance and try to manipulate God into doing what we want Him to do to make our lives better. Jephthah did this. He valued victory over everything else and attempted to manipulate God through a rash and tragic vow. The minor judges did this as well—desiring prominent political positions instead of right standing with God.

We have only one throne of priority in our lives, and we choose who occupies it. Is it you or God?

GROUP STUDY

INTRODUCTION

"Oh God, if you do this for me, I swear I'll do *[fill in the blank]* for You forever!"

All of us have made promises to God in exchange for an immediate favor from Him. Our promises are exorbitant, and we rationalize that God would definitely be getting the better end of the deal if He'd only do *this one little thing* for us.

The problem with such promises is that they're empty. Oh, we *may* fulfill them, but that's highly unlikely. But our fulfillment of the promise isn't the issue, and it's certainly not what has God's attention. Such promises only mask what's going on in our hearts—manipulation.

When we pledge divine exchanges, we're trying to manipulate God into doing something we want. We're trying to control Him and morph Him into the magic genie we make Him out to be in our minds, as if He's under the spell of those He *created*.

DISCUSS

- Describe a time when you attempted a divine exchange with God—making Him a promise in return for something you wanted.
- What did you want God to do?
- What did you pledge to do for Him in return?
- What did He do?

THE WORD

If ever a dire vow was made in Scripture, it came from the mouth of Jephthah, Israel's eighth judge. Having been appointed head over the people by the elders of Gilead (in a less-than-inspired way, at that), Jephthah presumed the battle against the Ammonites rested in his hands.

What he failed to recognize (due to blatant ignorance, blind ambition, and consuming paganism) was that God already conceded to use him as judge, ensuring victory for Israel over the Ammonites. Had he tuned into God and His will, he would never have made his infamous vow:

> "Jephthah made a vow to the Lord and said, "If You will indeed give the sons of Ammon into my hand, then it shall be that whatever comes out of the doors of my house to meet me when I return in peace from the sons of Ammon, it shall be the Lord's, and I will offer it up as a burnt offering."(Judges 11:30-31)

- What about this vow indicates Jephthah was being rash?
- What indicates he was trying to manipulate God?

What happened as a result of his vow to God?

> "When Jephthah came to his house at Mizpah, behold, his daughter was coming out to meet him with tambourines and with dancing. Now she was his one and only child; besides her he had no son or daughter...at the end of two months she returned to her father, who did to her according to the vow which he had made... (Judges 11:34, 39)

Not only does Jephthah make a completely unnecessary vow, he follows through with it—murdering his own daughter! The irony is thick, for if Jephthah had a good relationship with God and been theologically versed, he would have realized that God's law in Leviticus 27:1-3 gave him a way out:

185

"Again, the Lord spoke to Moses, saying, 'Speak to the sons of Israel and say to them, "When a man makes a difficult vow, he shall be valued according to your valuation of persons belonging to the Lord. If your valuation is of the male from twenty years even to sixty years old, then your valuation shall be fifty shekels of silver, after the shekel of the sanctuary."

DISCUSS/ACTION

Exchange vows made to God consistently fall under the umbrella of impulsive, uninformed, and manipulative attempts to cater to our desires rather than submit to His. Jephthah valued winning the battle so much, he risked everything to get it. He thought he knew what was best for him more than God did.

- What's one thing in your life you can't stand the thought of losing?
- If God took it away from you this week, how do you think your faith would be impacted?

The thought of losing what we love most is terrifying, but it could reveal what really captivates our hearts—what we treasure more than God.

- This week, let's change our vows. Instead of using God to get what we want, let's commit to asking Him what *He* wants, surrendering to and obeying His will. Will you attempt praying this way this week?

PRAY

WEEK EIGHT:
Follow Your Heart?

Judges 13:1-16:31

PERSONAL STUDY QUESTIONS

1. Who does God give Israel into the hands of when they fall back into sin? (13:1)

2. How long are they in oppression this time? (13:1)

3. What hardship does Manoah's wife experience? (13:2)

4. Who appears to her? (13:3)

5. After telling her that she'll have a son, what does he tell her about her son's lifestyle that will set him apart? (13:4-5)

6. What does Manoah do when he hears about his wife's encounter with the angel? (13:8)

7. Who does the angel appear to the second time? (13:9)

8. Does Manoah realize that he's speaking with an angel of the Lord? (13:16)

9. It's hard for us to imagine speaking with God through His angel and not knowing it. Manoah probably should've realized it early on, for the angel's appearance was "very awesome," not like a regular man. But he didn't, and neither do we.

Hebrews 13:2 tells us that we should not "neglect to show hospitality to strangers, for by this some have entertained angels without knowing it." Isn't that amazing? We can interact with God's angels without even realizing it!

Unlike Manoah, we shouldn't necessarily recognize them when we see them, for they appear in very human-like form. But we *should* extend grace, honor, and respect to every individual, because God is present with all of us—angel or not.

Christ once revealed truths about the end times to His disciples in Matthew 25:35-40, saying "'For I was hungry, and you gave Me something to eat; I was thirsty, and you gave Me something to drink; I was a stranger, and you invited Me in; naked and you clothed Me; I was sick, and you visited Me; I was in prison, and you came to Me.' Then the righteous will answer Him, 'Lord, when did we see You hungry, and feed You, or thirsty, and give you something to drink? And when did we see You a stranger, and invite You in, or naked, and clothe You? When did we see You sick, or in prison, and come to You?' The King will answer and say to them, '*Truly I say to you, to the extent that you did it to one of these brothers of Mine, even the least of them, you did it to Me.*'"

We are Christ's representatives to everyone on earth, and we are supposed to treat people as we would if He were present with us in the room. Who do you find difficult to treat kindly? How do these passages help you recommit to kindness and being an agent of God's grace in their lives? How can you go about showing His love to them from now on?

10. What happens to the offering Manoah and his wife give to the Lord? (13:19-20)

11. When Manoah finally realizes he spoke with an angel of God, what's his response? (13:22)

12. How does his wife reassure him that his fears will not come to fruition? (13:23)

13. What does the wife name her son? (13:24)

14. What does Samson see (and subsequently desire) in Timnah? (14:1)

15. What is his parents' response to his request? (14:3)

16. What happens on their way down to Timnah near the vineyards? (14:5-6)

17. What does Samson find on his return trip to Timnah? (14:8)

    • What does he do with it? (14:9)

18. What wager does Samson make with the men of Timnah? (14:12-13)

19. Who do the men enlist for help to solve the riddle? (14:15)

    • How do they threaten her?

20. Does Samson reveal the answer? Why? (14:17)

21. How does Samson secure his end of the wager? (14:19)

22. What happens to his wife? (14:20)

23. When Samson returns to his wife later, what does her father tell him? (15:2)

24. What does Samson do in his anger? (15:4-5)

25. What do the Philistines do in response? (15:6)

26. How does Samson respond to their retaliation? (15:8)

27. Why do the Philistines camp against Judah? (15:9-10)

28. How many men go to collect Samson for the Philistines? (15:11)

29. What does Samson make them promise him before surrendering? (15:12)

30. When the Philistines take custody of Samson, what happens? (15:14-15)

31. What does Samson ask for in his first recorded prayer? (15:18)

32. Where does Samson travel to next? (16:1)

33. Who does he visit there? (16:1)

34. What do the citizens of the city plan to do to Samson? (16:2)

35. What does Samson do that night? (16:3)

36. Who does Samson fall in love with in the valley of Sorek? (16:4)

37. When the lords of the Philistines discover the relationship, what do they propose to her? (16:5)

38. How many times does Delilah ask Samson what the secret to his strength is? (16:6-17)

39. When Samson awakes the last time, he acts as he did the other times before. Why? What did he not realize? (16:20)

40. God removed His Spirit of anointing from Samson, and he had no clue. This is one of the most depressing verses in all of Scripture, but we shouldn't fear it happening to us. Again, the Holy Spirit permanently resides in those who accept Christ as their personal Lord and Savior. That means that He never leaves us, never forsakes us, and never abandons us.

We may experience times in life when God doesn't seem close to us (and this can happen for numerous reasons), but we can always stand assured that He is close to us always. We may move away from Him, but He never leaves us.

When is the last time you set aside a moment to savor God's presence in your life and thank Him for it? Will you do so now? Pray that He will continue revealing Himself to you and allow you to experience His presence in addition to intellectually knowing He's there.

41. What do the Philistines do to Samson once they captured him? (16:21)

42. Why do the Philistines gather together to celebrate? (16:23-24)

43. What does Samson ask the boy to do for him? (16:26)

44. How many people are gathered together for the celebration? (16:27)

45. What does Samson ask God for? (16:28)

46. What's the very last act of Samson? (16:29-30)

47. How long did Samson judged Israel? (16:31)

COMMENTARY

The last minor judge account leads us to the last major judge story, that of Samson. If you have any church background, you may be familiar with Samson. You probably envision a beast of a man, standing with flowing dreadlocks like Goliath's precursor. It's easy to imagine a mammoth picking off Philistine hordes like a child step on ants.

You may also recall a certain woman named Delilah, the seductress who ends Samson's dynamic career. Many emotions arise at the mention of Delilah, and none of them are pleasant.

With so many elements of this story swirling in our minds, it's easy to let preconceived notions and biases taint the narrative. Before we begin, let me encourage you to approach this account with a blank slate. Remembering the degeneration based on previous chapters, let's dive into this familiar story and ask God to reveal the depths of its truth in ways we've never experienced before.

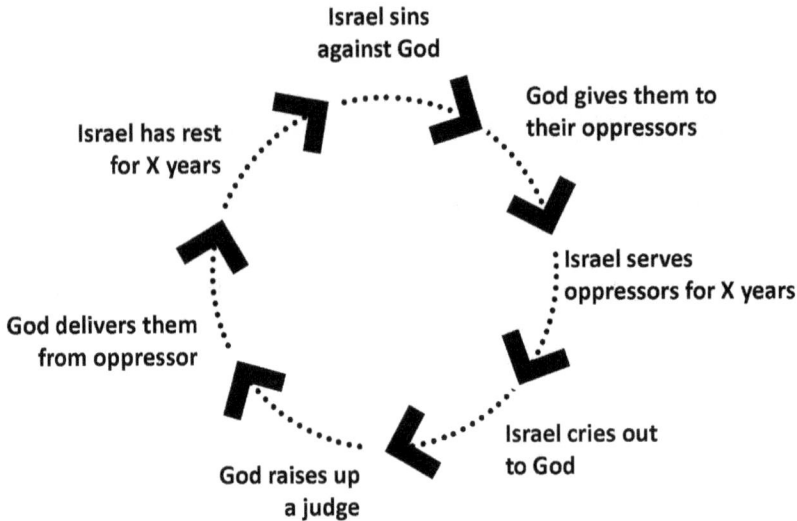

Samson's story (like every other major judge) begins with an ode to Israel's spiritual failure: "the sons of Israel again did evil in the sight of the Lord" (13:1a). I can almost hear the exasperated sigh of the author as he pens the word "again." Yes, believe it or not, the Israelites turn away from God *again*. Apparently their obsession with being like other nations has now completely blinded them to the fact that it's wrong. That, or they've grown so accustomed to their behavior that they're apathetic. Regardless, they throw themselves in the pit of sin once again.

The Lord, per usual, gives them into the hands of an enemy (13:1). This time it's the Philistines, and they oppress Israel for forty years. Unlike several other judge accounts, the Israelites do not cry out to God for deliverance; at least, there's no record of them doing so. Perhaps it's understood, or perhaps God just can't stand their infidelity anymore. But He acts anyway, setting a plan in motion to deliver them…again.

He begins His plan with a married, childless couple from the tribe of Dan (13:2). The husband is Manoah and the wife remains anonymous. Since women were considered lower-class at best, personal property at worst, it's not surprising that many women are anonymous in ancient texts. Scripture names several women (i.e., Deborah and Jael), confirming God's elevated view of women despite cultural tendencies to demote them. But still, some women remain without recorded name, as is the case of Manoah's wife.

In addition to being nameless, she is also barren. Being barren today is brutal, yet we have the medical technology to determine possible contributing factors. Back then, a woman's value was associated with the number of children she bore, so being barren carried extra weight and was often thought to be a curse from God.[105]

This barren couple seems to live an unremarkable life, but all that's about to change. On an ordinary day in their ordinary life, an angel of the Lord turns their world upside down. He appears to Manoah's wife and tells her something that will change their lives forever.

He begins with a seemingly harsh statement, "Behold now, you are barren and have borne no children" (13:3a). Thanks, Mr. Angel Man! Her barrenness haunts her daily, tainting every aspect of her life. She doesn't need a complete stranger to remind her of her predicament!

This appearance is likely another theophany; the angel of the Lord is probably Jesus taking on the form of a human. Though, we know the angel retained some glorious aspects, because she describes him as having an appearance like that "of the angel of God, very awesome," to her husband later on (13:6).

The angel's comment about her barrenness sets the stage for what he's about to reveal: she would conceive and give birth to a son (13:3). This situation occurs multiple times throughout God's Word. Sarah, Rachel, Hannah, Elizabeth, and more were all barren and miraculously gave birth to children after a special encounter with the Lord. Manoah's wife joins a list of astonishing births and, just like the rest, the child to be born would serve a specific purpose in God's story.

After stunning her with a revelation of her impending pregnancy, the angel gives her specific instructions for the child's care. While she is pregnant, she is not to drink wine or any strong drink; nor is she to eat anything unclean (13:4).[106] Her abstinence from wine would pave the way for a distinct vow that would be placed on her son's life. The angel tells her that

> No razor shall come upon his head, for the boy shall be a Nazirite
> to God from the womb; and he shall begin to deliver Israel from
> the hands of the Philistines (13:5).

The Nazirite vow is introduced and described in Numbers 6. This vow would be made by someone (male or female) who wanted to dedicate himself to the Lord for a specific amount of time. While under the vow, he would refuse to eat or drink anything from the vine, including wine, grape juice, grapes, or even foods containing the seeds of the grape. He was also to refrain from consuming any other strong drink or vinegar.

Following the restriction of drink, a person under the Nazirite vow also couldn't cut his hair. During the days of his vow, no razor was permitted to touch his head. When the vow was finished, a special ceremony would commence, in which his hair would be cut off and offered to God.

The final restriction for a person under the Nazirite vow was to stay away from the dead. While this wouldn't seem like a difficult rule to follow, it was to some degree. A Nazirite couldn't touch anything or anyone that was dead—human or animal. Killing a bug would be a no-no (which would be awful for me!). Also, if a family member died during the vow, he couldn't touch them. Touching the dead made someone unclean, and certain ceremonies were required for cleansing in order to be in right standing with God again. Nazirites needed to refrain from it altogether. If he failed, his vow would be over.

Scripture never reveals a specific length of time for Nazirite vows to last, leaving us to conclude that it was decided by the individual. When he would complete the time period of his vow, he would present an offering to the Lord. This offering would include one year-old lamb, one ewe, one ram, a basket of unleavened cakes, unleavened wafers, a grain offering, and a drink offering. The priest would present it all before the Lord, and the Nazirite would then shave his head and place the hair on the fire under the sacrifice of peace offerings. After all the ceremonial instructions were complete, the Nazirite was permitted go back to normal life (killing bugs, eating grapes, etc.).

While the angel doesn't elaborate on all the specific instructions to Manoah's wife, the fact that he tells her the basics confirms the Israelites' serious ignorance of God and His law among the Israelites. The simple components of the vow should have been common knowledge among His people; but as we've noticed, their hearts are far from Him.

When the angel completes his instructions, he leaves and the woman goes to tell her husband what has happened. (Don't know about you, but I'd certainly be freaking out!) She recounts three points to her husband (3:6-7):

1. She had been visited by "a man of God"
2. She would conceive and bear a son
3. Their son would be a Nazirite to God

Her description of the "man of God," reveals that she doesn't know exactly who he was, even though she assumes he's a divine being. She doesn't know where he came from, nor did the angel inform her of his name. All she knows about the angel is that he is a heavenly being. She's close to the truth but doesn't quite comprehend it.[107] She then excitedly tells her husband of the angel's promise that they would have a son. Great news indeed! Not only would they have a son, but he would be special—a child dedicated to God as a Nazirite from birth.

Her recount of the conversation adds and subtracts a couple of facts. First, she adds that the child would be a Nazirite from the womb *to the day of his death*. While she's not necessarily wrong, it's interesting that she perceives this. I wonder if she's so excited about the angel's revelation that she's committing herself to obeying his rules for the rest of her life and helping her future son do the same.

Along with adding the timeline, she neglects to mention that the child was never to cut his hair. Some believe this is understandable, since cutting the hair represented the end of the vow, and Samson would be under it his whole life.[108] I find it hard to concur, though, since he was never to drink wine or touch anything dead through the end of his life, either—yet she states both of these to Manoah. This may have been an oversight on her part, or perhaps it foreshadows the means of Samson's demise.

The last oversight of the wife is Samson's role: Israel's deliverer (at least, he would begin to deliver them) from the Philistines. This seems like quite an important component, but for some reason, she neglects to mention it. We can only speculate as to why. Perhaps it slips her mind in the flurry of excitement (though if she's anything like me, she would've remembered in the dozen or so retellings of the event later!). Maybe she mirrors Israel as a whole, not seeing a need for deliverance. The author doesn't record Israel crying out to God, so perhaps they've grown content with the Philistine rule and don't crave relief.

Regardless, Manoah is aware of the revelation (the part he was told), and his reaction is less than admirable. Instead of taking his wife at her word, he decides to get independent confirmation of the situation. He prays and asks God to "let the man of God whom You have sent come to us again that he may teach us what to do for the boy who is to be born" (13:8). Um, Manoah, the angel already revealed this information! Maybe he doesn't trust his wife. Or possibly, in his machismo, he's insulted that the angel didn't come to him first, so he refuses to believe it until he hears it first-hand.

God listens to Manoah and sends His angel again. But He doesn't cater to Manoah's demands entirely (we cannot force God's hand). Instead of appearing to Manoah, the angel appears to his wife again as she is sitting in a field (13:9). As soon as she sees the angel, she runs to retrieve her husband, saying "the man who came the other day has appeared to me" (13:10). Manoah stands up and follows his wife to the angel (13:11).

When they stand before him together, Manoah asks if he is indeed the man who appeared to his wife previously (13:11). The angel confirms, and Manoah wants to know what the "boy's mode of life and his vocation" will be (13:12). By asking this, Manoah admits to believing that the boy will be born. He's not questioning that a son will be born, or even that he will be a Nazirite as his wife had said. Rather, his question reveals his compulsion to be in control. While he may genuinely want to know what the boy's vocation will be (confirming that his wife hadn't told him), this isn't something that should matter much, especially in light of the impending miraculous birth.

The angel doesn't fall for Manoah's attempt at control. He answers indirectly, telling him that the woman should heed what he already revealed to her (13:13). Then He reiterates his previous instructions—that she shouldn't eat or drink anything from the vine or any other unclean thing (13:14). But he says nothing of the boy or his vocation. If God deemed a revelation to his wife sufficient, Manoah should agree.

Manoah then asks him if they could detain him in order to prepare a young goat for him (13:15). Are Gideon bells ringing in your head? This account is very similar to Gideon's. Gideon asks the angel to wait as well, except he desired to bring an offering, not just a meal. As with Gideon, the angel tells Manoah that he will wait, but will not eat their food. Instead, he recommends that they prepare a burnt offering for the Lord (13:16).

At this point, Manoah still doesn't realize that he's speaking with an angel of the Lord, which may explain his next question. Instead of rushing to prepare an offering, Manoah asks the angel's name (13:17). He claims that he wants to know so he and his wife can honor him when his words come to pass. If Manoah really wanted to honor him, he would've done so that moment, not wait until his words come to fruition. This is nothing but another attempt at control—"the divine name cannot be had on demand or taken in vain;" God cannot be manipulated.[109]

The angel refuses to comply with Manoah's request, and instead asks him, "Why do you ask my name, seeing it is wonderful?" (13:18). The angel's name isn't actually "Wonderful," as John or James are names. Rather, the word "wonderful" used here "describes God's knowledge as being incomprehensible and unattainable."[110]

Out of questions (and perhaps realizing the angel won't be manipulated), Manoah follows the angel's advice and prepares an offering of a young goat and grain (13:19). While the offering burns, the angel performs wonders as Manoah and his wife observe (13:19). The "wonders" are unknown, but whatever they were, they leave the couple mesmerized. When the flame torches the altar and licks the sky toward heaven, the angel ascends in the flame of the altar. Can you imagine seeing *that*? Manoah couldn't either, and he did see it!

The angel leaves, never again to appear to Manoah or his wife (13:21). Only then does Manoah realize they'd spoken with the angel of the Lord. Manoah's quite dense in the head, echoing the state of Israel in reference to God and spiritual matters. His wife recognized divinity, even if she didn't fully comprehend the gravity of it. But Manoah neglects to perceive the angel's deity, even after seeing him perform wonders and disappearing in a flame!

When Manoah finally realizes he encountered divinity, he trembles in fear, convinced he and his wife will die because they've seen God (13:22). His reaction is similar to Gideon's back in chapter 6, who also fears death when he realizes he's seen the Lord. Both men are irrational in their fear and incredibly ignorant. While they had seen deity, they had *not* seen God face to face. What witlessness to think they saw Him without immediately recognizing Him and then dying from awe-struck astonishment?

Manoah's wife recognizes the irrationality. In response to his fear, she points out:

> If the Lord had desired to kill us, He would not have accepted a burnt offering and a grain offering from our hands, nor would He have shown us all these things, nor would He have let us hear things like this at this time (13:23).

Duh, Manoah. If God really wanted to kill you, don't you think He would've by now? Also, why would He reveal His plan for your family's life if He planned to kill you before any of it was realized? Crazy. Though we're hardly ones to judge. If I saw an angel of God, I can't say how I'd react. My prayer is that I would be close enough with God beforehand that reason and logic wouldn't fly out the window. But who knows?

In due time, Manoah's wife gives birth to a son, and she names him Samson (13:24). The choice of this name is both fascinating and disheartening. Fascinating because the text tells us his mother named him, not his father. In a hierarchal culture, this turns traditional expectations upside down.

The disheartening aspect of his name is that it means "sun." That's not so bad in itself, but when we realize that it was a popular Canaanite name at the time,[111] it confirms Israel's idolatry yet again. Israelites are even naming their children after Canaanites! The people they were supposed to wipe out have now become their namesakes. Even more discouraging is the fact that his mother refuses to give her son a Hebrew name even though she spoke with an angel of the Lord and experienced a rather miraculous birth. The son who's divinely appointed by God to deliver Israel from the Philistines begins his life with a pagan name.

Despite his unfortunate name, Samson grows up and is blessed by the Lord (13:24). The Spirit of the Lord begins to stir in him, no doubt readying him (at least in part) for his role as judge in Israel (13:25). Samson is the only judge in the book who receives a call of God before his birth and is set apart for Him throughout the duration of his life. He has every advantage available to him (minus theologically sound parents, perhaps), and readers can't help but have great expectations for his life and judgeship. If only our expectations were ever upheld in this maddening book!

Samson's first recorded action of his adult life is his visit to Timnah (14:1). Timnah was a town originally allotted to the tribe of Dan, but it may have merged with the tribe of Judah at some point.[112] When the Philistines took over Israel, they occupied Timnah. But it must've been a relatively peaceful occupation, because Samson doesn't seem to experience any difficulties coming and going from there.

MEDITERRANEAN SEA

BENJAMIN

JORDAN RIVER

• TIMNAH

• ZORAH

• ASHKELON

P H I L I S T I A

• GAZA

J U D A H

DEAD SEA

↑
NORTH

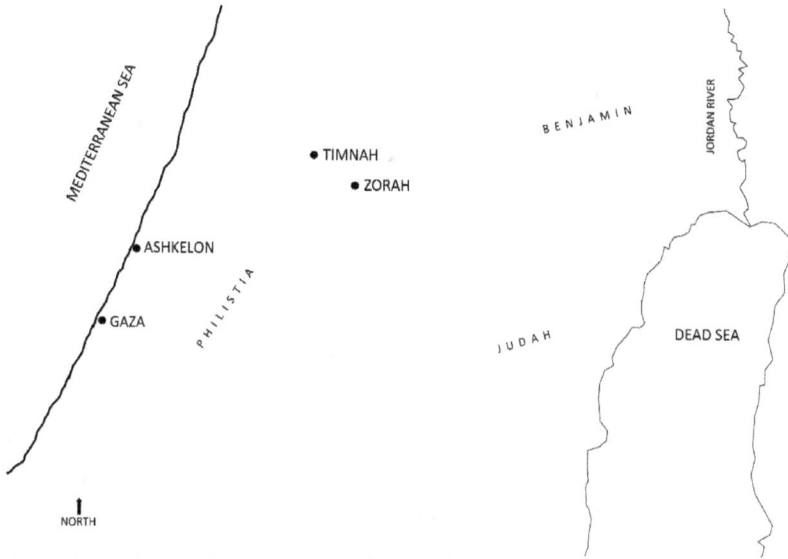

We discover rather quickly that Timnah itself isn't all that exciting; but someone living there is, at least to Samson. On one of his visits, Samson sees a Philistine woman living there and decides he wants her as his wife. The fact that he *sees* her is quite important and speaks to what occupies Samson's heart. Samson, like the other judges, serves as a microcosm of Israel as a whole. While he should be leading Israel toward God and righteousness, he busies himself fulfilling his own desires. Because she *looks* good to Samson, he wants her. His decision to make her his wife is void of trivial factors like commitment and viable faith, being based only on what looks good to him—what can satisfy what he wants.

He returns to his parents and informs them of his decision to marry the Philistine woman in Timnah (14:2). Even he admits that his desire for her is based on her looks. This attraction is purely physical, which is not the best foundation for a relationship! He then tells his parents to get her for him as a wife.

More so than today, marriages then were contracts between two families and before God. These contracts (or covenants), like any other legal contract, contained payments, stipulations of the agreement, and the penalties that would ensue should the contract be breached.[113] Marriages were taken very seriously, and Samson's parents know this well.

They aren't exactly thrilled that Samson wants to marry a Philistine. They even try to dissuade him, saying, "Is there no woman among the daughters of your relatives, or among all our people, that you go to take a wife from the uncircumcised Philistines?" (14:3). Unless they experienced a serious change of heart, it's doubtful their motivations are theology-driven. They probably just want to preserve their national heritage, which is ironic, since they have no problem prostituting themselves with surrounding cultures. They also probably remember the angel's words: that God would use Samson to begin delivering Israel from the Philistines. How could marrying a Philistine possibly fit into that plan?

Samson remains undeterred and tells them once again to get the woman for him, because she looks good to him (14:3). With three references to sight within as many verses, it doesn't sound like logical thinking drives Samson's decisions (not a fabulous character trait for a judge called by God).

The author pauses the narrative to include an omniscient clause that lets us peek into God's plan with this marriage situation. While it's not ideal, God plans to use Samson's marriage as an occasion to rise against the Philistines (14:4). We don't know what's going to happen, but with that preview, we can assume the marriage won't have a happy ending.

On their way to Timnah, Samson and his parents get separated for a reason unknown to us. While they're apart, Samson comes across a young lion (14:5). Since God doesn't want Samson dead yet, He anoints him with His Spirit afresh. Samson tears the lion apart "as one tears a young goat though he had nothing in his hand" (14:6). Tearing a young goat doesn't exactly sound easy to me, so I can only imagine what a feat tearing a lion apart limb from limb would be.

While I'd be tempted to brag about such a stunt, Samson neglects to tell his parents what happened. Under his Nazirite vow, touching a dead animal (which includes being the agent of its death) meant undergoing ceremonial rituals for cleansing. If he told his parents, they probably would've insisted on those cleansing rituals. But Samson is about to get married and decides he doesn't have time for such nonsense, so he keeps his mouth shut and continues on to Timnah. Apparently, "God and His law are not as important to Samson, who only wants what is 'right' in his eyes."[114]

When Samson arrives in Timnah, he speaks with the woman and confirms yet again that she looked good (14:7). Got to make sure it wasn't just a fluke the first time, I suppose. But it wasn't, so he still wants to make her his wife. After making the necessary arrangements for engagement, Samson and his parents head home.

Later on, Samson and his parents make the journey back to Timnah for the wedding. Along the way he turns aside to see if the lion carcass is still there (14:8). It is, and he notices that a swarm of bees had taken up residence in the corpse. The sight takes Samson by surprise, and understandably so. Flies and maggots, not bees, usually inhabit corpses. Most likely, "this carcass dehydrated quickly, eliminating putrification, and in no time at all provided a hospitable environment for bees not only to live but also to produce their honey."[115]

Breaking his vow once again, Samson scrapes honey from the swarm for a little snack. When he returns to his father and mother, he gives them some as well, not informing them of the source of their tasty treat (14:9). Keeping this secret from his parents makes them unclean as well. God provided Israel with strict dietary and sanitary laws to keep them healthy and safe. Eating food from an unclean source would require them to go through rituals in order to be clean before God once again. Samson clearly has no problem defiling himself, yet with this act we learn that he doesn't care much for others, either.

They continue down to Timnah and make a feast for the wedding, as young men customarily did (14:10). When the Philistines notice what's going on, they bring thirty men to celebrate with Samson as groomsmen of sorts (14:11). The lack of Samson's extended family and friends may indicate their disapproval of the marriage. But since Samson doesn't care one bit about anything (or anyone) except himself, he hardly misses the companionship, with his luscious new wife waiting for him. He helped himself to sweet honey despite being contaminated; now he's about to do the same with a Philistine woman.

When the men gather around Samson, he proposes a riddle to them (14:12). If they solve the riddle within the seven-day wedding celebration (and we get stressed out over a one-day celebration!), he would supply them each with garments—linen wraps and a change of clothes. But if they couldn't solve the riddle, they would each have to give him the same (14:13). The riddle is:

> Out of the eater came something to eat,
> And out of the strong came something sweet (14:14).

Normal individuals would be dumbfounded by such a riddle, and the groomsmen are no exception. When three days go by and they realize they're getting nowhere, they turn to Samson's bride for help (14:15). However, they don't exactly do so in a friendly manner. With egos bruised, they threaten to burn down her house with her and her father in it if she doesn't divulge the answer.

So begins the nagging. Highly motivated, Samson's wife begins pestering him for the answer to the riddle. She whines and complains and weeps—anything to get him to fess up. At one point, he asks her why he should tell her, since he hadn't even told his parents. He clearly is overflowing with love and respect for his new bride (14:16)!

She continues weeping before him until he can't stand it anymore. On the seventh day, he tells her the answer just to get her to shut up (14:17). In turn, she reveals the answer to the men, who are quick to approach Samson with their newly acquired nugget of gold:

> What is sweeter than honey?
>
> And what is stronger than a lion? (14:18)

Samson knows the answer came from his wife, and he's not pleased. In a fit of rage he says, "If you had not plowed with my heifer, you would not have found out my riddle" (14:18). Nice, Samson. You're barely married and you're already calling your wife a cow! But again, Samson's concern is hardly for her comfort. She doesn't compare to his compulsion to get what he wants.

Seething with rage, he leaves and travels to Ashkelon. The Spirit of the Lord comes upon him again, and he slaughters thirty men. Then he retrieves their goods and clothes and brings the clothing—probably still dripping with blood—to the men who "solved" his riddle. Still furious, he leaves his bride in Timnah and travels back to his father's house (14:19). When his bride's father sees him leave, he makes a careless decision by giving her to Samson's best man as a wife (14:20).

When Samson simmers down, he heads back to Timnah with a young goat for his wife (15:1). While this certainly isn't a gift I would appreciate, in ancient times it served as the equivalent of a box of chocolates.[116] In that case, it doesn't sound so bad. Samson is excited to be with his wife, but the feeling won't last long. When he approaches her home, her father refuses to let him in, saying, "I really thought that you hated her intensely; so I gave her to your companion." Knowing he's in trouble, he offers Samson an alternative, "Is not her younger sister more beautiful than she? Please let her be yours instead" (15:2). Nice dad!

But Samson will have none of it. He wants the first woman who was pleasing to his eyes, not her sister! His rage ignites once again, and he tells them, "This time I shall be blameless in regard to the Philistines when I do them harm" (15:3). This statement reveals quite a bit about Samson. It's first an admission of guilt. When he got angry with the thirty men of his wedding party, he murdered thirty completely uninvolved people. (Notice they're not *innocent*. God wants the Philistines destroyed, so they're definitely guilty, just not of a particular crime relating to Samson). Samson admits that his revenge wasn't justified in that act. Even though they cheated, their actions don't demand the murder of thirty men as retribution. Second, Samson's response reveals his apathy. Despite his awareness of his guilt, he simply doesn't care what's right or wrong. All he cares about is what he wants and what feels good to him.

The last insight we receive from his statement foreshadows what's to come: Samson will harm the Philistines again. Because he feels justified this time (whether or not it's legitimate), we expect this act to be far more gruesome and intense than the former. We won't be disappointed.

Sampson goes to a nearby field and catches three hundred foxes (here we are thinking strength is his only skill; he must've been fast too!). Next he takes the foxes and ties them together tail to tail. In the middle of the ties, he places torches and sets them on fire (15:4). For animal lovers, Samson's act is wretched enough; no need to read further. But it gets worse.

With the scent of charring flesh following them, the horde of foxes runs through the Philistine grain fields (15:5). Back in chapter 15:1 we read that this is the time of the wheat harvest, so the Philistines have just begun collecting the grain that's been growing. Samson's stunt burns up all the crops—the standing grain, vineyards, and groves. Everything is consumed by his tirade, leaving the Philistines without sufficient food for the coming season.

When the Philistines discover the culprit of this heinous act, they're enraged and decide to fight fire with fire (literally). But they don't retaliate directly with Samson. Instead, they seize his (ex-) wife and her father and burn them both (15:6). The anonymous wife and her father receive the same fate as the Philistine crops, ironically fulfilling the threat the groomsmen made against her in regard to Samson's riddle weeks before.

After learning of his wife and father-in-law's deaths, Samson promises revenge on the men. Like a child, he feels compelled to have the last word, though he does vow to quit the revenge cycle after this round of vengeance (15:7). What he doesn't realize is that revenge is impossible to control without God, the Ultimate Judge. When we take revenge into our own hands, we put ourselves in God's place[117] and erroneously believe that life will be peachy-keen again after justice is served.

Samson thinks this will be the last act of vengeance on his part. While that may sound admirable and a good use of restraint, that's a superficial understanding of the situation and Samuel. As long as he is his own god, he will fail and fall into his own cycles of degeneration, including that of revenge.

He'll also continue to grow arrogant. He already seems to be a rather egotistical fellow, which is ironic since the only attribute worthy of potential arrogance (his strength) comes solely from the Lord. He's abusing and taking credit for the miraculous gift the Lord gives him. The blessed child scorns the blessing by using it all to serve only selfish purposes. The fact that God uses it for His glory despite Samson's obvious motivation blunders is a remarkable testament to His grace.

This "last" act of revenge proves more brutalizing than either of the former. Samson goes against the Philistines and strikes them "ruthlessly with a great slaughter" (15:8). We're not told how many die that day, but we can reasonably deduce that the details are better left unspoken. He now has serious blood on his hands—blood that could have been justified should he have reached out to God and followed His lead against the Philistines via proper channels. But he didn't, and now he's an outlaw of sorts. He moves to the cleft of the rock of Etam, perhaps to avoid immediate reprisal from the Philistines and to confirm his position of having the last word.

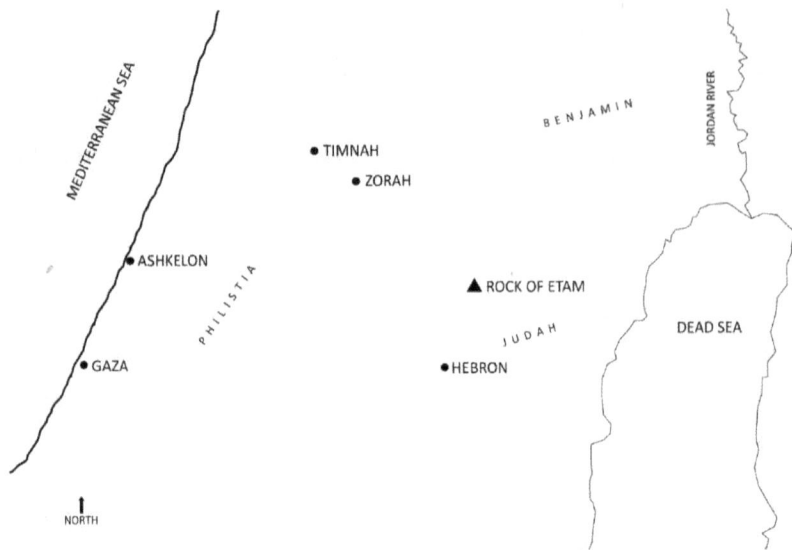

But the Philistines aren't giving up. They can't. One Israelite is undermining all the Philistines, which is impeding their control over Israel. If they can't keep one man under control, how can they possibly hope to manage a nation?

Even though the Philistines take issue only with Samson, their lack of virtue brings others into the fight. They've already murdered Samson's wife and father-in-law; now they turn their attention to Israel, particularly the tribe of Judah. They camp in Judah and spread out over Lehi (15:9). The name "Lehi" means "jawbone" and is a play on words for what's about to transpire between the Philistines and Samson.[118]

The men of Judah desire peace above all else and ask the Philistines why they have risen against them (15:10). To their knowledge, they haven't done anything wrong. They've been under the Philistines' thumb for almost two decades; surely they've figured out how to cohabitate with them without ruffling their feathers.

In reply, the Philistines inform Judah that they want Samson bound and delivered to them so they could exact revenge on him (15:10). If it wasn't so sad, the feud between Samson and the Philistines would be comical.

They're acting like children—he took my lollipop so I'm going to take his toy truck! The level of maturity squats deeper with each interaction. To think it could all have been avoided had Samson not used an impossible riddle to pick a fight.

Is a situation in your life spinning out of control? Has what started as a tiny disagreement now exploded into raging conflict, threatening to end a good friendship? The "innocent" flirting at the office has spiraled into a heated affair—your family doesn't know and the guilt is overbearing. Take some advice from Samson's life—end it now. If you need to, apologize. Mend the situation; ask for forgiveness; move on. Don't let things get worse. In the future, suffocate the seed of sin before it has time to grow!

Stuck in the middle of raging enemies, Judah believes the Philistines' request is reasonable, so they send men to seize Samson—three thousand men, to be exact (15:11). They head toward the rock of Etam, find Samson, and ask him two questions right up front: "Do you not know that the Philistines are rulers over us?" and "What then is this that you have done to us?" Just as Samson's words reveal much about him, these two questions expose the condition of Judah's hearts as well.

Beginning this book, we see Judah as noble warriors who follow God and conquer nearly all their allotted land. Now they get stuck in the middle of a theological summersault—upside down and unable to get right again. Their reminder to Samson that the Philistines rule over them is both a description and prescription. It describes their situation (the Philistines are, in fact, ruling over them). But it also serves as a prescription of apathy: they take no issue with the Philistines' rule and have no intention of doing anything about it. This reminds us of the strategic absence of a cry from Israel at the beginning of this cycle in chapter 13. Israel sins against God and gets conquered, but they grow comfortable in their captivity.

Israel slid away from God and have grown comfortable in their imprisonment. Freedom doesn't even enter their minds as a possibility anymore. Samson is the perfect leader to defeat the Philistines, but the

Israelites are blind to it. If Samson had fought for them, it's doubtful any Israelites would have had to fight at all! He can kill hundreds by himself; the rest of Israel can serve as his cheerleaders. But instead of entreating him to join forces and defeat the Philistines, the Israelites remind him of the way life is—the Philistines are ruling; and it's best (and easiest) to keep it that way.

The second question solidifies the vacancy of their bravado. Rather than stopping with a reminder of the Philistines' rule, they accuse Samson of harming them. God forbid Samson act in a way that threatens their way of life and makes it more difficult for them.

This throws us back to the pages of the wilderness after the Exodus (a story God reminds Israel of several times in the book of Judges, in fact). After ten miraculous plagues (including our familiar locust plague) and a climax of a sea parting, God delivers His people from the oppression of Egypt and gets them on their way to the Promised Land. The people of Israel were thrilled, but only for a short time. Soon they began complaining, claiming that life was better for them in Egypt! They couldn't grasp the concept of freedom because they were so used to their chains.

That's precisely what's happening again. Israel finds themselves in chains once more but has zero desire of deliverance. A glaring chance of freedom stares them in the eyes. His name is Samson, but their chains act as a blindfold. They can't see the means of deliverance standing directly in front of them.

Of course, this is all lost to those in the story. Samson doesn't miss a beat defending himself and carries out his childish behavior by declaring, "As they did to me, so I have done to them" (15:11). In other words, "they started it!" What a whiner, aptly following Israel's long history of grumbling. The irony is that Samson is in the Promised Land that his forefathers never could enter because of their sin. If earlier generations could have foreseen such behavior by those who eventually occupied the Promised Land, they surely would have been appalled.

Undeterred, the Israelites tell Samson their plans. They intend to bind and deliver him to the revenge-thirsty Philistines (15:12). Surprisingly, Samson agrees to their plan as long as they promise not to kill him. They concede to that stipulation, tie him up with two new ropes, and make their way toward the Philistines (15:13).

Upon entering Lehi, the Philistines hoot and holler, confident of their impending victory against the infamous Samson (15:14). What they don't factor into the situation is God. Once again, God isn't finished with Samson, so He anoints him mightily with His Spirit. I love the description of his escape from the ropes:

> The Spirit of the Lord came upon him mightily so that the ropes that were on his arms were as flax that is burned with fire, and his bonds dropped from his hands (15:14).

The ropes might have been made of Jell-O as far as Samson is concerned! They basically disintegrate and fall from him like fluttering feathers. In a swift motion, Samson grabs the closest resource available—the jawbone of a donkey (he's not doing well with his Nazirite rule against touching dead things!), and unleashes hell-bent fury on the Philistines. As the sun blisters down above them, Samson executes one thousand men (15:15). The town (Lehi, "jawbone") lives up to its namesake in a morbid way, and Samson completes yet another execution of vengeance.

We'd be remiss not to pause and note the similarity between this account and that of Shamgar, Jael, and the Thebez tower woman in previous chapters. Each of these people used a weapon directly available to them on short notice, and God gave them victory. Of course, Samson is the only one under the Nazirite vow, and touching a bone from a corpse once again requires that he undergo ceremonial cleansing. But who has time for that? Samson decides that he doesn't; surely his inconceivable victory gets him a pass. Not so wise, Samson; though wisdom seems to have stretched its wings and flown away long ago.

In a spirit of giddiness (perhaps topped with a dollop of bewilderment caused by exhaustion), Samson recites an impromptu verse of victory, perhaps to onlookers surrounding him:

> With the jawbone of a donkey,
> Heaps upon heaps,
> With the jawbone of a donkey
> I have killed a thousand men (15:16).

After finishing his little jingle, Samson throws the jawbone on the ground and renames the town Ramath-lehi, meaning "the high place of the jawbone" (15:17). When his nerves settle down a bit, Samson realizes that he's parched. He subsequently transforms from a child to a child drama-queen.

In his first recorded prayer, Samson complains:

> You have given this great deliverance by the hand of Your servant, and now shall I die of thirst and fall into the hands of the uncircumcised? (15:18)

Oh, how telling this short prayer is of the heart of Samson. As noted before, Samson is not ignorant of God and His anointing on his life. His parents undoubtedly told him of his special calling, and it's been confirmed over and over again. However, instead of using this knowledge for good and to move toward God; he uses and abuses it to get his own way. He admitted guilt before, but in the same breath admitted his apathy. He *knows* what's right and what God wants; he just doesn't care.

With this recent thousand-man slaughter, Samson is intellectually aware that the deliverance was accomplished by God, not himself. But he admits this only to God. He neglects to mention God's involvement in his little victory stanza or in the presence of others. But now that he wants something, of course it's God who gave him victory!

This admission is scarcely spoken before a complaint rises like uncontrollable bile from the same mouth. If God can give him such a great deliverance, can He not provide His "servant" some water? While the word "servant" is hardly consistent with Samson's perspective of self, that's not what is most striking about his question. In an embarrassingly childish manner, Samson whines that he'll simply die if he doesn't get water soon! And worse, maybe he'll even fall into the hands of the uncircumcised Philistines too. Seriously, Samson? He doesn't seem to catch the irony in his words. He takes no issue in *marrying* a Philistine, but now he uses his scorched tongue to scorn their inferior status.

This thirst complaint reminds us of Israel's similar complaint in the wilderness after the exodus. When Israel enters the desert,

> They thirsted there for water; and they grumbled against Moses and said, "Why, now, have you brought us up from Egypt, to kill us and our children and our livestock with thirst?"[119]

Perhaps Samson is merely trying to fill his forefather's expert whining shoes. Unknown to Samson, another man will come, displaying the same entitled, thankless, and self-absorbed attitude. Jonah is most famous for his three-day, all-expense paid trip inside the belly of a fish, but what most don't realize about Jonah is his incredulous self-absorption. Nonetheless, God uses him to bring the news of salvation to a bunch of "uncircumcised" people living in Nineveh. But because Jonah hates the people of Nineveh, he's enraged at their repentance. He throws a temper tantrum that competes voraciously with any two-year-old, saying "Therefore now, O Lord, please take my life from me for death is better to me than life" (Jonah 4:3). Unlike Samson, who used death as a dramatic conclusion, Jonah *wants* to die because he doesn't get his way!

All these examples serve as good news for us. If God can use these men in spite of their deep seeded flaws, He can use us too! God's patience with us expands vast like the universe, and with each new day, He gives us mercies afresh.

God's patience extends to Samson in the midst of his rant as well. He splits the "hollow place that is in Lehi so that water came out of it" (15:19). The hollow place mentioned here literally reads "mortar," a word typically used to describe "a hollowed stone or deep wooden bowl in which, for example, olives were crushed to produce oil."[120] Water pours out and Samson drinks to his fill, feeling revived and reenergized. He names the hollow place En-hakkore, which can be interpreted as "the spring of the one who calls," or "the spring of the one who names."[121]

Samson then arises and judges Israel for twenty years.

--

Sometime during his judgeship, Samson travels to Gaza (16:1). Gaza is the "southernmost of the five principle Philistine cities, although, with its strategic position on the trade-routes from Egypt to western Asia, it had a history going back to a period long before the Philistine occupation."[122] It seems similar to Timnah in that people travel in and out without much trouble; Samson certainly doesn't have issue in entering.

When he arrives, his eyes get him in trouble again. He sees a harlot who's pleasing to the eyes, and he decides to help himself to her services (16:1). Samson's life seems to be marked by the presence of women, four specifically. This is number three. First is his mother, who although anonymous, plays a prominent role in his life. Next is his wife, whom we don't know much about. Although she doesn't seem super-influential, she does manage to conjure up some serious consequences from the conflict instigated between the Philistines and Samson because of her. The third woman, a harlot, remains anonymous like the previous two. We learn next to nothing about her, but due to her occupation, we can imagine she's a less-than outstanding moral character. She's pretty, and that's all Samson cares about, per usual.

When the Philistine Gazites learn that Samson is within their city, they surround the city gates and lie in wait (16:2). They plan to ambush and kill him when he exits the city the following morning, hoping he'll be in a stupor after his late-night escapades with the harlot. But Samson has no intention of staying until morning. The perfect gentleman, Samson stays with the harlot until midnight, then gets up to leave (16:3).

Arriving at the gate, he supposedly notices the men lying in wait for him. Or perhaps he heard whispers of their plan before he left the woman's house. Regardless, he will not be played the fool. He grabs hold of the doors of the city and puts them on his shoulders for a little road trip (16:3). While this does not sound all that impressive, it is when we realize the enormity of these doors.

Cities back then were as deemed as strong as their surrounding walls and gates. In order to enter the city, people would pass through "elaborate gatehouses that were often two or three stories high, with guardrooms flanking the tunnel-like opening."[123] They were enormous fortifications, wide enough for chariots to ride on top of.

The doors of such a gate were massive (see illustration). They reached the heights of the walls they protected— again, two to three stories tall. But Samson doesn't just grab the doors. The doors are attached to the two posts that hold them together, along with horizontal bars that adorn them. These doors with their accompanying accessories weigh at least four to five hundred pounds.[124] Samson pulls Gaza's doors, posts, and bars clear out of the ground then carries them on his back all the way to the mountain opposite of Hebron (16:3).

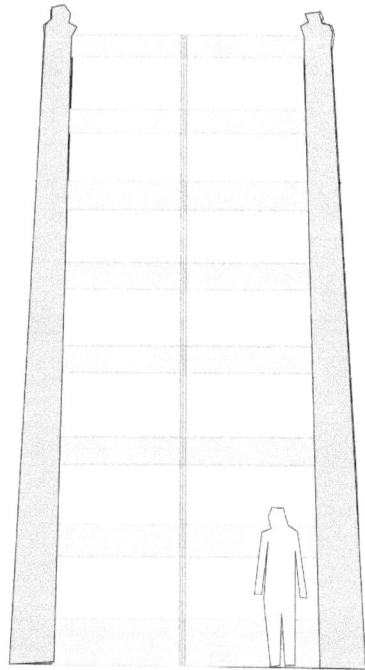

Scholars debate the distance Samson

travels with the gates on his shoulders, mainly because the text isn't clear. Due to the ambiguity of the language, some believe that Samson carries the gate "toward" or "in the direction" of Hebron. If this is the case, Samson may have carried it only a short distance before dumping it.[125] Others take the text more literally, advocating that Samson travels most of, if not the entire, distance between Gaza and Hebron with the doors on his back. If this is true, Samson travels nearly forty miles with a several-hundred-pound load on his back.[126]

Regardless of the distance, Samson's feat still drops the jaws of those who see and hear about it. Carrying 400-500 pounds *any* distance is impressive, and I wouldn't be one bit surprised if it was the nearly forty-mile stretch between Gaza and Hebron. Samson is someone to be reckoned with; how foolish of the Gazites to think they could have killed him in an ambush! His massacre of the 1,000 men with a donkey's jawbone should have dissipated that thought; but now they *know* they don't stand a chance against him. They'll have to be far more creative in their plans to eliminate this particular threat against the Philistines.

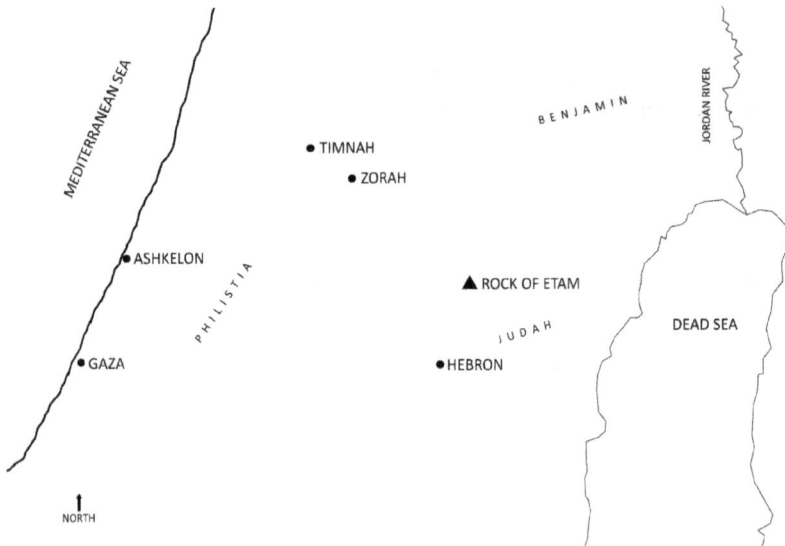

They don't have to wait long.

Samson travels to the Valley of Sorek, where he finds the fourth, last, and only named woman in his life (16:4). Zorah, the birthplace of Samson, overlooked the Valley of Sorek, which was the "most direct route from the hill country near Jerusalem to the Philistine plain."[127] There he finds the scandalous Delilah.

When the Philistines discover Samson's relationship with Delilah, their interest is riled. This could be the way they bring Samson down! The lords (or leaders) of the Philistines approach Delilah when Samson isn't around. They offer her a proposal:

> Entice him, and see where his great strength lies and how we may overpower him that we may bind him to afflict him. Then we will each give you eleven hundred pieces of silver (16:5).

Their offer presents us with several insights. First, (and contrary to nearly every artistic rendition of Samson's person), he is not a humongous Goliath-type figure possessing chiseled layers of bulging muscles. If such an imposing figure was the one disrupting the Philistines' way of life, they would not have been looking for the *secret* of his strength. It would have been obvious. Samson most likely looked like an average man, making his feats that much more dumbfounding.

Next, their proposal brings to mind the one made between Samson's groomsmen and his wife. Except instead of threatening Delilah with death as the groomsmen did, the lords try a different tactic: bribery (perhaps they're weary of death and destruction?). They offer her eleven hundred pieces of silver each, which was quite an impressive number (16:5). There are the five Philistine lords, so the total number would have been 5,500 pieces—more than three times the weight of gold accrued by Gideon after the Midianite king victory.[128]

This is a *huge* amount of money. The average wage of a day laborer was ten shekels a year, making this amount equivalent to 550 years' worth of wages.[129] To give us a better grasp, it would amount to about $16,500,000 to the average American who earns an annual salary of $30,000. Considering inflation and other monetary changes over the course of time, it took Judas the promise of only thirty pieces of silver to betray Jesus. This amount totals only four months' wages back then, or the equivalent of $5,000 today. That's a pretty disgusting comparison. Our Savior is betrayed for an amount that could purchase a new bedroom set of furniture or an old, clunky car. Samson, on the other hand, is a sorry excuse of a man and is betrayed for an amount that could provide comfortable lifestyles for several dozen people.

After the Philistines offer the enormous amount of money that leaves dollar signs in Delilah's eyes, they propose a plan that reveals their intentions. They tell Delilah they want to capture and afflict Sampson. If Delilah cares for him at all, it should make her squirm a bit; though we get no glimpse of her hesitation.

As far as we can tell, Delilah immediately confronts Samson to find out the secret to his strength (16:6). The money is simply too good to pass up. She, like Samson, is catering to the eyes of her lust, and even though it's not sexual, she, too, cares only about herself.

What's fascinating about Delilah's inquiry of Samson is her directness. Like the Philistine lords, Delilah doesn't disguise her intent. She tells him bluntly, "Please tell me where your great strength is and how you may be bound to afflict you" (16:6). Really, Delilah? She could have left out the affliction part easily enough! She could've dressed it up with some seduction, or at least lied as to why she wants to know. But no, she tells him what she wants to know and why she wants to know it!

Her directness suggests either a total lack of shrewdness (playing a dumb blonde role) or that Samson is intoxicated. Otherwise, she's completely mad, having lost all mental capacities in light of the wealth she's about to amass. It's likely that Samson may be slightly inebriated when Delilah asks him. While the text hasn't directly told us that Samson broke the second component of his Nazirite vow (not consuming alcohol), he's most likely no stranger to the vine. We find him in vineyards twice in chapter 14, and wedding ceremonies hardly commenced without the merriment that accompanied drinks. Since Samson cares only about what pleases him, drinking probably plays a role in his pursuit of pleasure.

Instead of laughing at her and leaving (as he should have), Samson answers her—though not with transparency (16:7). He sees an opportunity to play games with Delilah, and we've already seen with the groomsmen that Samson enjoys games. He tells her that if he's bound with seven fresh cords that have not been dried, then he will become weak and like any other man.

When he falls asleep, Delilah has the Philistine lords deliver the cords according to his specifications (16:8). She binds him herself. With the Philistines lying in wait in the inner chamber, she yells, "The Philistines are upon you, Samson!" Samson shoots up, snapping the cords as easily a single blade of grass (16:9). He sends the Philistines running for their lives, and his secret remains protected.

But Delilah doesn't give up. She once again confronts Samson, saying, "Behold, you have deceived me and told me lies; now please tell me how you may be bound" (16:10). She points out that Samson lied to her and now politely asks for the truth. Although she leaves out the affliction part, she still tells him that she plans to bind him with an understood intent to harm him.

Andy Stanly, the senior pastor of North Point Community Church, once discussed this scene in a sermon. He asked the question on everyone's mind: "Could a man really be that stupid?" Delilah just proved that she couldn't be trusted. Surely Samson notices and knows her intentions. What Andy said next caused the audience to erupt in laughter: he admitted that men really *are* that stupid, especially when it comes to women! They don't think clearly (or at all) in the presence of beautiful women—particularly a woman they're mesmerized with. Being a woman, I don't understand this phenomena, but I'll trust the men who say otherwise.

Samson answers her, though again with deceit, continuing his little game. He tells her that if he's bound tightly with new ropes that have never been used, he'll become weak and be like any other man (16:11). Never mind that new ropes didn't work before when Judah handed him over to the Philistines. Maybe she hadn't heard that story.

Delilah acts on his word, even though she may not entirely believe him. She takes new ropes and binds him once again (16:12). But after yelling that the Philistines have come upon him, she's seriously disappointed with what happens. Samson jumps up and snaps the ropes from his arms as if they were made of bubbles. He defends himself and manages to keep his secret safe.

She turns to him yet again, accusing him of lying to her until now and demanding that he tell her the truth of how he may be bound (16:13). Albert Einstein defined insanity as "doing the same thing over and over again and expecting different results." Delilah seems to be infected with a bout of the crazies because she's not altering her strategy.

The answer comes with deceit, but this time Samson gets dangerously close to the truth. He tells her:

> "If you weave the seven locks of my hair with the web [and fasten it with a pin, then I will become weak and be like any other man." So while he slept, Delilah took the seven locks of his hair and wove them into the web] (16:13).[130]

By saying anything about his hair, Samson is playing with fire. He knows that his hair is the only unbroken part of the vow, and he deduces that cutting it would result in his demise. But he tells her this anyway.

Two types of looms were used to weave—vertical and horizontal. Weaving was an important industry in the region, based on the large numbers of loom weights archeologists discovered in the area.[131] The text gives us no indication of which type is used to weave Samson's hair, but since the author doesn't seem to think it's important, it's of little consequence to us as well.

When Delilah finishes weaving his hair, she cries out to Samson again with warning that the Philistines are upon him. When he wakes up, he pulls out the pin and goes after them as he has two times before (16:14).

By this point, Delilah is frustrated. She knows he's been playing games with her, and she's been a good sport. But the money is real and she's tired of waiting. She then says:

> How can you say, "I love you," when your heart is not with me? You have deceived me these three times and have not told me where your great strength is (16:15).

Delilah plays the love card—highly ironic since she clearly loves him only as a venue for retrieving hordes of money. Despite her obvious manipulation and intentions, she is the only woman Samson claims to have loved. She has him under her spell and backs him into a corner with this new strategy. This plea is absent of her typical stated intentions of binding him or having him afflicted; but by now it's an understood component.

Samson doesn't cave, at least, at first. But she's relentless and pesters him again and again, day in and day out (16:16). Our memories ring back to his wife pestering him about the riddle during their wedding celebrations. He should've learned his lesson then. But Samson's obsession with self-pleasure leaves no room for the inconvenience of a woman's nagging. He gets annoyed to the point of death and decides he's had enough.

Caving, he tells her

> all that was in his heart and said to her, "A razor has never come on my head, for I have been a Nazirite to God from my mother's womb. If I am shaved, then my strength will leave me and I will

become weak and be like any other man" (16:17).

As Andy Stanley says, men can really be that stupid, and Samson proves it. Knowing what would happen if he revealed the truth, Samson tells Delilah anyway, confirming once again his priority of personal comfort over God and the purposes He ordained for Samson's life.

This rash act reminds us of Jephthah in part, but it's particularly similar to Esau's account in Genesis 25. Esau and Jacob are twins. Esau, the big, manly hunter, holds the favor and love of his father. Isaac. Jacob, the small, frail, domestic one, is loved by his mother, Rebecca. One day Esau comes home from working in the field and is famished. Jacob has been cooking stew, and its delectable aroma causes Esau's stomach to roar with hunger. Esau asks Jacob for some stew, but Jacob shrewdly refuses unless Esau surrenders his birthright to him. (Birthrights were a major deal back then, not something any firstborn son would give up willingly.) But Esau is driven by the lust of his stomach, not rational thought, so he agrees to give his younger brother his birthright in exchange for a bowl of soup.

Such selfishness and an obsession with comfort leads to terrible decision-making skills. Both Esau and Samson exchange life-altering advantages for a moment of temporary peace and pleasure. These men blind themselves to all logic and reason because they're driven by momentary desires. This isn't a perspective one falls into overnight, by the way. These men spent years catering to their every whim, not denying themselves anything they wanted. Due to this fierce lack of self-discipline, they place themselves in precarious situations that are impossible to unwind.

This time, Delilah knows Samson told her the truth (woman's intuition, perhaps?) (16:18). She sends and calls for the Philistine lords, assuring them that this time their efforts will pay off. They personally accompany their men, money in hand.

Delilah eases Samson to sleep on her lap and calls for a man to come shave his head (16:19). This is the only time she doesn't act against him herself.

We probably shouldn't read much into it, though it's possible she's feeling the slightest bit of remorse for what she's about to do. Perhaps she knew the previous occasions weren't going to be successful because she detected his dishonesty. Knowing it wouldn't work, she had no problem acting on his lies personally. But this time, she's planning to collect her money, understanding it will be the last time she'd see Samson, at least as a free man.

While she didn't cut his hair, the text states that "she began to afflict him, and his strength left him" (16:19). The affliction mentioned here is quite obscure, especially since she would have hardly done him harm until she was absolutely certain his strength had left him.[132] But perhaps she is that confident he told her the truth and she tests his lack of strength somehow before he's fully awake.

Irrespective, Samson's strength is gone. While it happens in direct correspondence with the shaving of his head, his hair is not the actual reason he possessed strength during his life. The hair merely represents something, or rather, Someone, who keeps Samson anointed with His Spirit and capable of mighty feats of strength.

As with the previous three times, Delilah calls out in warning for Samson. He wakes up with a start and says, "I will go out as at other times and shake myself free" (16:20). But what he doesn't know proves to be the most depressing verse in the entire Old Testament:

But he did not know that the Lord had departed from him (16:20).

Samson has no clue his strength is gone. Perhaps he doesn't yet realize that his hair is cut, or maybe his arrogance won't let him believe that God would actually strip him of his strength in a confrontation with the Philistines. Most likely, he never truly felt God's Spirit upon him before. He may have been intellectually aware of God's presence, but his selfishness made him calloused toward God. The fact that he can't feel the difference between God's anointing and lack thereof speaks volumes of his spiritual state.

The judgeship role in this book is officially reversed. Rather than "the judges overthrowing the oppressor (Ehud vs. Eglon), the judge is undone by the oppressor's hired gun."[133] The Philistines seize him and immediately gouge out his eyes (16:21). Gouging eyes was a common ancient Near Eastern custom in military dealings with enemies (remember the thumb and toe removal from Judges 1). By blinding their enemies, conquerors humiliated them and prevented them from being able to take up arms again or flee.[134] In addition to blinding their captives, they would also force them to do menial tasks usually performed only by slaves or women.[135] This increased the humiliation factor and was convenient since tasks like grinding didn't require sight.

With blood oozing from his uninhabited eye sockets, Samson is taken to Gaza and bound with bronze chains before being placed in the millhouse to grind grain (16:21). The irony of the location (Gaza) doesn't escape us. Just a short time previously, Samson visited a harlot there and stripped the city of their fortified gates in a display of strength that shook the knees of onlookers. Samson returns to Gaza now as a blinded prisoner, void of God's Spirit, just like the men surrounding him.

Presumably, a bit of time elapses as Samson performs his grinding duties. His hair begins to grow back, though no one seems to notice (16:22).

The lords of the Philistines decide to hold a celebration in honor of Dagon, their god, for delivering Samson into their hands (16:23). Remember Jephthah's argument in chapter 11 with the king of Ammon? He advocates that gods deliver battles and victories into the hands of their worshippers. Thus far, Israel stands as the true and living God's chosen people. Even though experiencing bouts of captivity due to their sin, their God is the only one alive and in sovereign control. But this fact is lost on the Philistines as they abide by the normal customs of the day—worshipping their idol, Dagon.[136]

When the Philistines see the great and mighty Samson defeated and blind, they proclaim,

> Our god has given our enemy into our hands,
>
> Even the destroyer of our country,
>
> Who has slain many of us (16:24).

Samson is then brought out for their amusement and jesting (16:25). In their celebration, they thoroughly enjoy mocking the one who aggravated their lives for so long. The man who single-handedly slew thousands of Philistines and utterly destroyed acres of crops now stands incapacitated and at their mercy. No doubt the Philistine lords are giddy with their new expensive toy.

Samson is led by a boy (he is blind, after all) and placed between two pillars. These pillars would have supported the house (or temple) of Dagon as key foundational pieces. In a seemingly innocent request, Samson asks the boy to place his hands on the supporting pillars so he could rest against them (16:26). By displaying weakness in needing to rest, Samson puts the boy at ease, making him comfortable to cater his request. Little does he know it will be the last act of his life.

With his arms leaning against the foundational pillars, the author pauses to describe the scene with further detail. We're told that the house is full of men, women, and the lords of the Philistines. Additionally, about 3,000 men and women are on the roof looking down on Samson, joining in the celebration from above (16:27). Thousands and thousands of people are gathered—all enjoying their long-awaited lofty positions above Samson.

Samson's second and final recorded prayer occurs at this point. He cries to the Lord,

> O Lord God, please remember me and please strengthen me just this time. O God, that I may at once be avenged of the Philistines for my two eyes (16:28).

Even in a suicidal plea, Samson remains steadfast in his selfishness. While he does speak with God, it's for his own purposes. Like Jephthah before him, his only prayer to God is an attempt to manipulate Him into doing what he wants. His motivation is revenge for his eyes, not to display God's power or to deliver Israel. His previous vow of "quitting" his vengeful acts is now a smothered memory in the distant past.

Grasping the two foundational pillars, Samson cries, "Let me die with the Philistines!" and pushes with all his might (16:29). The pillars come crashing down in his last display of bulging strength. Even though there's no mention of the Spirit anointing him, God clearly does so, for no man could have managed such a feat on his own. The temple tumbles down and everyone within it perishes.

Though Samson dies thinking he exacts his revenge on the Philistines, the surviving Philistines from other towns most likely hold a different perspective. Just as their "god" delivered Samson into their hands, now Samson's God delivers them into his hands. While Samson may have been too blind to see God's sovereign hand, there's a good chance the Philistines did, at least in part. God is glorified even through Samson's incredulous self-absorption.

The last ironic twist of Samson's life is pointed out by the author: Samson kills more in his death than he ever did in his life (16:30). The judge born with every conceivable advantage is the only one who fails to deliver Israel. Every other judge had significant disadvantages, yet all of them managed to free Israel from their enemies. But not Samson. He slaughters many, but like the angel said in the prophecy to his mother, Samson only *begins* to deliver Israel. Samson, "the strong man of the book, reveals himself as essentially the weakest, weaker than any of his predecessor judges, for Samson is subject, a slave to physical passion—the lowest kind of subjugation."[137] His selfishness prevents him from accomplishing what he could have, if he had simply followed God and placed Him on the throne of his heart.

Word of the catastrophe spreads fast. His father's household and brothers come to Gaza to retrieve his body. They bury him between Zorah and

226

Eshtaol in the tomb of Manoah his father (16:31). Samson's judgeship is brought to an end after twenty years, though because he failed miserably, there's no mention of peace for Israel. The Philistines still rule.

--

Samson's life leaves a sour taste in our mouths. He's certainly no champion, and his life echoes the deteriorating depravity of Israel as a whole. One commentator wisely notes, "Samson's struggle between loyalty to his parents and erotic attraction to foreign women is [a reflection] of the struggle of…his nation between religious devotion to YHWH and attraction to foreign cults."[138] Samson aptly models Israel's depravity, both shunning God and striving after what looks good to them. Israel has developed an addiction to following their heart rather than God's, and their last judge only fuels their addiction, moving them further away from God than when they began.

As with other judges, God uses Samson to accomplish His purposes despite his anemic faith. While Samson should hardly be our role model, we should note that he *did* know God's plan for his life. Despite actions to the contrary, he was aware of God's movement in and through his life (as evidenced in his prayers). He knew his strength came from God, and he knew that God used it to disrupt the Philistines' oppression over Israel.

God used Samson's miniscule amount of faith in great ways for His glory. Even if Samson never publically thanked or credited God for his victories, the people knew who to credit (an unavoidable conclusion in a highly theistic society), and God got the glory.

GROUP STUDY

INTRODUCTION

"Follow your heart" is an overused prescription in our culture, and it's extraordinarily misguided. According to Scripture, our hearts are "more deceitful than all else and...desperately sick; who can understand it?" (Jeremiah 17:9). Doesn't sound like something we should follow!

Yet we do...all the time, and much to our own demise. Following our hearts usually means following our emotional impulses—something we desire and "have to have," to the neglect of wisdom, logic, rational reasoning, and God's Word.

DISCUSS

- Share a time when you decided to "follow your heart" in a situation or relationship despite warnings not to.
- What did you do?
- What should you have done?
- What were the consequences?

THE WORD

While most notoriously known for his unmatched strength, the trend that plagued Samson's life for the worst was his unrelenting choice to follow his heart. Samson's primary concern throughout his entire life was himself— what *he* wanted and thought was good in *his* sight.

- Take a minute to discuss Samson's life (Judges 14:1-16:31). What circumstances and decisions in his life reveal his preoccupation with self above all else?

One of the most depressing verses in the book of Judges (and the entire Bible, for that matter) reads:

> She said, "The Philistines are upon you, Samson!" And he awoke from his sleep and said, "I will go out as at other times and shake myself free." **But he did not know that the Lord had departed from him.** (Judges 16:20)

- Why is this verse (particularly the bolded portion) sad?
- Why do you think Samson didn't realize that God (and his strength) had departed from him?

DISCUSS/ACTION

The biggest problem with following our hearts is that it leaves little room for following God's. As Christians, our goal is to become like Jesus; but that can't happen if we're distracted by selfish pursuits and temporarily satisfying impulses.

Samson had every advantage imaginable—set apart from birth, the recipient of great mercy from God, and endowed with unfathomable strength—yet he died having never followed God. He spent his entire life missing the point of life entirely—knowing God, becoming more like Him, and helping others do the same.

- What's currently keeping you from following God's heart when it's not aligned with yours?
- Do you struggle using the gifts, skills, talents, and abilities He's equipped you with to pursue His agenda, not just yours?
- How can you better use your gifts to make His desires (namely, the gospel) a reality in your life and the lives of others?

PRAY

WEEK NINE:
The Measure of Success

Judges 17:1-18:31

PERSONAL STUDY QUESTIONS

1. Where does Micah live? (17:1)

2. What does he admit to his mother? (17:2)

3. What's his mother's unusual reaction? (17:2)

4. What does his mother do with the returned money? (17:3-4)

5. Who does Micah make his priest? (17:5)

6. Where does the Levite come from? (17:7-8)

7. What does Micah offer him? (17:10)

8. Verse 17:13 reveals the Micah is convinced God will prosper him because he secured a Levite priest for his household. Though with different circumstances, we often do the same. We think because we volunteer or don't cheat on taxes or don't cheat on our spouses, we magically accrue God's favor and material blessings.

The problem with this perspective is that it completely contradicts God's Word. First, we cannot control God or manipulate Him into blessing us. Second, material blessings aren't necessarily indicative of His favor, though it can be (there are lots of wealthy people in this world who are anything but moral). Lastly, God promises trials, not an abundance of blessings, in this life. This isn't our true home (heaven) so we shouldn't expect life on this earth to look like it.

Take a moment to check your motivations. Are you doing good works in order to get something from God or because you love God? If He took everything away from you, would you still praise Him?

9. How many men does Dan send to spy out land? (18:2)

10. How do they recognize the Levite? (18:3)

11. What do they ask him to do for them? (18:5)

12. How does the Levite respond? (18:6)

13. What city do the spies travel to? (18:7)

14. What do they report to their brothers about the city when they return? (18:9-10)

15. How many Danites set out for their conquest? (18:11)

16. Where do they stop along the way? (18:13)

17. What do they do at their stop? (18:17)

18. How do they respond when the Levite tries to stop them? (18:19)

19. Who tries to stop the Danites as they leave? (18:22-23)

    • Are they successful? (18:25-26)

20. What do they do to the city they originally set out for? (18:27)

21. Why couldn't the city put up much of a fight? (18:28)

22. What do the Danites rename the city? (18:29)

23. What do they do with the items they stole from Micah? (19:30-31)

COMMENTARY

As we discovered in the beginning of this book, Judges has two introductions. Apparently, our author appreciates balance, because he finishes the book with two conclusions as well. While we've finished our study of the major and minor judges, the story of Israel's history at this time isn't yet complete.

Rather than concentrating on individual leaders of Israel, the author gives us a glimpse into daily life of typical Israelites in the final chapters. He does this to reveal what life was like for them at the time—that most everyone, not just those surrounding the judges and/or the judges themselves, was spiraling into depravity and faithlessness

After Samson's death, we're introduced to a man named Micah (17:1). Nothing remarkable is mentioned about Micah; he's not from a dominant tribe, nor is he called to lead Israel in any significant way. He's simply an ordinary man going about an ordinary life.

Micah is from the tribe of Ephraim and lives there with his family. We learn rather quickly that he is not a man of integrity. We meet Micah amidst a conversation he's having with his mother, which begins with a confession: Micah admits to stealing eleven hundred pieces of silver from her (17:2). That particular number should sound familiar; it's the amount Delilah received from each of the Philistine lords.

Before we give Micah a break for confessing on his own volition, we learn that the only reason he admits guilt is because his mother uttered a curse against the person who stole her money (17:2). Afraid of the curse (whatever it was), Micah confesses, hoping to avoid the ramifications of the curse. Faith Failure #1: Micah fears the curse more than he fears God. Thievery has never been permissible with God, but Micah doesn't care. He, like so many before and around him, cares only about himself. When the money will cause him more harm than good, he surrenders it to his mother and is willing to accept the consequences if it means avoiding those of the curse.

Normal individuals would expect his mother to be upset at this revelation. After all, her son is an adult and should know far better than to act so treacherously against his own family. But shockingly, his mother responds by saying, "Blessed be my son by the Lord!" (17:2). While it's possible that his mother is a lunatic, the more likely explanation is that she's trying to reverse the curse she uttered before she realized who the thief was. She doesn't want to punish her son; he's her baby boy! So she does what she can to appease the situation.

As soon as he returns the full amount to his mother, she dedicates the entire amount to the Lord (17:3). If she'd stopped with that intent, it would have been refreshingly wonderful. But we've learned not to get our hopes up in this book. Instead, his mother says she'll dedicate the silver so her son can "make a graven image and a molten image" (17:3). Faith Failure #2. Idolatry has transformed into a full-blown addiction in Israel, not just a practice they dabble in every once in a while.

Contrary to her word, she takes only 200 of the silver shekels (less than one-fifth of the total) to make into graven and molten images. Her actions don't match her words, and her words weren't admirable to begin with!

This deception reminds us (at least in part) of Ananias and Sapphira's story in Acts 5. They sold a piece of property and told the apostles they were dedicating the entire amount to God and His church. But they were lying, trying to look good, and kept a portion of it for themselves. What's ridiculous about their story (along with Micah's mother's), is that they weren't compelled to give any money in the first place! Since they were under no obligation to give at all, they certainly could have given a portion and been honest about it. But they weren't, and it cost them their lives.

Micah and his mother commit idolatry without thinking twice about it. She takes the silver to the local silversmith so he can craft idols for their household (17:4). How convenient!

The graven and molten images are set up for display in Micah's home. Faith Failure #3. In addition to these images, Micah has a shrine, ephod, and other household idols (17:5). The new idols seem to fit nicely with the collection he already has. His idolatrous setup "reflects the primary function of temples/shrines in the ancient world—a residence for deity."[139] The shrines would be used to serve the family, an attempt to gather divine assistance in life situations like conception, childbirth, protection against natural calamities, and the fertility of flocks and fields.[140] Of course this stands starkly against God and His instructions for worship. God desired to be worshipped formally in His tabernacle back then, not through shrines of idols set up in individual homes.

When Micah's shrine gets big enough for his liking, he consecrates his son to fulfill the role of priest (17:5), which is Faith Failure #4. The irony flows thick through the details of this account. Micah (whose name means "Who is like God?")[141] is trying to secure the favor of idols that are nothing but metal, stone, and wood. He does this to the detriment and disappointment of the true God who looks down on him, longing for a relationship. The God who can give him security and blessing is the only one Micah ignores.

At this point, the author reminds us that "in those days there was no king in Israel; every men did what was right in his own eyes" (17:6). While this seems obvious, considering the actions of both leaders and the common folk, it's nice to be reminded. This is not the way life is supposed to be for Israel. God desired so much more for them and gave them ample opportunity to grasp it. But time and again they refuse Him for inferior copycats that don't amount to more than a paperweight, much less a genuine and thriving life!

This reminder serves as a transition text for the next part of our story. We zoom in on another man—a Levite living in Bethlehem in Judah (17:7). (While he remains anonymous for the majority of the story, we learn his name is Jonathan at the end of chapter 18, so we'll refer to him as such from here on.) Bethlehem is not an official Levitical town, which makes us ask why he lives there. We learn later that he is a descendant of the Kohathite branch of Levites, which means he was supposed to be living in Ephraim, Dan, or western Manasseh, not Bethlehem.[142]

Even though a misplaced Levite doesn't seem like a major problem, it serves as further condemning evidence against Israel's faithlessness. If anyone was supposed to be following God with dedicated fervency, it was the Levites! The tribe of Levi had been chosen by God to serve Him as priests in the tabernacle. They carried great religious authority and were supposed to be experts in God's law. The fact that we have a wandering Levi pounds another nail into Israel's decree of guilt.

Jonathan leaves Bethlehem for reasons unknown (maybe he couldn't find sufficient priestly work in a town unsuited for priestly duties?). He heads toward Ephraim and stumbles upon Micah's house (17:8). Micah greets him and they begin chatting. Micah asks where he came from and Jonathan admits that he's from Bethlehem, though he's traveling in an effort to find a suitable place to live (17:9).

Every gear within Micah's brain thrusts into full operation mode—here's his opportunity to secure a priest, and not just a wanna-be priest like his son, Faith Failure #5. Micah proposes that Jonathan come to live with him as a father figure and priest to his household (17:10). He'd supply him with room and board, which would include ten pieces of silver a year, clothing, and necessary maintenance. Jonathan knows a good deal when he sees one, so he accepts Micah's offer (17:11).

Presumably, Micah deconsecrates his son and replaces him with Jonathan, who becomes his high priest and lives in Micah's house (17:12). He then makes a telling statement: "Now I know that the Lord will prosper me, seeing I have a Levite as priest" (17:13). Again with the irony, and Faith Failure #6. Micah's theology is so twisted, he believes that having a priest from the line anointed by Yahweh will somehow aid in his idolatrous shrine efforts. Micah's faith in God is miniscule, if it even exists.

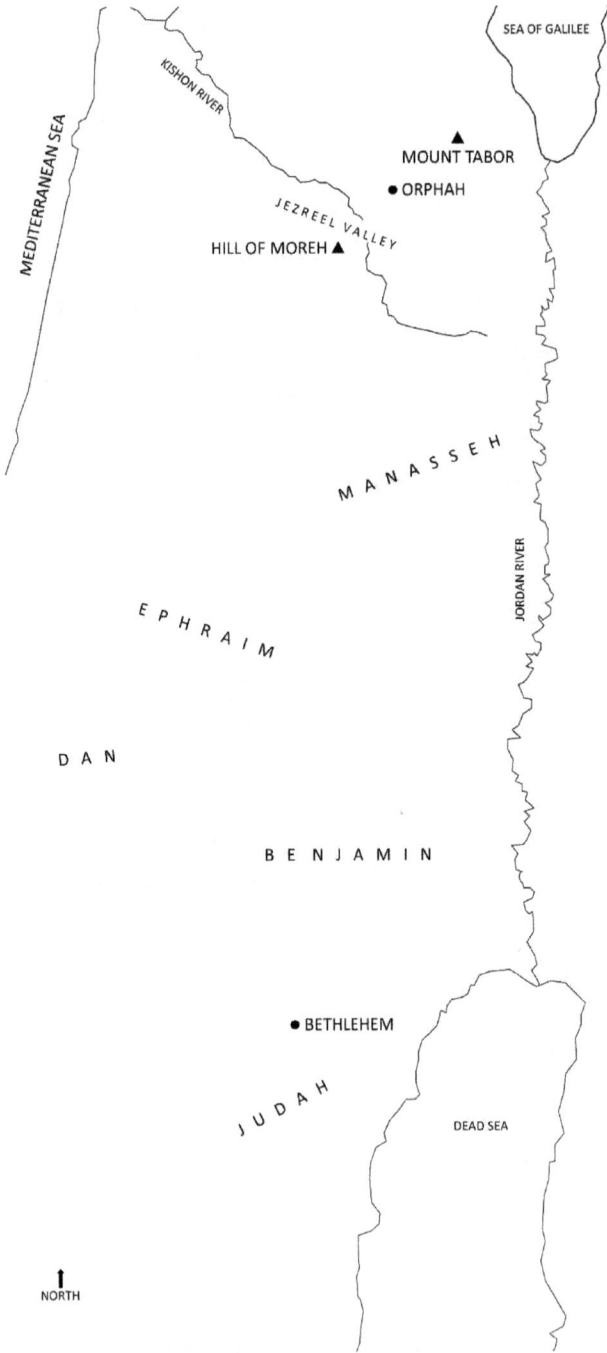

Actions reveal what occupies our hearts (Matthew 15:18-20). Micah claims to know God and even to be blessed by Him, but his actions prove the opposite. He doesn't know God any more than he knows how many stars blink in the sky. I fear that the majority of us pew-warmers today are like Micah. We claim to know and worship God, but are only occupying space, not worshipping, on Sunday mornings. Our lives are full of selfish ambition, not selfless pursuit of glory. We demote God in our hearts, which results in parched faith, uninspired lives, or worse—actions like Micah's that slap God in the face and bring others along with us. Let's strive to be faithful, not faithless—to pass tests of faith, not fail and flounder like Micah.

--

The author once again reminds us that Israel has no king at this time—no one to lead them in the ways of God and toward righteousness (Judges 18:1). Not that they should've needed one—God always desired to be their King. But since they are incapable of following anyone without flesh (and don't do a great job at that), their lack of a king is a bigger deal than it should be.

We now enter a new scene, which introduces a third party to the story. While Micah and Jonathan are happily playing "house" with their made-up shrine, the tribe of Dan grows restless in their lack of inherited land. They follow Jonathan's lead unknowingly, also looking for a place to settle down (18:1). If you recall from chapter 1, the tribe of Dan was the least successful in securing their inheritance, and now they're fidgety from waiting. Their restlessness is telling, because they *have* been told where their allotted land is.[143] But at this point, they have yet to occupy it, which reveals their lack of faith and drive to do so.

Instead of seeking God and His help in securing their land, Dan decides to act on their own. Sound familiar? Pretty much every story in this book contains examples of men who do the same. They send five men to spy out the land—reminiscent of the days of Moses, Joshua, and then Joseph from chapter one—all who sent spies to explore their land (18:2).

During their explorations, the Danite spies come across Micah's house. Apparently, his house was rather noticeable or in a great location, for it seems to attract lots of travelers! When they come near his house, they recognize the voice of the Levite, Jonathan (18:3). Most scholars believe it is Jonathan's southern accent that is distinguishable, not his voice specifically (Guess southern accents are everywhere!).[144] Thus, they didn't know Jonathan personally, though they would've recognized his heritage or previous geographical residence from his accent.

The Danites approach Jonathan and ask him three questions (18:3): who brought him here, what is he doing here, and what does he have (that's keeping him here)? There's little reason to believe they have any devious motivations behind their questions. Jonathan tells them of Micah's generous offer—having hired him and making him his priest (18:4).

Satisfied with his answer, they tell him to ask God whether they will be prosperous on their journey (18:5). Again, they're asking God's opinion late in the game, desiring confirmation of plans they already made rather than asking what His plans are. But that's just the first problem with this inquiry. The far more pressing (and basic) one is that they've already been told the location of their land![145] God told them where their land would be, but they didn't like it—too many enemies, too much work. So they venture off to find land that looks good to them.

We follow the Danites' footsteps often. While we may grasp intellectually that God is not our personal magic genie, we don't approach Him as if He's much else. Most of us pray only when we want something. If He doesn't give us want we ask for, we grow bitter, disappointed, depressed, lethargic, or we ignore Him completely. We question, doubt, and/or dismiss Him as a cosmic liar or incompetent fool. We deceive ourselves into thinking we know better than He does. A little tip for you: that never works out well!

Dan wants God to bless the plans they made without Him, and they expect Jonathan to acquiesce. Unfortunately, Jonathan doesn't disappoint.

Jonathan tells them to go in peace, for their journey has the Lord's approval (18:6). This "revelation" has little, if any, basis in reality. Jonathan doesn't seek God any more than the Danites did. He has been playing the role of priest with Micah, and he's learned something in his practice—it's far easier to tell someone what they want to hear, even if it's not the truth.

Once again satisfied with Jonathan's words, the Danite men depart and head to a town named Laish (nowhere near their originally allotted land). The author describes Laish as a town filled with

> People who were...living in security, after the manner of the Sidonians, quiet and secure; for there was no ruler humiliating them for anything in the land, and they were far from the Sidonians and had no dealings with anyone (18:7).

We can imagine Laish as an oasis amidst a land ridden with conflict. They're a peaceful people; no one bothers them, and they keep to themselves in return. The people of Laish interpret their isolation as a measure of security, taking no further cautions against unforeseen attacks.[146]

When the Danite spies return to their brothers, they give a good report (at least according to them). They confirm that the land they saw is very good—spacious, lacking in nothing, and an easy target (18:9-10). Pleased with the report, the Danites gather six hundred armed men and set out to conquer their new self-promised land like bullies ganging up on the class nerd (18:11).

On their way, they camp at Kiriath-jearim in Judah before moving on to Micah's house (18:12-13). The five spies inform the soldiers that there are idols, an ephod, a graven image, and a molten image in the houses that stands before them (18:14). That information gets the soldiers' attention, and they decide to act on it.

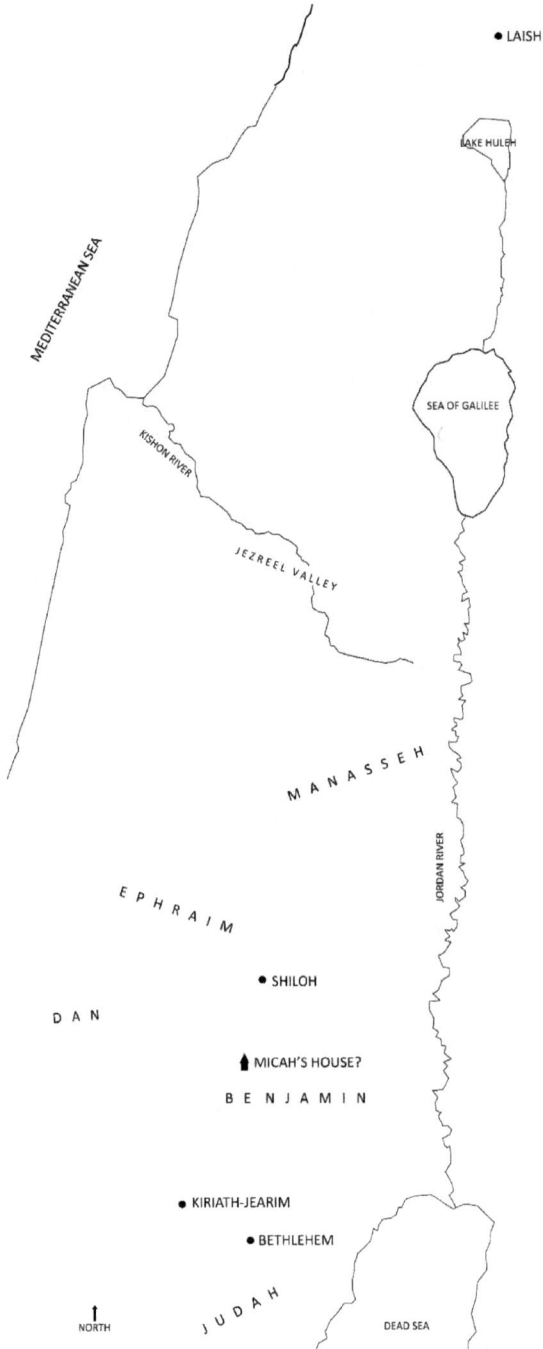

LAISH

LAKE HULEH

MEDITERRANEAN SEA

SEA OF GALILEE

KISHON RIVER

JEZREEL VALLEY

MANASSEH

JORDAN RIVER

EPHRAIM

● SHILOH

DAN

⌂ MICAH'S HOUSE?

BENJAMIN

● KIRIATH-JEARIM

● BETHLEHEM

↑ NORTH

JUDAH

DEAD SEA

Like the spies before them, the soldiers turn aside to Micah's house (18:15). The armed force visits Jonathan and ask him of his welfare while remaining by the entrance of the gate (18:16). Meanwhile, the five spies begin confiscating the items in Micah's shrine (18:17). When Jonathan notices, he confronts them (18:18). They immediately tell him to be silent and come with them (18:19). After all, it's far better to be a father and priest to an entire tribe instead of just one man and his household!

The cunning Levite seizes this new opportunity and accepts their offer with gladness. He even helps them steal Micah's idols (18:20). His position just increased a thousand-fold in significance, at least in his mind. He probably thinks he's the luckiest Levite in all of Israel!

The Danite soldiers pack up their newly acquired goods in a strategic line with little ones, livestock, and valuables in front of them for protection should they be attacked (18:21). They begin resuming their journey but are interrupted by Micah and his neighbors (18:22). Feigning ignorance (though not well), the Danites ask Micah and his friends why they have gathered against them (18:23). Stunned at what he's witnessing and more so by the absurd question, Micah responds,

> You have taken away my gods which I made, and the priest, and
> have gone away, and what do I have besides? So how can you say
> to me, "What is the matter with you?" (18:24)

While Micah's question is understandable and quite reasonable, it reveals his faithlessness once more. He's upset because they're stealing his gods from him. Micah asserts that because he made (created or brought into existence) the idols, he owns them. What he doesn't realize is that by admitting he made them, he's undermining their entire status as "gods." Nothing with self-asserting power can be crafted by human hands; the idea is ludicrous and defies common sense.

Similarly, if you or I hired a potter to mold a beautiful vase, we have caused the vase to come into being. But it's only a vase, not a god. However,

Micah makes his "vase" a god. He attributes divine powers to a lifeless object and then worships it. Yet Micah misses the lunacy in his actions because he's so consumed with being wronged by the Danites.

Despite being guilty, the Danites intimidate Micah and force him to stand down. They order him to be quiet and let it go unless he wants both himself and his family to die (18:25). Micah's scorned but not dumb. He lets them pass, knowing he stands no chance against them. With head hanging low, he heads back to his house, stripped of his prized shrine, idols, and personal priest.

The idols Micah used for God's blessing were, in reality, the curse that kept God's blessing away. Sure, he had a nice life with lots of stuff, but none of it meant anything without God—none of it bore eternal weight or significance. The downpour of God's favor saturates us when the umbrella of idolatry is removed, but Micah's too despondent to pay any attention. Losing his idols should have driven Micah closer to God, but alas, he grows depressed by the lies idolatry has fed him for so long.

While Micah sulks, the Danites continue their journey and make it to Laish (18:27). Thinking they have accrued extra blessing and guaranteed success from God because of their new idols and priest, they attack the town. Because Laish is a peaceful people who keep to themselves, they are destroyed without much of a fight. Dan slaughters the people with the sword then burns the city.

Satisfied with their success, they rebuild the city and live in it (18:28). They rename the city Dan after their patriarchal father and are quick to erect their own shrine, using Micah's gods and priest (18:29-31). Jonathan settles himself into his new position, thinking he's become quite the successful priest. He is, after all, a priest for an entire tribe of Israel! He starts a family and his descendants remain priests of Dan until the day of their captivity. (The captivity mentioned here is most likely that by Tiglath-pileser III of Assyria in 734 B.C.)[147]

Concluding this story is the epitome of irony: "So they set up for themselves Micah's graven image which he had made, all the time that the house of God was at Shiloh" (18:31). The true and anointed house of God exists and is located at Shiloh during this time. That's where the Danites (and the Levite and Micah) should have worshipped and sought after God. But this escapes their notice and/or concern. They think they're successful when in reality, they're a culmination of failure. Not only have they disobeyed God in the pursuit of unapproved land, but they also steal, murder, and commit flagrant apostasy by building a shrine of idols. They are the epitome of failure, but in their deprived state of mind, they perceive themselves to be successful and incredibly blessed by God.

--

While several components of this story are applicable to our lives, a major theological principle is that of the true measure of success. Genuine success is loving God and becoming more like Him. That's why we exist—to exalt Him and become more like Jesus. In the process, He takes care of everything else. He teaches us how to love and serve others and provides for our every need, perceived or not. As long as we focus on Him and put Him on the throne of our hearts, we're successful in His eyes. His eyes' perspective is the only one that matters.

But when we take our eyes off Him, we flounder in our depraved and finite perceptions. Micah, Jonathan, and the Danites display this with disturbing clarity. Micah steals from his mother, thinking money will secure success in his life. But his mother's curse threatens that status, so he confesses. He then pursues success by erecting a shrine with multiple idols and graven images. When that's complete, he's surprised by an extra "blessing" of his very own priest! Now he's convinced that success is his, since he surely has God's hand of favor on his life.

Jonathan the Levite isn't content with life in Bethlehem, so he sets out for a better one. He unexpectedly receives a fabulous offer—he can be the "high priest" of an entire household. What a position and title! But he never anticipates an even greater offer from the Danites. Now he's the priest of a tribe and has surely accomplished great success with God's blessing on his life.

The Danites grow anxious from not having a land of their own, so they go and find one that will be easy to conquer. Along the way, they steal idols and a priest to make their own, thinking such items will increase their status and blessing. To their knowledge they do, for they destroy a sleepy town and murder all the inhabitants. Surely they have God's blessing and favor, for they are immensely successful in the world's eyes.

All three parties are grossly unaware of God's definition of success because they're blinded by selfish ambition. Their blindness leads them to believe they are blessed by God, for their lives look good on the outside. What a grave fallacy.

God's blessing is not synonymous with material goods or heightened status. While those may be indications of God's blessing, they certainly aren't guarantees of His approval on our lives. Consider Tim, an incredibly rich man who attends church and believes his life is as good as it gets. The only issue is that Tim has been committing adultery against his wife of thirty years. But the affair makes him happy and, since his finances continue increasing, he assumes God's fine with it.

Or what about Grace Community, a local church? Their numbers have skyrocketed lately, and people keep flooding the doors for weekend services. Surely God's hand of blessing is upon them! The tiny problem of the pastor preaching guised heresy is no big deal. The sermons make people feel good, so it's all right. They're successful and keep growing, certain they have God's favor upon them.

Both of these examples are fictitious but represent legitimate ways people erroneously believe they have God's favor and blessing on their lives. Because they appear successful, they assume their little "sins" are acceptable.

God must believe they're super-special, so they continue on in their ignorance and theological retardation.

God considers us successful if we love, glorify, and become more like Him. Notice that these goals are completely independent of anything material. While they impact every facet of our lives, these goals don't necessarily coincide with physical blessings. Nor do physical blessings necessarily indicate the progress of our discipleship. A starving child with mud-caked cheeks in Zimbabwe may have more of God's favor than a multi-millionaire businessman in Chicago.

God wants our hearts aligned with His. The actions of Micah, the Levite, and the Danites reveal that their hearts were far from God; thus, they are not successful in His eyes. How about you? Take some time to evaluate your heart and life this week. Do your pursuits and desires align with God's? Are you using what He's given you for His glory or your own?

GROUP STUDY

INTRODUCTION

> "It is not your business to succeed, but to do right.
> When you have done so the rest lies with God." C.S. Lewis

In a culture obsessed with success and appearances, it's no wonder we're constantly pressured to get ahead, no matter what the cost. The end goal of success justifies the means of getting there, even if the means aren't always the most moral of endeavors.

DISCUSS

- Have you ever compromised your morals and values to get ahead (at work, in relationships, etc.)?
- What was the situation?
- Who was affected?
- What was the result?

THE WORD

The world defines success very differently than God does, and as we all know, appearances can deceive. Though some may reach enormous success materialistically, that's not an automatic indication of God's blessing on their lives.

Three characters described in the first conclusion of Judges mirror worldly success (erroneously thinking it's the result of God's blessing), despite having little regard for integrity and following God.

Micah: steals money from his mother and uses it to build a cult shrine. He assumes God's blessing continues on his life when he finds a "priest" for his idolatrous shrine.

The opportunistic Levite: appears successful in his vocation with Micah and even gets a promotion with the Danites, also believing God's favor was upon him.

The tribe of Dan: seeks success as well, even if it comes at the cost of disobedience to God.

- What other details of these stories reveal selfish motives rather than godly ones?

The passage concludes with another depressing statement:

> The sons of Dan set up for themselves the graven image; and Jonathon, the son of Gershom, the son of Manasseh, he and his sons were priests to the tribe of the Danites **until the day of the captivity of the land**. So they set up for themselves Micah's graven image which he had made, **all the time that the house of God was at Shiloh.** (Judges 18:30-31)

- How long did their apostasy last (**bold**)? Why do you think that is significant?
- What's particularly ironic about the last statement (**bold**)?
- Do you think they were aware of their apostasy or blinded by pride in their apparent success?

DISCUSS/ACTION

The only worthwhile measure of success (and true blessing from God) is declared in God's Word—what He deems right in His eyes. If Micah, the Levite, and the Danites had been at all concerned for God and His Word, they would've realized that worldly success is not synonymous with God's

249

blessing, and it's not worth pursuing if it doesn't advance God's kingdom.

- How do you struggle with measuring success in your life?
- What do you think success would look like in God's eyes?
- What can you do this week to merge the two?

PRAY

WEEK TEN:
Follow Me?

Judges 19:1-21:25

PERSONAL STUDY QUESTIONS

1. Where does the Levite live? (19:1)

2. Where is his concubine from? (19:1)

3. What does his concubine do to him? (19:2)

4. What does the Levite intend to do when he sees her? (19:3)

5. What's her father's reaction to the Levite's arrival? (19:3-4)

6. How many times does her father detain him? (19:4-8)

7. Where does the Levite's servant want to spend the night? (19:11)

8. Why does the Levite refuse? (19:12)

9. Where do they end up staying the night? (19:14-15)

10. Who offers to take them in? (19:16-21)

11. Who surrounds the house while they are celebrating? (19:22)

12. What do they want to do to the Levite? (19:22)

13. How does the old man respond to their request? (19:23-24)

14. Do the men listen to him? (19:25)

15. What does the Levite do to escape them? (19:25)

16. What do the men do to his concubine? (19:25)

17. What does the Levite find at the doorway when he wakes up and prepares to leave? (19:27)

18. What does he do when she doesn't respond to him? (19:28)

19. What does he do when he arrives home? (19:29)

20. How does Israel respond? (19:30)

21. Where does Israel assemble together? (20:1)

22. Does the Levite accept any responsibility for the fate of his concubine when he testifies to the elders of Israel? (20:4-7)

23. Is Israel united in their plans for retribution? (20:8, 11)

24. What do they ask Benjamin to do? (20:12-13)

25. How does Benjamin respond? (20:13-14)

26. How many people does Benjamin gather for battle? (20:15)

27. How many men fight for the rest of Israel? (20:17)

28. Who inquires of God before battle? (20:18)

29. How does God respond? (20:18)

30. Who wins the battle that day? (20:21)

31. Sometimes God doesn't answer our prayers the way we think He should. His answers include "no," "not yet," and "yes, but in a different way," more than we'd like.

    Is there something you've been asking for to no obvious avail? Does He seem silent? Are your prayers in alignment with what He tells us is important in His Word? Should you consider adjusting them to make sure they are?

32. When Israel inquires of God the second time, what does He say? (20:23)

33. Who wins the battle the second day? (29:25)

34. When they inquire of God a third time, what does He say? (20:28)

35. Who wins the battle the third day? (20:35-36)

36. How many Benjamites escape? (20:47)

37. What else does Israel destroy? (20:48)

38. What oath did the men of Israel take against Benjamin at Mizpah? (21:1)

39. Why does Israel weep before the Lord? (21:3)

40. What camp didn't originally participate in the battle? (21:8-9)

41. What do the tribes of Israel do to them? (21:10-12)

42. How many virgins do they capture? (21:12)

43. What does Israel tell the remaining 200 Benjamites without wives to do? (21:19-22)

44. After the Benjamite men do so, what does everyone do? (21:24)

COMMENTARY

The first conclusion of Judges leaves our hearts heavier than all the stories preceding it. If only it would be the low point of the book. Every time we think Israel has hit rock bottom, our disappointment surges to greater depths. But rest assured, Israel is going to reach the bottom of their pit in this conclusion. The verdict against them will officially be made on the basis of the evidence we've accumulated so far.

Our story begins with another repetition of Israel's state: "In those days, when there was no king in Israel..." (19:1). The "everyone did what was right in his own eyes" part is absent from the text, but not from our minds. It's an assumption the author intends for us to make, and he confirms it with the story he's about to recount. Israel is without a leader, so they decide to make leaders of themselves. Shocking that it won't turn out to be a wise choice!

We're then introduced to another Levite, though this one resides in the hill country of Ephraim, not Bethlehem (19:1). Just having read of Jonathan, our hearts are immediately on guard against this new Levite. Even though he's supposed to be one of the moral and godly ones, we don't get our hopes up. But, contrary to our expectations, he starts on a positive note (albeit brief). Ephraim is actually a legitimate place of residence for a Levite.

Jonathan and this Levite's account are linked (other than both being Levites) by the mention of Bethlehem. While this new Levite doesn't reside in Bethlehem like Jonathan did, he does have a concubine who lives there (19:1). Unlike others who've had concubines in our studies (Gideon, Jair, etc.), this Levite seems to only have a concubine, for there's no mention of a wife. He certainly could have been married to another woman, but this story only focuses on the Bethlehemite concubine.

Concubines were women typically considered legal, second-ranked wives. They were more easily divorced and "generally began as servants or slaves and were legally elevated to their status with the consent of the husband's full-status wife or wives, without bringing them a dowry."[148] Their primary purpose was to provide the husband more children or simply to serve as an official sexual partner.[149] Not a role I'd jump in line for, but it was a common reality for many women back then.

This particular concubine (unnamed like several other women in this book), apparently isn't a fan of her husband because she cheats on him. Then she leaves him and returns to her father's home in Bethlehem (19:2). She remains there four months before her husband comes to fetch her.

We're not told why the Levite waits four months before retrieving his concubine. Maybe he thinks she'd return voluntarily then gets impatient. Or perhaps he was trying to decide if she was worth his time, since she played the harlot against him. Regardless, he ultimately determines to bring her back, so he packs up his servant and a pair of donkeys and travels to Bethlehem (19:3).

His plan is to "speak tenderly" to her, possibly in an effort to woo her back. This suggests that he may bear some guilt about their separation. She may have had an affair, but clearly he isn't upstanding in his innocence either.

When he arrives, they make amends and she brings him into her father's house (19:3). Her father is quite happy to meet him, for he assumes the Levite is giving his daughter a second chance. Affairs are so commonplace today, they're barely considered scandalous. But back then, they were disastrous and disgraced the entire family of the guilty. The concubine's father hopes to erase his family's disgrace, so he shows elaborate hospitality to the Levite over a three-day period (19:4).

Satisfied with his welcome, the Levite prepares to leave on the fourth day after his arrival (19:5). But his father-in-law isn't ready to let him go, so he encourages him to stay and enjoy a meal before he departs. The Levite agrees and partakes in another impromptu feast at his father-in-law's expense (19:6). As the sun descends to let the moon take over, the father insists that they stay one more night. After much urging, the Levite yields to another night but is resolute in leaving the next morning (19:7). I would personally find this irritating, but the Levite obliges, though not for long.

Early the next morning, the Levite wakes up ready to go, but once again, his father-in-law presses him to enjoy one more meal (19:8). Vexed, but presumably hungry, the Levite accepts his invitation, so they eat and drink. The sun once again begins to wane in the sky, but the Levite isn't fazed by the lateness of the day. He rises to leave only to be interrupted yet again by his father-in-law. The father pleads for him to remain one more night in a display of excessive (and annoying) hospitality (19:9). The Levite will have none of it, though. He packs his donkeys and departs from the house with his servant and concubine (19:10).

Traveling back then was difficult enough without the added dangers that nightfall invited. The Levite, concubine, and servant make it as far as Jebus before the sun begins to set, and his servant suggests they turn aside in order to rest there for the night (19:11). Jebus, which is six miles from Bethlehem, is synonymous with Jerusalem, although it is not a residence of Israelites yet.[150] Because of this, the Levite refuses to stop there for the evening (19:12). Instead, he wants to continue to Gibeah or Ramah, where Israelites reside (19:13).

The sun sets on them as they near Gibeah, so they decide to stay there that evening (19:14-15). Gibeah is a town within the tribe of Benjamin, so the Levite feels secure and confident in his choice. Typically, visitors would wait in the open square of the city until someone invited them in. The open place was most likely located just within the city gates and used as a meeting place for judicial, business, and social purposes.[151] The Levite's group encounters a problem, though: no one is coming to invite them in! Rude!

Without options, they continue waiting until finally, an old man enters the city from his daily work in the fields (19:16). Like the Levite, he is from the hill country of Ephraim but is staying in Gibeah. When he sees the Levite and his company, he asks where they are headed and where they came from (19:17). The Levite tells him they are just passing through from Bethlehem and are heading toward his home in a remote part of the hill country of Ephraim.

He also mentions (maybe to induce the old man's guilt?) that no one has offered to take them in (19:18). Assuring the old man they have sufficient supplies for themselves and their donkeys, the Levite wryly forces the old man to show them hospitality (19:19).

Apparently the old man never planned to leave them in the street. He insists they come with him and let him provide for their needs according to the hospitality traditions of the day (19:20). A man of his word, he supplies their donkeys with food and washes his guests' feet before serving them food and drinks (19:21).

In the midst of enjoying themselves, they hear pounding at the door

258

(19:22). The house has been surrounded by the men of a particularly abject breed. The author describes these men as "worthless fellows," just like the men Abimelech hired to follow him and those who surrounded Jephthah during his outcast days.

With fists beating the door, they demand that the old man bring out his male guest so they could rape him (19:22). What? Who are these people besides evil with a side of crazy? Some scholars suggest their request reveals more than twisted sexual desires. They claim that it's also an issue "of power (the men of Gibeah wish to express their power over the Levite) and honor (the men of Gibeah wish to bring dishonor and shame upon the Levite)."[152] I tend to agree, since any act of rape (hetero- or homosexual in nature) betrays a desire for control and exercise of power.

What a hospitable welcome from fellow Israelites! The servant probably wants to choke his master for not listening to him back at Jebus. They surely would have received a better welcome than this, even if they were ignored.

Frantic, the old man (responsible for the well-being of his guests) discourages the men from acting so wickedly. He reminds them that the Levite is his guest and thus is under the cloak of his protection (19:23). While this would have been an excellent argument, he knows the men are beyond listening. Even still, his next actions are completely unjustified.

The old man offers the worthless fellows an alternative to the Levite:

> Here is my virgin daughter and his concubine. Please let me bring them out that you may ravish them and do to them whatever you wish. But do not commit such an act of folly against this man (19:24).

If ever a statement revealed a person's heart, it's this one from the old man. Surely he's joking. What human being could possibly offer his own daughter to be ravaged by vicious men? How could such a disgusting thought even pass through his mind, much less his mouth?

The author could rest his case against Israel here and now with a unanimous jury verdict of guilt. It's so corrupt, it's almost surreal. But God is not finished bringing charges against Israel; the situation grows direr.

Since the men aren't listening to the old man, the Levite takes action. He grabs his concubine and thrusts her into the wicked hands groping at the doors, then manages to shut the door behind him. To his surprise and relief, his plan works. The men seize, rape, and abuse the concubine all night long (19:25). Hours of torture, demoralizing debasement, and more physical pain than she ever imagined possible are afflicted upon her. While unwritten, her screams probably resound throughout the town of Gibeah. But no one will confront an unruly mob consumed by evil. Thus, the neighbors bear as much guilt as her husband; everyone is guilty of the putrid sin that's rotting their souls.

When the sun begins breaking up the darkness, the men dump the concubine and head home. Barely alive, she drags herself to the old man's house and falls at the doorway, unable to continue (19:26).

Thinking the worst is over, we're hit with another wave of nausea. The Levite wakes up! What is implied when someone wakes up? That he was sleeping! How could he possibly have slept while his concubine is being brutally raped by a violent gang of men? How dare he go on as if nothing happened, ignoring her cries of agonizing pain and torture?

This "man of God" is certainly a man of the devil. He can't possibly possess a soul with any moral attributes left. He's as disgusting as they come, even if he didn't brutalize her himself. Her blood is on his hands. And to think he just left her father's home, whispering sweet words to her so she'd come back to him!

Our repugnance of him almost makes us wretch when we see what he does next. After waking from his restful sleep, he lazily opens the door and sees his concubine lying at the doorway with her hands on the threshold (19:27). Instead of rushing to her side and extending her care (he could at least pretend he was up all night in absolute worry), he audaciously tells her to get up so they could continue their journey. Is this seriously happening? Yes. And it should make us writhe.

This is just one example of what sin mutates into when we let it reign in our lives. Remember, sin is anything and everything that usurps God on the throne of our hearts. If we've ever been tempted to think our "little sin" isn't that big of a deal, this shows us how wrong we are. We may evade serious consequences at first, but this is where sin leads if left unchecked.

When the concubine doesn't answer (how could she? She's either unconscious or dead), he picks her up and puts her on a donkey (19:28). When they get home he enters his house and grabs a knife. He then slices her into twelve pieces, limb by limb (19:29). The text is ambiguous about her condition before her dismemberment. It's possible that she was clinging to life and her husband murders her. Or she could have died sometime between Gibeah and Ephraim. His act disturbs us regardless, and her blood is still on his hands.

Angry (perhaps mostly because of the inconvenience), he sends her body parts to different territories of Israel. His goal is to wake up Israel from their moral lethargy and get them enraged at what's taken place. It's quite ironic, however, "that the one who issues such a call for justice is himself so selfishly insensitive and self-involved in the crime itself."[153] The Levite is looking for attention, and that's exactly what he gets.

Everyone who received a piece of the concubine's dismembered body declares:

> Nothing like this has happened or been seen from the day when the sons of Israel came up from the land of Egypt to this day. Consider it, take counsel and speak up! (19:30)

While it's technically accurate that Israelites have never received body parts via courier, the sin precipitating the body parts is not unfamiliar as they claim. But the author (and Levite, presumably) knows that focusing on individual sin is far more gripping than speaking of a nation's sin collectively. Our minds wash out large-scale information because it's difficult to grasp. But give us a story that's focused on one individual and we eat it up—or in this case, grow enraged.

Israel is sufficiently infuriated by such an obvious and gross act of sin, so they call a counsel together to discuss how to deal with the situation. The sons of Israel from Dan to Beersheba assemble "as one man to the Lord at Mizpah" (20:1).

Irony weaves this entire book together but takes a prominent role in these final chapters. Until this point, Israel has never assembled together with such unity. Sin tends to encourage disunity and broken tension between Israel and God, and between the tribes of Israel themselves. Now, because one man decides to showcase the evil poisoning Israel, the nation comes together as if they've never been apart. They act as one man and are determined to purge the evil from their midst.

Standing in front of an assembly of hundreds of thousands, the leaders of Israel address the Levite and ask him for his testimony of what happened (20:2-3). The Levite responds:

> I came with my concubine to spend the night at Gibeah which belongs to Benjamin. But the men of Gibeah rose up against me and surrounded the house at night because of me. They intended to kill me; instead, they ravished my concubine so that she died. And I took hold of my concubine and cut her in pieces and sent her throughout the land of Israel's inheritance; for they have committed a lewd and disgraceful act in Israel. Behold, all you sons of Israel, give your advice and counsel here. (20:4-7)

While the majority of his account is true, he neglects to mention several facts, some crucial. First, there's no mention of his slave, though that's not dire. Next, while the men of Gibeah may have killed him, that wasn't their intention. Though admittedly awful, they claimed only to want to rape the man in order to exercise their power and dominance over him. Their intent was to terrorize him, not murder him. The latter may have ended up occurring if they got their hands on him, but it certainly wasn't a foregone fact.

Next and crucially, the Levite leaves out every shred of evidence that points to his guilt. He says what the men did to his concubine, not the fact that he shoved her out the door! Also, he lets them assume the men killed her. Again, the text isn't clear whether she was dead or not that morning. But if she wasn't, it wouldn't be beneath the Levite to conceal his guilt further and heap more blame on the men of Gibeah. Oh, they were guilty, but he just as much.

As soon as he finishes speaking, the assembly arises as one man and prepares to take action (20:8). This is mistake number one. The elders of Israel should know better than to take one man at his word. The law in Deuteronomy 19:15-19 clearly states that

> A single witness shall not rise up against a man on account of any iniquity or any sin which he has committed; on the evidence of two or three witnesses a matter shall be confirmed. If a malicious witness rises up against a man to accuse him of wrongdoing, then both the men who have the dispute shall stand before the Lord, before the priests and the judges who will be in office in those days. The judges shall investigate thoroughly, and if the witness is a false witness and he has accused his brother falsely, then you shall do to him just as he had intended to do to his brother. Thus you shall purge the evil from among you.

Israel intends to purge the evil from among them; but that's the limit of their lawfulness. Listening to the Levite as one witness is good but definitely not sufficient. Even if every word out of his mouth was true, it still wouldn't be enough. They are supposed to have at least one other witness to collaborate his story, in addition to launching a thorough investigation into the matter. They do neither. If they had, they might have realized that the Levite should be punished as well. The horrific story still to come attributes guilt to the Levite and Israelite elders just as much as the men of Gibeah.

The Levite has cunningly enticed their emotions in his appeal, making them oblivious to the law they're supposed to be observing. He's lit a match and thrown it into a puddle of gasoline. He feels wronged by the men of Gibeah: they have, in fact, destroyed a perfectly good sex partner. So he manipulates Israel into quenching his thirst for revenge. Little does he know (or perhaps he does and doesn't care) that his little stunt would cost the lives of thousands of Israelites, nearly wiping out an entire tribe.

Also interesting to note is that this nameless, non-judge Levite elicits more manpower through his crafty antic than any other judge in the book. Four hundred thousand soldiers gather at his beck and call, driven to a near frenzy by his inadequate testimony. The people who once only wept at an angel's indictment of their sins are now moved to action, but by a schemer.[154]

The Levite then disappears. The "convener and manipulator of the assembly will not be present to give an account or be held responsible for what now transpires."[155] We never hear of him again; he vanishes as soon as his plan is set into motion.

In a fit of rage, the elders ignore due process and decide to exact justice in a rash manner by going up against Gibeah (20:9). Continuing their unified front, they tell each tribe to select 10 percent of their men to supply food for those who attack Gibeah in Benjamin (20:10). The author reminds us yet again that the men are united as one, ready to carry out the elders' plan (20:11).

Before launching an attack, Israel sends messengers to the tribe of

Benjamin, asking how they could've allowed such wickedness to transpire within their tribe (20:12). Then they make demands: they want Benjamin to draw out the men who committed this heinous act so they could be put to death, and thus remove the wickedness from Israel (20:13).

Unlike Jephthah, who at least tries to resolve potential war amicably, Israel decides their only mercy will be to refrain from taking the entire tribe of Benjamin to war. They don't ask Benjamin to verify the facts, nor do they leave justice to be carried out within their own tribe. Instead, they approach Benjamin with pounding fists, not unlike the worthless men who committed the egregious crime in the first place—with no warning and no options.

With such a brash approach, it's not surprising that Benjamin doesn't react well. They refuse to listen to their brothers, pride getting in the way of their willingness even to investigate (20:13). Israel angered them by hurling accusations at them; they're certainly not going to bow to their request after having been so deeply disrespected.

Just as Israel united as one man, Benjamin unites and gathers 26,000 men to Gibeah (20:14-15). Gathering there seems to be a strategic move, as they subtly (but strongly) refuse to accept Israel's accusations by defending the city.

Out of their army, 700 men were choice warriors, left-handed and able to "sling a stone at a hair and not miss" (20:16). Pretty impressive, and most certainly not the kind of people I'd like to face in battle. They could take me out like David did Goliath without even getting close! But even if all 26,000 men were of the same caliber as their impressive cavalry of 700, Benjamin is still at a major disadvantage. Their numbers amount to only 6.5 percent of Israel's army, making victory nearly impossible (20:17).

The next passage describes three battles that transpire between the Israelites and Benjamin. Neither side is willing to work out their issues amiably, so war is inevitable. Another gross irony to note: Israel descends to civil war amidst outside oppression. Israel is surrounded and occupied by the pagan nations, yet instead of driving them out, they turn to fight each other. It's as if they're saying, "Time out, God. We know You want us to drive out these wretched people and live amazing and peaceful lives with You, but we're not quite ready. We need to take care of something really quick—oh, and it just happens to be civil war." Not brilliant, Israel.

BATTLE ONE

Israel arises and travels to Bethel to inquire of God (what a novel concept!). Bethel, meaning "house of God," lies near Mizpah, where Israel gathered originally. Since Mizpah has a longstanding history as an anointed sacred site in Israel,[156] the choice to inquire of God at this location makes sense.

They ask God who should go up first against the Benjamites (20:18). Notice they don't ask God *if* they should go up against the Benjamites or if He had a better idea about how to resolve their conflict. Nope. They simply assume their choice of civil war is the best. Also, this question is nearly identical to the one asked in chapter 1, when Israel wants to continue the momentum Joshua established against the Canaanites. In both instances, Israel asks God who should go first, and interestingly, God answers both the same: Judah.

Israel camps against Gibeah the next morning and marches out to battle against the Benjamites stationed there (20:19). In a remarkably short time, Benjamin crushes their Israeli brothers, killing 22,000 men in one afternoon (20:20-21). That's nearly the equivalent of the entire number of Benjamite soldiers! Stunned, Israel retreats, marking the end of battle one. Benjamin: 1; Israel: 0.

BATTLE TWO

Beaten down and greatly discouraged, Israel weeps before the Lord the rest of the afternoon (20:23). When evening comes, they inquire of Him again, asking if they should go up a second time against Benjamin. The Lord answers by telling them to go up again.

When the second day dawns, Israel rises against Benjamin again, per the Lord's instruction (20:24). Their spirits are probably lifted and their confidence high as they march against their brothers. Unfortunately, their confidence won't last long. In a similar manner to the day before, Benjamin spites Israel again, slaughtering 18,000 men (20:25). That's a total of 40,000 men Benjamin has killed, dropping Israel's army from 400,000 to 360,000 without any significant losses of their own. Israel retreats before more are killed, drawing an end to battle two. Benjamin: 2; Israel: 0.

BATTLE THREE

Demoralized, Israel gathers together at Bethel to weep before the Lord. They fast the remainder of that day until evening, offering multiple burnt and peace offerings to the Lord (20:26). They simply can't figure out what went wrong. How could they be losing? Had they been paying attention, they would have realized that God never told them they would win—only that they should go to battle. Again, Israel never asked about the validity of the war at all; they only assume God is on their side. They were gravely mistaken.

Israel inquires of the Lord a third time, this time with extra emphasis (20:27). The Ark of the Covenant is present with them, along with the grandson of Aaron, Phinehas, who serves as a priest (20:28).[157] Armed with a legitimate priest and the Holy Ark of the Covenant, Israel asks God if they should go up again or cease their battle against Benjamin. This is the first time the Israelites leave room for not battling against their brothers. Their arrogance and frenzied emotions left no room for the possibility of being wrong before. Too bad it took the loss of 40,000 lives to cast doubt in their minds.

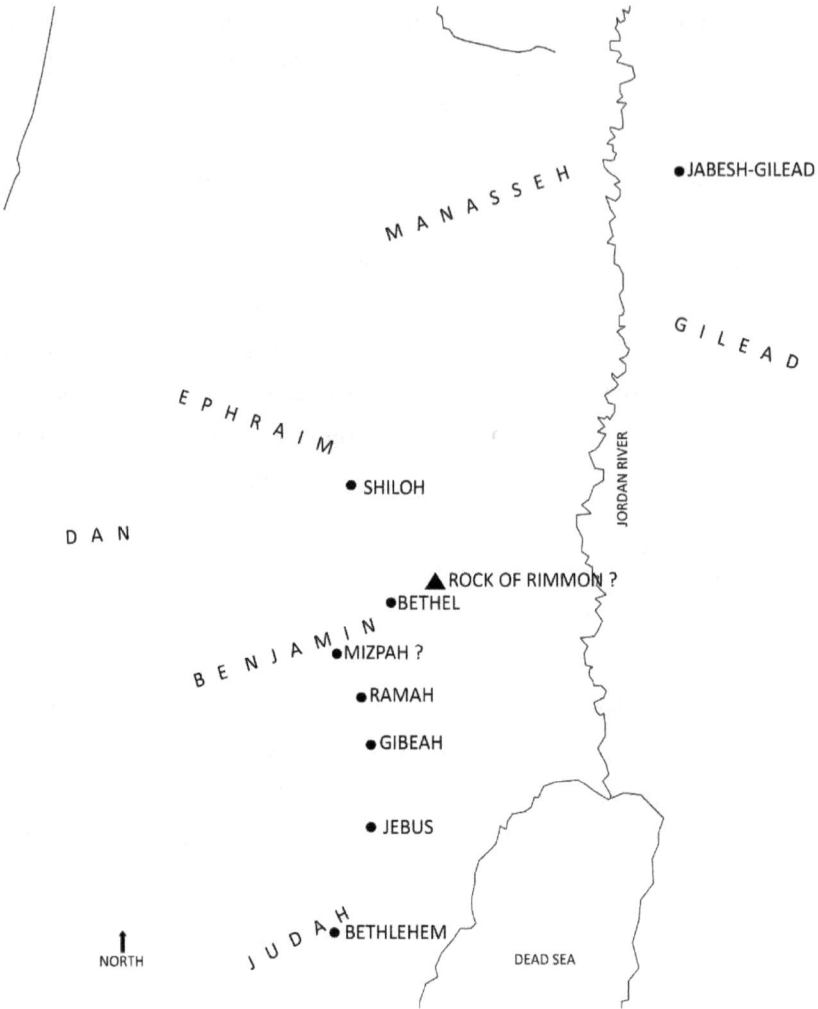

God repeats His command to go up, this time with a guarantee of victory (20:28). He promises to deliver the Benjamites into Israel's hands. Israel responds with obedience (which is quite refreshing to see in this book), and sets an ambush around Gibeah.

With the third day here, Israel begins the battle as they have before—arraying themselves against Gibeah (20:29-30). (From this point to the end of the battle, the sequence of events is unclear. The author repeats several progressions, making it chronologically difficult to follow. Verses 33-36a seem to give a condensed version of the battle account; leaving 36b-48 a more detailed rendition.[158] The ensuing recollection of the account recalls the major points, though admittedly not every detail is according to chronological order.)

The Benjamite soldiers leave Gibeah to pursue Israel along the highways and in the fields, killing about thirty men almost immediately (20:31). Their instant success fuels their egos, and they think victory is once again certain. What they don't know is that the Israelites plan to draw them away from the city on purpose, feigning retreat (20:32).

Keeping a portion of their troops in Baal-tamar (precise location unknown, but close to Gibeah),[159] Israel sets an ambush for the Benjamites heading that way (20:33). Meanwhile, another ten thousand Israelites are sent to camp against a defenseless Gibeah (20:34). The battle now becomes fierce and God strikes down Benjamin before Israel (20:35).

Israel continues to lure the Benjamites away from Gibeah, simultaneously sending their reserves to ambush it and destroy everyone within the city walls (20:36-37). Before deploying that day, Israel had decided on a sign: when smoke arose from Gibeah, it was meant that victory is near (20:38). When Gibeah is struck down, Israel sets it on fire, and smoke rises like insurmountable pillars in the sky (20:40).

Both Benjamites and Israelites realize the gravity of the situation, and Benjamin gets scared (20:41). They realize they've been beaten, and in a last-ditch effort, they try escaping by way of the wilderness (20:42). Six hundred men manage to escape, but the rest are killed directly in battle or indirectly in their attempt to flee (20:43-47).[160]

Fueled by rage and the adrenaline of victory, Israel turns against Benjamin even more by destroying other cities. They pulverize them, killing the cattle and everything else within sight. After thoroughly ravaging them, they set the cities on fire in a last act of spite (20:48).

269

--

Caving to their rash impulses leaves Israel in a predicament that rivals Jephthah's vow. Sobering up from their bloodlust, Israel realizes that they've effectively wiped out an entire tribe of Israel. The twelve tribes are now the eleven tribes, and the ironic part is that there's no guarantee they even killed the original offenders. There's a possibility (albeit small) that some of the worthless fellows who committed the original crime are a part of the remnant that escaped. We also assume the Levite is alive and well somewhere, having entirely avoided the civil war he instigated.

The 600 remaining Benjamites escape to the Rock of Rimmon, so maybe there's hope. If they can repopulate the Benjamites, the twelve tribes would remain whole. It's a good plan, but one with a serious problem. When Israel originally gathered at Mizpah, they took a vow not to allow any of their daughters to marry the Benjamites (21:1). The irony never ceases, does it? Israel refuses to abide by God's command not to marry Canaanites, but when they make up their own rules about intermarrying—within their own tribes—it's as enforceable as laws of nature.

Stuck, Israel once again weeps bitterly before God until evening (21:2-3). In the midst of their groaning, they ask why this has happened, why one tribe has all but been extinguished. I don't know, Israel, maybe it has something to do with the fact that *you* just wiped them out!

The day after, Israel wakes up early to sacrifice burnt and peace offerings to God (21:4). Then someone has an idea. Did anyone originally fail to come up with them against Benjamin (21:5)? Presumably Israel had taken another vow when in Mizpah. The second vow stated that any tribe, city, place, etc. that didn't accompany Israel to fight against Benjamin would surely be put to death. If they could find someone who didn't, they could kill them and keep the virgins to give as wives to the Benjamites so they could repopulate their tribe.

Israel clearly wasn't listening for God or His input when they spent all that time weeping before Him and offering sacrifices. They've lost their minds. In an effort to save and repopulate a tribe they destroyed, they're now willing to wreak havoc on another Israelite city. Are they that dense? Apparently so.

Someone discovers that Jabesh-gilead is guilty of not sending anyone to join Israel's forces originally, probably because they (commendably) wanted nothing to do with a civil war (21:8-9). If Jabesh-gilead's intentions were noble, they're now the cause of the greatest distress they'll ever experience. Israel sends 12,000 valiant warriors to their city with clear instructions to kill all the inhabitants except virgin girls (21:10-11). *All* inhabitants includes women and children, by the way—a despicable and odious act for Israel even to consider doing against their brothers, much less carry out.

But they do. Within a miniscule amount of time, Israel slays every inhabitant of Jabesh-gilead except 400 young virgins. Kidnapping the distressed young women, they bring them to the camp at Shiloh in the land of Canaan (21:12). Remember from the first conclusion that the house of God was standing in Shiloh at this time, making this gathering location highly disconcerting. Israel is blatantly ignoring (and detestably sinning against) the God who's right there!

Israel then sends the "good" news to the 600 remnants of Benjamin: they can come out of hiding. Israel won't hurt them; in fact, they have 400 wives to give them so they can repopulate their tribe (21:13). While it may sound good to Benjamin, can you imagine what this situation must have been like for these young women? They most likely witnessed the murder of their family members and friends—mothers, fathers, brothers, sisters, aunts, cousins, best friends, and domestic chore mates. They hear their screams when they sleep and can't help but visualize the atrocities every time they close their eyes. These women are traumatized and now are subjected to rape since their marriages are hardly of their own volition.

But Israel's sin is not yet complete. It should be, but their propensity for evil apparently won't allow it yet. Even if you lack math skills as I do, you'll likely notice a slight discrepancy in numbers. Four hundred virgins are not enough for six hundred men. Israel notices this too and feels compelled to devise another plan (21:14-18).

The elders of Israel have to come up with a way to secure two hundred wives for the remaining Benjamites that doesn't violate the oaths they took. Someone remembers a certain festival that takes place at Shiloh every year, and an idea sparks in their minds (21:19). At these festivals, people would dance—people including young virgin girls. They instruct the wifeless Benjamites to:

> Lie in wait in the vineyards, and watch; and behold, if the daughters of Shiloh come out to take part in the dances, then you shall come out of the vineyards and each of you shall catch his wife from the daughters of Shiloh, and go to the land of Benjamin (21:20-21).

Basically, the elders are reducing these young women's value to that of fish. While the girls are enjoying the festival, carefree and dancing, the Benjamites were to pounce on them and catch them as they would fish in water. Whatever girl they "caught" would be his wife and would travel back to Benjamin with him as he rebuilt his life with his fellow brothers.

The scene is ludicrous and the elders are coming full circle. This situation began as outrage against the men of Gibeah for "catching" and raping the Levite's concubine. Now it's transformed into a court-ordered mandate for Benjamites to catch and rape young women. They're asking the Benjamites to repeat the initial offense, only 200 times worse!

Clueless to their own depravity, the elders craft a plan for the fathers of the kidnapped girls. Should a father complain, they would "encourage" them to step down voluntarily, since Benjamin needs wives. They shouldn't worry, either. Because they didn't knowingly surrender their daughters, they wouldn't be guilty of breaking their oaths (21:22).

The Benjamites follow the orders. While the girls danced, they each grab one and carry her away (21:23). Everyone is happy (or at least "guilt-free," according to their own estimation) except the 600 innocent women who have to live traumatized for the rest of their lives. The situation has reversed entirely—the payment for one woman's life and one Levite's thirst for revenge is the death of over 60,000 men, women, and children, and lives of virtual slavery (much like the original concubine) for 600 young women. Was it worth it? Israel seems to think so, for they disperse to their homes immediately after (21:24).

The author concludes with the statement that sums up the book quite thoroughly:

> In those days there was no king in Israel; everyone did what was right in his own eyes. (21:25)

--

Despite the absence of a judge in this last story, leadership is present, along with the muscle of those who follow. The Levite was supposed to be a moral and theologically sound leader of Israel. Levites were priests and were called by God to lead His people into His truth in accordance with His laws. As the story aptly reveals, the Levite fails miserably in his calling as priest, husband, son-in-law, God-follower, and upstanding citizen in general. He's consumed with self-preservation and uses manipulation to launch a civil war, all to quench his thirst for revenge (reminding us of Gideon). Without hesitation, he replaces God as the leader, harming countless others in his wake.

The elders of Israel follow him and subsequently lead Israel into a civil war that nearly eliminates a tribe in Israel. Failing to follow God and His pre-ordained laws of justice, they grip the gavel and exact justice their own way. Even realizing their mistake doesn't push them toward God. Instead, they make matters worse. Ignorantly stubborn, they craft plans to "fix" the situation they so royally messed up. Not surprisingly, their plans make matters worse again. Now a tribe is all but annihilated, cities are demolished, thousands have been murdered, and hundreds of families are left robbed of daughters.

When we make ourselves our own leaders, we throw our lives in disarray. But like all other sin, our chaotic messes don't remain confined to us—they impact everyone around us, and not for the better. God gives us the ability to choose who we'll follow, and our decisions carry great weight. Just as we mirror those we follow, others mirror us.

Who do you choose to follow—God or yourself? Who do you influence? Are you leading those around you toward God or away from Him?

GROUP STUDY

INTRODUCTION

We don't like to admit it, but we're all followers. We all look up to, shadow, and walk in the proverbial footsteps of people we admire. Subsequently, we all *have* followers—our friends, children, families, and coworkers. Someone is always watching, always gauging their behavior by the direction of ours.

DISCUSS

- Who do you look up to/admire?
- Why?
- Who looks up to you? Who do you have influence over?

THE WORD

Israel struggled immensely with proper role models. Instead of remaining faithful to God and their covenant with Him (the ideal Leader), they prostituted themselves after idols and pagan cultures—inevitably leading them astray. The concluding chapters of Judges leave much to be desired. In them we see Israel floundering in their cycle of degeneration, reaching rock bottom morally, socially, spiritually, politically, and behaviorally.

A selfish Levite follows *his* ideals of morality and abuses everyone around him, leaving a brutalized concubine and civil war in his wake. The elders of Israel (who were supposed to lead Israel in God's ways) follow *their* ideas of vengeance instead of God's protocol of justice, nearly wiping out an entire tribe of Israel.

The issue underlying all of Israel's problems is summed up in the last verse:

In those days there was no king in Israel; everyone did what was right in his own eyes. (Judges 21:25)

- Why do you think having a king (a moral, godly one) would have made a difference for Israel?
- What's the problem with making yourself your own leader?

DISCUSS/ACTION

The most terrifying aspect of the book of Judges (so aptly revealed in the last passages) is how far, fast, and fully we can fall, left to our own vices. We degenerate when we follow anyone but God, and our failures don't occur in a vacuum. Our choice of leaders impacts everyone around us. Our choices influence others' lives and faith.

- Think about who you choose to surround yourself with on a regular basis (your most intimate relationships).
- Are they people pursuing God with all their heart and might?
- Is there anyone you should consider distancing yourself from?
- Or anyone you should pursue a deeper relationship with?
- How can you be a better influence on those around you as you seek to follow God (*not* following in Israel's footsteps)?

PRAY

Conclusion:
Final Thoughts

I hope you have enjoyed your study in Judges. More than that, I pray God used this study to rejuvenate your soul and catapult your faith to levels you never dreamed possible. While Judges isn't the most joyful book in the Bible, it profoundly reveals the depth of human depravity apart from God. If He doesn't reign on the throne of our hearts, our lives go haywire in a chaotic web of debauchery and idolatry, even if it's not initially obvious.

In a culture that's consumed with self-gratification, we aren't far removed from the moral pulse of Israel during the time of Judges. Divorce rates are higher inside the church than outside it, abuse is skyrocketing, and church attendance declines rapidly every year. The moral heartbeat of our culture has dropped to a near-lethal state, and books like Judges serve as a defibrillator to get it beating again.

We have to be honest and take a thorough look into the mirror of our own hearts before change will happen. Like those leading Israel, our government leaders doesn't see the need to become more like Jesus and let Him reign. But that is hardly an excuse for believers not to strive after Him. God has blessed this generation with brilliant theologians and pastors who lead with hearts like His. Let's turn our attention to these men and women and follow them as they follow Christ.

Change begins with us—with taking God at His Word and making Him the priority in our lives. As Christ followers, we are His disciples, "little Christs" who seek to become like Him more and more every day. This happens only through relationships that are fueled by His Word: first, our relationship with God, and then our relationships with people. When these relationships are grounded in and fueled by God's Word, the blossoming of our tiny seedlings of faith is inevitable.

Let's learn from Israel's mistakes in Judges. Let's say yes to God and no to rationalizations that tempt us to stray (like Othniel). Let's exercise wisdom and build arsenals of faith against the enemy through daily prayer and steadfast commitment to Christ (an area Ehud could've done better in). Let's seize each opportunity God presents to us by being aware of them and seeking them out (like Deborah and Jael). Let's place God on the rightful throne of our lives so the colors of our hearts match the ones we're portraying to the world around us (unlike Gideon). Let's get in the Word and let it consume us, eradicating our ignorance (unlike Jephthah). And finally, let's commit to following God's heart and match our desires with His (unlike Samson).

Seek first His kingdom and righteousness. Love Him with all your heart, soul, mind, and strength, and love others as yourself. While you won't be perfect, you will nourish your faith. And as we've seen, He makes the impossible a reality through those who honor Him in this way.

APPENDIX A:

"Heroes" of Hebrews

The Judge "Heroes" of Faith in Hebrews

Four of our major judges appear again in Scripture, and in quite the peculiar location. Gideon, Barak, Jephthah, and Samson are mentioned in a chapter known as the "Hall of Faith" in Hebrews 11. Hearing the title of that chapter, our ears perk in curiosity. None of these men stand as prime examples of faith, much less as "heroes" we should emulate. How do we reconcile their presence in this chapter with what we've learned about them in Judges? Let's find out together.

Hebrews 11 describes patriarchs and others who display intense acts of faith and are honored by God accordingly. Opening the chapter is a definition of faith: "Faith is the assurance of things hoped for, the conviction of things unseen." In other words, faith takes God's promises for tomorrow as a reality we embrace today. Faith takes God at His Word, and the rest of the chapter showcases men and women who did precisely that.

The author of Hebrews takes us on a journey through the historical narratives of the Old Testament to reveal men and women of old who display faith in ways we admire. First is Abel and the faith he showed through his sacrifice—one that sparked events leading to his death. Next is Enoch, who expressed so much faith in life that he never died! He was simply carried away straight to God when his time on earth came to an end.

After Enoch, we read about Noah and the faith he exercised in building the ark, quite the ridiculed action since it had never rained before. Abraham comes next with his numerous acts of faith—acting on God's Word even though he never fully experienced the promises declared for him and his family. His wife, Sarah, also displayed faith and conceived in her late years.

Their son, Isaac, blessed his sons, Jacob and Esau, by faith, and Jacob blessed all his sons in faith when he was about to die too. Joseph, one of Jacob's sons, showcased huge amounts of faith in his life as well as in his death, confident that God would keep His Word and lead Israel out of Egypt one day.

Moses' faith began with his mother, who hid him in the reeds against Pharaoh's orders to murder all Israelite boys. As Moses grew in stature, he also grew in faith and was used by God to deliver Israel in one of the greatest stories of deliverance the world has ever known. Israel expressed faith in the wilderness and as they began conquering the Promised Land under Joshua's leadership, as did Rahab, who chose to believe Israel's God rather than her country's own idols.

After recounting these men and women, the author realizes that continuing would yield a book much larger than the one he intends to write. So he concludes his faith chapter like this:

> And what more shall I say? For time will fail me if I tell of Gideon, Barak, Samson, Jephthah, of David and Samuel and the prophets, who by faith conquered kingdoms, performed acts of righteousness, obtained promises, shut the mouths of lions, quenched the power of fire, escaped the edge of the sword, from weakness were made strong, became mighty in war, put foreign armies to flight. Women received back their dead by resurrection; and others were tortured, not accepting their release, so that they might obtain a better resurrection; and others experienced mockings and scourgings, yes, also chains and imprisonment. They were stoned, they were sawn in two, they were tempted,

they were put to death with the sword; they went about in sheepskins, in goatskins, being destitute, afflicted, ill-treated (men of whom the world was not worthy), wandering in deserts and mountains and caves and holes in the ground. And all these, having gained approval through their faith, did not receive what was promised, because God had provided something better for us, so that apart from us they would not be made perfect.[161]

Since so many men and women serve as wonderful examples of faith, why does the author include Gideon, Jephthah, Barak, and Samson, who exuded such miniscule glimpses of faith in their lives? The answer is simple: because ultimately, like other examples, any faith they did express was implanted by God and then used for His glory.

We do not come to faith unless God first draws us (John 6:44). It's impossible to harvest faith on our own because we are dead in our depravity apart from Him. Only when He begins wooing us do we awaken to His truth through the gospel, and only then are we able to respond to His invitation in faith.

Faith originates in God and is present within those whom He calls, even if it's not always obvious. Most examples the author uses in this Hebrews chapter showed serious lack of faith and blatant disobedience to God in their lives. Abraham lied twice about Sarah being his wife, David was a murderer and adulterer, Jacob manipulated others as easily as he drew breath, Moses was a murderer and disobeyed God, and Rahab was a lying prostitute. While their actions were used by God in huge ways to accomplish His purposes, these men and women were not squeaky perfect by any means.[162]

The point of this chapter is to reveal and confirm what God can do with the tiniest fleck of faith imaginable. Jesus said that if we have faith the size of a mustard seed, nothing will be impossible for us (Matthew 17:20). Mustard seeds are *tiny*, only 1-2 millimeters in size. Credit cards are one millimeter in thickness, so that's how tiny we're talking.

If we possess even that tiny amount of faith, God can and will accomplish mesmerizing feats in and through our lives. Barak, Gideon, Jephthah, and Samson were far from morally sound, as we have seen. But each of them possessed a mustard seed of faith, which God used to smite Israel's enemies. God is the one being praised by the author of Hebrews in this passage, just as He is in Judges. He is the one who caused the magnificent acts to occur. Doing so through faulty humans showcases His glory that much more.

What hope we have as well! We don't have to live up to the pedestal we put our heroes of faith on. God uses normal people like you and me to move mountains through faith. If He can use the miniscule faith of the judges, He can certainly use ours too!

The point of application for the Hall of Faith is written in the following verses and holds the key to proper interpretation:

> Therefore, since we have so great a cloud of witnesses surrounding us, let us also lay aside every encumbrance and the sin which so easily entangles us, and let us run with endurance the race that is set before us, fixing our eyes on Jesus, the author and perfecter of faith, who for the joy set before Him endured the cross, despising the shame, and has sat down at the right hand of the throne of God. For consider Him who has endured such hostility by sinners against Himself so that you will not grow weary and lose heart.[163]

Yes, we can look up to men and women of old who served God and exercised great faith. But the reason they're so great isn't because of what they did, it's because of who they placed their faith in—God! Faith is only as dynamic and powerful as the object we put it in.

In order to follow their example (and prayerfully surpass them) in faith, we must do as the author says and fix our eyes on Jesus. We must run toward Him and place Him on the throne of our hearts every day and in every facet of our lives. He is the one who initiates, grows, matures, and perfects our faith; He is the one who should receive all glory, honor, and credit. He uses broken, selfish, and thoroughly faulty people to accomplish His purposes—all the more reason to praise and bless His name! We can participate in His glorious plan of redemption just like people in the Old Testament (including Judges) could. Hallelujah!

APPENDIX B:
A Little Note About Ruth

Any book on Judges would be remiss not to include a least a brief note about Ruth, the book following Judges in the Old Testament. While Judges leaves us sober in our heightened awareness of depravity, Ruth shines brightly with rejuvenating hope. In a "refreshing way, the book provides an antithesis to the incessantly negative message about the conditions in Israel during that time"[164] by bursting forth God's light through someone who remained faithful against all odds.

Ruth is a magnificent love story about a young woman named Ruth who selflessly follows the God of her mother-in-law. During the time of the judges, a man named Elimelech takes his wife, Naomi, and two sons to the land of Moab because there was a famine in the land of Judah (where they had lived previously). When they arrive, they find wives named Orpah and Ruth for their two sons. They live in Moab about ten years before tragedy strikes their family. In a short amount of time, Elimelech and both of his sons die, leaving Naomi and her two daughters-in-law alone.

At Naomi's urging, Orpah returns to her family in hopes of starting a new life. But Ruth refuses to leave Naomi, telling her the now-famous lines "Where you go, I will go, and where you lodge, I will lodge. Your people shall be my people, and your God, my God. Where you die, I will die, and there I will be buried."[165] Naomi caters to Ruth's wishes and they return to Naomi's former home in Judah.

Without money or resources (it's not as if women could go out and get a job in those days), Ruth volunteers to collect grain from nearby fields so they could eat. Back then, owners of fields were mandated to leave some produce/grain behind during harvest so the poor could glean some food for themselves. This helped the economy tremendously and required poor citizens to participate in earning their food.

Naomi blesses Ruth for wanting to go, and she gives her permission. One day, as she's gleaning in the fields, she catches the eye of the landowner, Boaz. Naomi realizes that Boaz is a kinsman-redeemer for Ruth, meaning that he is eligible to become her husband since hers had passed away. But there's a problem. One man in the family is in line before Boaz and rightfully has claim to Ruth if he wants. In a shrewd deal, Boaz presents the opportunity to him, but he refuses.

Boaz' dream comes true and he marries Ruth, the faithful Moabitess. (Yes, it's quite ironic that a Moabite woman is more faithful to God than the Israelites are at the time!) They end up having children, one of whom is named Obed, who becomes the father of Jesse, who becomes the father of David—as in King David. King David becomes a father, and through his descendants of many generations is born another man who would change the world—Jesus.

In the midst of the darkness and depravity of Israel during the time of the Judges, one brilliant light bursts forth. God uses the steadfast faith of a lowly widow to continue the line of His one and only Son, who would accomplish the greatest act of redemption the world has ever known.

Every redemption story in Judges is but a blurry foreshadow of the glory that will come when Jesus Christ is born and embodies the gospel of God. Even when the world seems dark around us and we can't see two feet in front of us, God is alive. Not only that, He's working and moving to draw us and others closer to Him. As long as we have breath, He's writing our stories as a part of His big story of redemption. He uses us regardless of the size of our faith, but let's be encouraged to embrace Him as Ruth did, not like the judges. Let's place Him on the throne of our hearts so we can be used that much more in His gospel and story!

Bibliography

Albright, W.F. *Archaeology and the Religion of Israel* (John Hopkins Press, 1953).

Boiling, Robert G. *Judges: Introduction, Translation and Commentary* (Garden City, NY: Doubleday, 1975).

Boiling, Robert G. "In Those Days There Was No King in Israel." In *A Light Unto My Path: Old Testament Studies In Honor of Jacob M. Myers,* (Philadelphia: Temple University Press, 1975).

Block, D.I. *Judges, Ruth* (Nashville: Broadman & Holman, 1999).

Burney, C.F. *The Book of Judges* (New York: KTAV, 1970), 349; and George F. Moore, *Judges* (Edinburgh: T & T Clark, 1895).

Chisholm Jr., Robert B. *A Commentary on Judges and Ruth* (Grand Rapids, Michigan: Kregel Publications, 2013).

Cundall, Arthur E. and Leon Morris. *Judges and Ruth* (Downers Grove, Illinois: Inter-Varsity Press, 1968).

Davis, Dale Ralph. *Such a Great Salvation: Expositions in the Book of Judges* (Grand Rapids, Michigan: Baker Book House, 1990).

Deffinbaugh, Bob."Strong Women, Weak-Kneed (Wimpy) Men." Published December 7th, 2009, accessed March 18, 2014.

https://bible.org/seriespage/strong-women-weak-kneed-wimpy-men-judges-41-24.

> "The Dark Days of Israel's Judges," 2009, accessed November 2014. https://bible.org/seriespage/4-ehuds-gut-reaction-or-no-guts-no-gory-judges-35-31.

Douglas, J.D. and Merrill C. Tenney, editors, *Bible Dictionary* (Grand Rapids, Michigan: Zondervan, 1987).

Goslinga, C. J. *Joshua, Judges, Ruth* (Grand Rapids: Zondervan, 1986).

Herrick, Greg. "Baalism in Canaanite Religion and Its Relation to Selected Old Testament Texts," (July 2004). Accessed March 6, 2014. https://bible.org/article/baalism-canaanite-religion-and-its-relation-selected-old-testament-texts.

Instone-Brewer, David. *Divorce and Remarriage in the Bible* (Grand Rapids, MI: Eerdmans, 2002).

Keil, C.F. *Joshua, Judges, Ruth* (Grand Rapids: Eerdmans, 1950).

Marcus, D. "The Bargaining Between Jephthah and the Elders (Judges 11:4-11)." *JANES* 19 (1989).

Mobley, Gregory. *The Empty Men: The Heroic Tradition of Ancient Israel* (New York: Doubleday, 2005).

O'Connell, R.H. *The Rhetoric of the Book of Judges,* (Leiden: Brill, 1996).

Pfeiffer, Charles F. *Baker's Bible Atlas* (Grand Rapids, Michigan: Baker Books, 2003).

Stone, Ken. *Sex, Honor, and Power in the Deuteronomistic History* (Sheffield: Sheffield Academic, 1996).

Walton, John H. general editor, *Zondervan Illustrated Bible Background Commentary: Joshua, Judges, Ruth, 1 & 2 Samuel* (Grand Rapids, MI:

Zondervan, 2009).

Wood. Leon J. *The Holy Spirit in the Old Testament* (Eugene, Oregon: Wipf and Stock Publishers, 1998).

Younger, Jr., K. Lawson *The NIV Application Commentary: Judges, Ruth* (Grand Rapids, Michigan: Zondervan, 2002).

Endnotes

[1] Psalm 98

[2] K. Lawson Younger, Jr. *The NIV Application Commentary: Judges, Ruth* (Grand Rapids, Michigan: Zondervan, 2002), 21.

[3] John H. Walton, general editor, *Zondervan Illustrated Bible Background Commentary: Joshua, Judges, Ruth, 1 & 2 Samuel* (Grand Rapids, MI: Zondervan, 2009), 105.

[4] Walton, *Bible Background Commentary*, 108.

[5] Walton, *Bible Background Commentary*, 107.

[6] Walton, *Bible Background Commentary*, 107.

[7] "Genocide." *Merriam-Webster.com*. Merriam-Webster, n.d. Web. 15 July 2014. <http://www.merriamwebster.com/ dictionary/genocide>.

[8] "Justice." *Merriam-Webster.com*. Merriam-Webster, n.d. Web. 15 July 2014. <http://www.merriamweb-ster.com/dictionary/justice>.

[9] For a more thorough discussion of absolute vs. relative truth, read Furby, *More than Words*, 96-101.

[10] For examples of the Canaanites' sin, study the rest of this book, other books in Scripture, or historical books recounting this time period. Canaanites would offer their children as sacrifices for their gods (murder), treat women as objects and rape them at will, and engage in a host of other atrocities.

[11] Genesis 15:12-16

[12] Walton, *Bible Background Commentary*, 107.

[13] See Habakkuk 2:18-20 for a punchy display of the absurdity of graven images and idol worship.

[14] Augustine famously quoted, "You have made us for yourself, O Lord, and our heart is restless until it rests in You."

[15] The term "Asherah" and "Asheroth" are used interchangeably depending on what version of the Bible is being used. "Asheroth" is used in the NASB and ESV; "Asherah" is used in the NIV, NKJV, NLT, and HCSB. Both refer to the same goddess.

[16] Greg Herrick, "Baalism in Canaanite Religion and Its Relation to Selected Old Testament Texts," (July 2004). Accessed March 6, 2014. https://bible.org/article/baalism-canaanite-religion-and-its-relation-selected-old-testament-texts

[17] Younger, *The NIV Application Commentary*, 101.

[18] Younger, *The NIV Application Commentary*, 105.

[19] Judges 3:6

[20] Read more about God's confined presence in 1 Kings 8:26-32

[21] Leon J. Wood. *The Holy Spirit in the Old Testament* (Eugene, Oregon: Wipf and Stock Publishers, 1998), 41.

[22] Caleb, Othniel's older brother, was approximately 85 years old during the initial conquest of Israel against the Canaanites of the Promised Land. At least 25 years had elapsed since that time, leaving Othniel around the age of 75-80 years old. Wood, Leon, *The Holy Spirit in the Old Testament*, 54.

[23] Wood, Leon, *The Holy Spirit in the Old Testament*, 41.

[24] Read Ephesians 1, particularly verses 13-14, for a more thorough understanding of the Holy Spirit's role in our lives.

[25] Arthur E. Cundall and Leon Morris. *Judges and Ruth* (Downers Grove, Illinois: Inter-Varsity Press, 1968), 75.

[26] Younger, *The NIV Application Commentary*, 115.

[27] Younger, *The NIV Application Commentary*, 117.

[28] Isaiah 46:8-13 is a great explanation and reminder of God's sovereignty and power.

[29] Genesis 22:18, 22:4; Psalm 22:27, 46:10; 67:2, etc.

[30] Robert Deffinbaugh, "The Dark Days of Israel's Judges," 2009, accessed November 2014. https://bible.org/seriespage/4-ehuds-gut-reaction-or-no-guts-no-gory-judges-35-31.

[31] Even though Ehud's account isn't the last mentioned (Shamgar's is), since he is the last major judge, the cycle resumes with him. We don't know how long Shamgar judged Israel or where or when he judged Israel. Remember, these accounts aren't necessarily chronological. The text resumes with Israel after Ehud, so we will as well.

[32] Dale Ralph Davis. *Such a Great Salvation: Expositions in the Book of Judges* (Grand Rapids, Michigan: Baker Book House, 1990), 72.

[33] Bob Deffinbaugh."Strong Women, Weak-Kneed (Wimpy) Men." Published December 7th, 2009, accessed March 18, 2014. https://bible.org/seriespage/strong-women-weak-kneed-wimpy-men-judges-41-24

[34] Younger, *The NIV Application Commentary*, 139.

[35] Othniel may have judged holistically too (in fact, he probably did); we're just not privy to such details since they lack in his account.

[36] 2 Corinthians 12:9

[37] Proverbs 21:1

[38] Deuteronomy 18:22

[39] Younger, *The NIV Application Commentary*, 139.

[40] Some translations (NASB, NIV, RSV, CEV) don't phrase her command literally because they know the question form would cause confusion. Other translations (ESV, KJV, NKJV, HCSB) leave it phrased as a question for readers to figure out. The problem with this is that readers would have to do major research to discover that the question is used as an idiom, not suggesting that Barak had previously heard about God's command.

[41] Deborah phrases her prophetic words as a question that can be taken literally or rhetorically. I'm inclined to believe the latter; but some scholars believe God had revealed Barak's task to him on a previous occasion. For the contrary view, read "Strong Women, Weak-Kneed (Wimpy) Men" by Bob Deffinbaugh available at https://bible.org/seriespage/strong-women-weak-kneed-wimpy-men-judges-41-24

[42] Deffinbaugh, "Strong Women."

[43] J.D. Douglas and Merrill C. Tenney, editors, *Bible Dictionary* (Grand Rapids, Michigan: Zondervan, 1987), 564.

[44] Charles F. Pfeiffer. *Baker's Bible Atlas* (Grand Rapids, Michigan: Baker Books, 2003), 107.

[45] Robert B. Chisholm Jr. *A Commentary on Judges and Ruth* (Grand Rapids, Michigan: Kregel Publications, 2013), 240.

[46] Chisholm, *Judges and Ruth*, 236.

[47] Cundall and Morris, *Judges and Ruth*, 94.

[48] Chisholm, *Judges and Ruth*, 238.

[49] Chisholm, *Judges and Ruth*, 238.

[50] Cundall and Morris, *Judges and Ruth*, 100.

[51] One example of this is found in Psalm 51: David's confession after committing adultery and orchestrating a murder. He says, "Against You, You only, I have sinned." David's sin impacted far many more than God, but he realizes that ultimately God is the one we sin against, and David apologizes for it outright.

[52] Exodus 10:5-6

[53] While the angel is mentioned in Deborah's song, we don't see him moving directly, only in a recapitulation of words.

[54] Cundall and Morris, *Judges and Ruth*, 104.

[55] Cundall and Morris, *Judges and Ruth*, 104.

[56] Douglas and Tenney, *Bible Dictionary*, 1008.

[57] Exodus 33:20. Several theophanies fill the pages of Scripture (i.e. Genesis 32:24-32). God also manifests His presence in natural elements like pillars of fire and clouds (Exodus 13:21). Some commentators believe the angel of the Lord is a separate entity from the Lord in this passage, but the text makes it difficult to justify. The Lord would have strong preeminence over the angel, yet when the angel disappears, Gideon is filled with fear and continues talking with the Lord. This suggests this is a theophany appearance, one that established a method of communication directly with Gideon even if the physical being didn't appear as a physical agent from this point forward (we're not told how God speaks with Gideon from this point on).

[58] Judges 6:13

[59] 2 Corinthians 1:22

[60] Chisholm, *Judges and Ruth*, 275.

[61] Younger, *The NIV Application Commentary*, 177.

[62] Douglas and Tenney, *Bible Dictionary*, 99.

[63] Romans 8:28

[64] Some commentators believe that the inclusion of Gideon's name here reveals his steadfast allegiance to God rather than an attempt to gain credit with God. See Chisholm, *Judges and Ruth*, 285. But from the surrounding text and the conclusion of Gideon's story, it seems most likely that Gideon is attributing credit to himself along with God—an action that precipitates an accumulation of arrogance later on, revealing his true colors all along.

[65] Cundall and Morris, *Judges and Ruth*, 113.

[66] Chisholm, *Judges and Ruth*, 285.

[67] Pfeiffer, Bakers Bible Atlas, 105.

[68] See Chisholm, *Judges and Ruth*, 287. Oreb and Zeeb were leaders of the Midianite army (comparable to Sisera in the Deborah/Barak account). But they were not the kings of Midian.

[69] For further evidence of Gideon's misguided decision making, see Younger, *The NIV Application Commentary*, 197-198.

[70] Douglas and Tenney, *Bible Dictionary*, 983.

[71] Cundall and Morris write, "The command of a father to his son to slay two kings in cold blood is indicative of the general standards of the age, which were not those of the New Testament. It would be accounted an honour for a youth to slay such important prisoners of war, and a corresponding disgrace for the captives themselves." 119-120.

[72] Younger, *The NIV Application Commentary*, 206.

[73] Cundall and Morris, *Judges and Ruth*, 124.

[74] Chisholm, *Judges and Ruth*, 311.

[75] Gregory Mobley. *The Empty Men: The Heroic Tradition of Ancient Israel* (New York:

Doubleday, 2005), 151.

[76] Cundall and Morris, *Judges and Ruth*, 127.

[77] Chisholm, *Judges and Ruth*, 314.

[78] Younger, *The NIV Application Commentary*, 224. See footnote.

[79] Cundall and Morris, *Judges and Ruth*, 130.

[80] Cundall and Morris, *Judges and Ruth*, 132. Also see W.F. Albright, *Archaeology and the Religion of Israel* (John Hopkins Press, 1953), 113.

[81] Younger, *The NIV Application Commentary*, 230.

[82] Younger, *The NIV Application Commentary*, 230.

[83] According to Joshua 19:17-23, Issachar's territory included: Chesulloth, Shunem, Hapharaim, Shion, Anaharath, Rabbith, Kishion, Ebez, Remeth, En-gannim, En-haddah, and Beth-pazzez. Their border ended at the Jordan and included sixteen cities. Nowhere is the hill country of Ephraim mentioned, causing us to pause at Tola's resident location.

[84] Younger, *The NIV Application Commentary*, 238.

[85] Douglas and Tenney, *Bible Dictionary*, 391.

[86] While several patriarchs had multiple wives, the practice is never condoned by God. In fact, stories with the inclusion of multiple wives/women only increase the drama and difficulty of life for the men of the families (see Abraham, Jacob, David, etc.)

[87] Cundall and Morris, *Judges and Ruth*, 137.

[88] Tob was a fertile land in Syria, located northeast of Jephthah's home, Gilead.

[89] D. Marcus, "The Bargaining Between Jephthah and the Elders (Judges 11:4-11)." *JANES* 19 (1989): 99.

[90] D.I. Block, *Judges, Ruth* (Nashville: Broadman & Holman, 1999), 355.

[91] Younger, *The NIV Application Commentary*, 255.

[92] Numbers 21:21-31

[93] Younger, *The NIV Application Commentary*, 256.

[94] Younger, *The NIV Application Commentary*, 257.

[95] Younger states, "it may seem odd to Western readers for sheep or cattle to come out of one's house. But the typical 'four-room house' of this period contained a room that housed animals." *The NIV Application Commentary*, 263.

[96] Cundall and Morris, *Judges and Ruth*, 152. Also see Douglas and Tenney, *Bible Dictionary*, 141-142.

[97] Chisholm, *Judges and Ruth*, 367.

[98] See Deuteronomy 7:1-6; Joshua 23:12-13

[99] Revisit Judges 2:5-6

[100] Younger, *The NIV Application Commentary*, 277.

[101] Douglas and Tenney, *Bible Dictionary*, 792.

[102] Younger, *The NIV Application Commentary*, 278.

[103] While the author of Judges doesn't reveal a remnant, the book of Ruth does. See Appendix B.

[104] Romans 1 & 2

[105] While several ancient texts verify this point, a simple study is the account of Jacob, Leah, and Rachel in Genesis 29-30. Leah's happiness and sense of identity came through her ability to bear Jacob children, though she learns she can't earn his love that way.

[106] For a list of unclean food items, see Leviticus 11

[107] Younger, *The NIV Application Commentary*, 288.

[108] Younger, *The NIV Application Commentary*, 289.

[109] Younger, *The NIV Application Commentary*, 291.

[110] Chisholm, *Judges and Ruth*, 398. Also see C.F. Burney, *The Book of Judges* (New York: KTAV, 1970), 349; and George F. Moore, *Judges* (Edinburgh: T & T Clark, 1895), 321.

[111] Cundall and Morris, *Judges and Ruth*, 160.

[112] Walton, *Bible Background Commentary*, 190.

[113] David Instone-Brewer. *Divorce and Remarriage in the Bible* (Grand Rapids, MI: Eerdmans, 2002), 4.

[114] Younger, *The NIV Application Commentary*, 302.

[115] Walton, *Bible Background Commentary*, 192.

[116] R.G. Boiling, *Judges: Introduction, Translation and Commentary* (Garden City, NY: Doubleday, 1975), 234.

[117] Deuteronomy 32:35

[118] Walton, *Bible Background Commentary*, 198.

[119] Exodus 17:3

[120] Cundall and Morris, *Judges and Ruth*, 173.

[121] Walton, *Bible Background Commentary*, 199.

[122] Cundall and Morris, *Judges and Ruth*, 173.

[123] Walton, *Bible Background Commentary*, 199.

[124] Walton, *Bible Background Commentary*, 200.

[125] C.F. Keil, *Joshua, Judges, Ruth* (Grand Rapids: Eerdmans, 1950), 418.

[126] C. J. Goslinga. *Joshua, Judges, Ruth* (Grand Rapids: Zondervan, 1986), 440.

[127] Pfeiffer. *Baker's Bible Atlas*, 110.

[128] Walton, *Bible Background Commentary*, 200.

[129] Walton, *Bible Background Commentary*, 200.

[130] Judges 13b-14a. The section in brackets are in Greek translations of the Bible; but not in Hebrew manuscripts.

[131] Walton, *Bible Background Commentary*, 202.

[132] Cundall and Morris, *Judges and Ruth*, 178.

[133] Younger, *The NIV Application Commentary*, 320.

[134] Walton, *Bible Background Commentary*, 202.

[135] Walton, *Bible Background Commentary*, 202.

[136] For more information of Dagan, see Walton's description in the *Bible Background Commentary*, 202.

[137] Younger, *The NIV Application Commentary*, 324.

[138] R.H. O'Connell, *The Rhetoric of the Book of Judges*, (Leiden: Brill, 1996) 224.

[139] Walton, *Bible Background Commentary*, 207.

[140] Walton, *Bible Background Commentary*, 202.

[141] Chisholm, *Judges and Ruth*, 448.

[142] Younger, *The NIV Application Commentary*, 339.

[143] Joshua 19:40-48

[144] Robert G. Boling, "In Those Days There Was No King in Israel." In *A Light Unto My Path: Old Testament Studies In Honor of Jacob M. Myers,* (Philadelphia: Temple University Press,1975), 263.

[145] Younger, *The NIV Application Commentary*, 340.

[146] Cundall and Morris, *Judges and Ruth*, 188.

[147] Walton, *Bible Background Commentary*, 211.

[148] Walton, *Bible Background Commentary*, 168.

[149] Walton, *Bible Background Commentary*, 168.

[150] Walton, *Bible Background Commentary*, 212.

[151] Cundall and Morris, *Judges and Ruth*, 195.

[152] Ken Stone, *Sex, Honor, and Power in the Deuteronomistic History* (Sheffield: Sheffield Academic, 1996), 75-79.

[153] Younger, *The NIV Application Commentary*, 358.

[154] Younger, *The NIV Application Commentary*, 376.

[155] Younger, *The NIV Application Commentary*, 370.

[156] Walton, *Bible Background Commentary*, 218.

[157] The Ark of the Covenant served to represent the presence of God. Strict rules surrounded its care, but God blessed those who respected and obeyed His statutes regarding it. For more information, read Exodus 25:14-22; 2 Samuel 6:2-17.

[158] Chisholm, *Judges and Ruth*, 504.

[159] Walton, *Bible Background Commentary*, 219.

[160] For a more detailed explanation of the seemingly mismatched numbers, see Chisholm, *Judges and Ruth*, 505-506.

[161] Hebrews 11:32-40

[162] It should also be noted that the author spends far more time (thus giving more honor) to men like Abraham and Moses than he does the judges in this chapter. He "does not intend for his readers to assume that all these individuals have the same spirituality, level of faith, and maturity." Younger, *NIV Application Commentary*, 326.

[163] Hebrews 12:1-3

[164] Younger, *The NIV Application Commentary*, 389.

[165] Ruth 1:16-17

www.ingramcontent.com/pod-product-compliance
Lightning Source LLC
Chambersburg PA
CBHW062037090426
42740CB00016B/2929